ADVANCE PRAISE

"Nancy Boyles's new book, *Classroom Reading to Engage the Heart and Mind*, will help teachers start conversations around social and emotional learning by using well-vetted picture books. Once again she writes what teachers want to know now, using literature that she has specifically selected on current topics students face daily. She creates an engaging template as the perfect resource for student responses, using strategies to help students reflect and connect to characters."

—Elizabeth Gilmore, Reading Specialist, Plainfield CT

"*Classroom Reading to Engage the Heart and Mind* is a beautiful text for any educator who longs for their students to be enlightened by literature and develop a deeper understanding of the story and of themselves. Nancy Boyles provides abundant selections of stunning literary stories as well as thought-provoking questions for teachers and students that help facilitate social and emotional competencies that are now recognized as an integral part of educating the whole child."

—Meg Morrison, School Adjustment Counselor, Mental Health Counselor, Mindfulness Teacher

"If you're in the field of education and you love a good children's book, then you know the positive impact of stories on students. Nancy Boyles's *Classroom Reading to Engage the Heart and Mind* takes all of the guesswork out of choosing quality children's literature and guides you to the right texts, lessons, and rigorous activities for all of the competencies of social and emotional learning."

—Bridget Vaughan, M.Ed., Children's Literature Professor, Literacy and English Language Arts Curriculum Coordinator

"After spending a career in the elementary classroom, I still have times when words fail me. Sometimes I struggle with how to express the deep, important ideas that make teaching less about grades and tests and more about the human condition. I've come to believe that picture books can stand in the gap. This book proves that picture books hold power. Children deserve to encounter and experience powerful stories to discover the power in themselves."

—Tanny McGregor, teacher and author of *Comprehension Connections: Bridges to Strategic Reading, Comprehension Going Forward: Where We Are and What's Next, Genre Connections: Lessons to Launch Literary and Nonfiction Texts,* and *Ink & Ideas: Sketchnotes for Engagement, Comprehension, and Thinking*

CLASSROOM READING
TO ENGAGE THE
HEART & MIND

Norton Books in Education

CLASSROOM READING
TO ENGAGE THE
HEART & MIND

200+ Picture Books
to Start SEL Conversations

NANCY BOYLES

W. W. NORTON & COMPANY

Independent Publishers Since 1923

Copyright © 2020 by Nancy Boyles

All rights reserved
Printed in the United States of America
First Edition

For information about permission to reproduce selections from this book, write to
Permissions, W. W. Norton & Company, Inc., 500 Fifth Avenue, New York, NY 10110

For information about special discounts for bulk purchases, please contact
W. W. Norton Special Sales at specialsales@wwnorton.com or 800-233-4830

Manufacturing by Sheridan Books
Book design by Anna Reich
Production manager: Katelyn MacKenzie

Library of Congress Cataloging-in-Publication Data

Names: Boyles, Nancy N., 1948- author.
Title: Classroom reading to engage the heart and mind : 200+ picture books to start SEL
     conversations / Nancy Boyles.
Description: First edition. | New York : W. W. Norton & Company, 2020. | Series: Norton books
     in education | Includes bibliographical references and index.
Identifiers: LCCN 2019030181 | ISBN 9780393714203 (paperback) | ISBN 9780393714210 (epub)
Subjects: LCSH: Picture books for children—Educational aspects. | Affective education.
Classification: LCC LB1044.9.P49 B68 2020 | DDC 372.45/2—dc23
LC record available at https://lccn.loc.gov/2019030181

W. W. Norton & Company, Inc., 500 Fifth Avenue, New York, N.Y. 10110
www.wwnorton.com

W. W. Norton & Company Ltd., 15 Carlisle Street, London W1D 3BS

1 2 3 4 5 6 7 8 9 0

This is a book about stories
Stories that engage the heart and mind
Stories we read aloud to children
And the stories of our own lives
For even when the story
Is a picture book
A good story invites us to journey back
Days or decades
Because that character's experience
Was so much like our own
Inside our classroom or beyond
And we grow socially and emotionally
Along with our students

This book is dedicated
To all the teachers and children
Lucky enough to hold these stories
In their hands
And in their hearts

CONTENTS

INTRODUCTION

Coming Home to Social Emotional Learning

With the publication of this book, I've come full circle. Way, way back in a time before Smart Boards (and even before white boards), when teachers still wrote with chalk on blackboards, I became a teacher. I graduated from my small liberal arts college with an elementary teaching certification in hand and lots of enthusiasm for my future in the classroom, but pitifully few skills. Even then, I wanted to specialize in literacy, but my coursework in the area had only consisted of a three-credit class that covered methods in both reading and math. There was a single textbook. The first half was devoted to math. You flipped it over and began anew for reading. I'm not making this up.

When I arrived at Boston University the following fall to pursue a Master's degree with a focus in literacy, I was not disappointed. The program was exactly what I needed, and I knew I would leave it prepared to hit the ground running. But early on I had to make a choice. I could take 36 credits of coursework, or I could take 30 credits and write a thesis for the remaining six credits. I decided on the latter, as I was an impoverished graduate student, and this was the less costly option.

I needed a topic. It was the 1970s and things like sensitivity training, affective education, and bibliotherapy were trending. Back then we had yet to invent the term *social emotional learning* (SEL), but educators were focusing a lot on the notion of a student's self-concept, an early effort toward some of the same goals now addressed through SEL. So I designed a study that explored the link between self-concept and children's literature. I had a passion for kids' books, and this seemed like a perfect way to connect the mind and the spirit.

I remember that the outcome of the study was positive. Children's feelings about themselves could indeed be impacted by the characters they met in books. And although now I might not vouch for the reliability of my fledgling methodology, my research set in motion a path I followed throughout my career: students' emotions matter, and our curriculum needs to reflect that idea.

I hope mine always did. But somewhere along that path, I took a fork in the road. It's not that I cared less about how children *feel*, but that I became similarly fascinated by how they *think*. If you were to know me only through my publications—books about comprehension strategies, writing scaffolds, close reading, and Depth of Knowledge—you might conclude that I was solely invested in the rigor of brainwork. In fact, some people are surprised to see my name attached to conference presentations about synthesizing social emotional learning and literacy.

I came back to this area because teachers and administrators began asking me: "What about social emotional learning?"; "Can you help us integrate SEL into our literacy curriculum?"; "How do you see SEL connecting to your work in comprehension?" I wasn't sure at first. The field of SEL had marched forward without me, and I had some catching up to do. But of course, social emotional learning *does* integrate easily with the work I've cared about for so long. It's a next step, another way of helping students transform their lives through the power of books.

Of course, there are many programs available that offer a comprehensive approach to social emotional learning. I couldn't design a better full-scale program than what these organizations provide. Likewise, there's a ton of research, and more available every day, addressing the theory and science behind SEL. But my niche, and the purpose of this book, is to help teachers make those research-based practices come alive in their day-to-day work with students—in particular through the power of stories.

Book Overview

There are two parts to this book.

Part I: Understanding Social Emotional Learning and Its Connection to Literacy has 2 chapters and **Part II: Teaching Social Emotional Skills Through Picture Books** includes five chapters.

In **Part I, Chapter 1: Why Social Emotional Learning and Why Now?** we begin with a call to action based on the urgent need for SEL, and an exploration of the classroom behaviors teachers see every day that validate this need. The chapter continues with research that suggests positive outcomes for students engaged in social emotional learning, as well as an explanation of policies and practices in place that support SEL. Next, I introduce the definition of social emotional learning provided by CASEL (Collaborative for Academic, Social, and Emotional Learning) and the CASEL framework, with competencies and focus areas that guide the remainder of the book. This chapter concludes with a discussion of the teacher skills needed to optimize SEL through a positive classroom climate.

Chapter 2: Social Emotional Learning Through Literacy starts by connecting SEL to best practices, including applying SEL to literacy standards, close reading, interactive read alouds, and Depth of Knowledge. Here I also introduce the questioning strategy I integrate into all later chapters called *Seven Thinking Boxes,* which links social emotional learning to comprehension through text-dependent questions. This chapter continues setting the stage for Part II by explaining the rationale for selecting books that engage the heart. It concludes with a list of all 240 titles across the SEL competencies.

The heart of this book is **Part II: Social Emotional Learning Through Picture**

Books. Chapters 3–7 dive into the five SEL competencies, one at a time, and all follow the same format. Each begins with an introduction to the competency and the focus areas. Then the focus area is unpacked, first with a definition of the focus as it relates to literacy, and after that, what it looks like in the classroom when it is going well, and when more support is needed. I provide reflection questions for teachers to ponder themselves or as part of a professional study group with colleagues.

Next, these chapters explain what to look for in books matched to individual focus areas, with an emphasis on the *message* in each story: What does this story say about self-confidence (for example) that is valuable for students to understand? I profile five books for each focus area, selected to represent five messages relevant to that category. The final book profiled under each heading also includes questions for each of the Seven Thinking Boxes, followed by a set of generic Box questions teachers can ask about *any* book addressing that focus. Woven throughout are composite stories from my classrooms over the years, and a few tales from outside the classroom, too.

An Appendix following Chapter 7, **Ten SEL Books for the Principal's Office**, suggests titles for those times when students get "sent to the principal" for social emotional reasons.

This book is meant to be a hands-on resource with lots of practical classroom applications. In a nutshell, here's what you'll find:

- The 5 SEL competencies, identified and explained
- 24 SEL focus areas, identified and explained
- 5 books profiled for each focus area, identified and explained—for a total of 120 profiles
- 5 additional books listed for each focus area—for a total of 120 supplementary books (That's 240 books in all)
- 24 question sets for the profiled books—one for each focus area
- 24 generic question sets to be used with any book—one for each focus area
- MANY classroom-ready charts and rubrics

What is it about a good story, even when the story is from a picture book, that inspires such a personal connection? I'm imagining the stories you will add to these lists that resonate with *you*. And I'm imagining (and hoping) this will be more of an "arm chair book" than a "desk chair book," a curl-up-with-a-cup-of-tea book. So, let the reading (and learning) begin.

CLASSROOM READING
TO ENGAGE THE
HEART & MIND

PART I

UNDERSTANDING SOCIAL EMOTIONAL LEARNING AND ITS CONNECTION TO LITERACY

CHAPTER 1

WHY SOCIAL EMOTIONAL LEARNING AND WHY NOW?

Everyone is talking about social emotional learning (SEL). Ten years ago, it was barely a whisper in education. Now it's a roar. SEL is a hot topic at conferences, the subject of countless journal articles and books, and the core of dozens of programs and initiatives in preschool through high school and beyond. Why?

The Urgent Need for Social Emotional Learning

The need for social emotional learning has always existed, though for more than a decade, schools have been laser-focused on new standards, measures of accountability, and everything cognitive: Can students achieve grade-level benchmarks? Can they demonstrate proficient thinking on performance tasks? Can they read on level by grade three?

Teachers recognized the trade-offs. Hammering away at literacy and math standards meant less time for the softer side of school—students' social and emotional development. And when students didn't meet academic standards, many schools doubled down so that reading and math consumed nearly the full day. Curriculum became prescriptive, with fewer occasions for personalization. Not only was recess a thing of the past, but gone too were social studies projects, science experiments, and other parts of the school day that involved social interaction. Still, the frenzy continued because it was those academic scores that appeared in reports and in the media.

In addition to the emphasis on accountability, pervasive environmental issues have continued to take their toll: substance abuse in some students' homes, poverty, hunger, and so forth. And for all students, there's the constant lurking threat of school violence. These and so many other circumstances collide, contributing to classroom behaviors that detract from learning, including:

- Too many disciplinary referrals
- Aggression
- Poor choices that impact the whole classroom
- Difficulty listening and following directions
- Distractibility
- Lack of engagement
- Unnecessary interruptions
- Lack of empathy for others' feelings
- Bullying
- Inability to manage anger
- Poor sportsmanship
- Inability to work in a group
- Difficulty accepting consequences

And this is the *short* list! During workshops, whenever I ask teachers how they know their students need to focus more on social emotional learning, their lists fill pages, and they'd willingly spend entire sessions giving examples. Indeed, the need for social emotional learning is clear, but is it worth it? The research says YES!

Research Support

Research suggests that SEL initiatives can make a difference in several ways. In 2011, the Collaborative for Academic, Social, and Emotional Learning (CASEL) along with other researchers published a meta-analysis of 213 social and emotional learning programs. The analysis indicated that students who participated in SEL programs showed improved classroom behavior, an increased ability to manage stress and depression, and better attitudes about themselves, others, and school. For example, at age 25, years after their program ended, SEL program participants noted fewer psychiatric and substance abuse problems and fewer arrests. Another study indicated that SEL program participants were 42% less likely to be physically aggressive in school. But gains go beyond social and emotional health. SEL programs also contribute to better academic performance. The meta-analysis also found that participating in a social emotional learning program translated to an 11 percentile-point gain in achievement (Durlak, Weissberg, Dymnicki, Taylor, & Schellinger, 2011).

A follow-up meta-analysis six years later examined results from 82 additional SEL interventions implemented from kindergarten to high school. This time, the news was even better. This research showed that more than three years after the last intervention, the academic performance of students in SEL programs was an average of 13 percentile points higher than students who didn't participate in SEL programs. This was an increase of two percentile points over the earlier study. The same analysis also showed more positive social behaviors, fewer conduct problems, and lower drug use (Taylor, Oberle, Durlak, & Weissberg, 2017).

Policy Support

I've always been an advocate of high standards, critical thinking, and challenging assessments, but the goal should not be academic rigor at the expense of social emotional development. We should seek to balance academic needs with social emotional needs, and I'm excited that the pendulum is currently swinging back toward the middle in the field of education.

In fact, social emotional learning is more than a good idea; it's a mandate. In all 50 states, SEL has been incorporated into preschool standards. Many states mandate SEL for grades K-12, as well. But we need to work hard to implement SEL as effectively as possible. Policies at the federal level contribute to these initiatives by providing funding for research and evidence-based practices. For example, the *Every Student Succeeds Act* (ESSA) works to assure that assessments measure SEL accurately.

Other organizations oversee a broad range of SEL initiatives. The National Commission on Social, Emotional, and Academic Development (NCSEAD) focuses on how to integrate SEL and academic development into school design, culture, teaching, and learning (The National Commission on Social, Emotional, and Academic Development, n.d). The Collaborative for Academic, Social, and Emotional Learning (CASEL) works with experts, schools, districts, and states across the country to drive research, guide practice, and inform policy. The CASEL website (https://casel.org/), a go-to resource for all things SEL, is chock full of amazing tools, including:

- *The CASEL Guide to Schoolwide SEL* that offers guidance on implementing high-quality SEL
- *CASEL's District Resource Center* with more than 500 resources that support high-quality district implementation

- *The CASEL Program Guide* that help schools select SEL programs from those currently in use throughout the country
- *The SEL Assessment Guide* that helps districts make decisions about selecting and measuring students' social emotional learning
- A free monthly electronic newsletter (https://casel.org/join-the-movement/) that keeps subscribers informed about recent developments in the field

Research-Based SEL Practices in Action

CASEL asserts that the best way to promote students' social emotional learning is through comprehensive, systemic, schoolwide initiatives. One characteristic common to almost all programs (of those described in the *CASEL Program Guide*) is *explicit* SEL lessons, some of which are even scripted. There is also often a family component; class meetings; role-play; and problem-solving and community-building activities. Most programs provide professional development and a focus on teachers' emotional health as well.

What is generally missing from these programs, however, is the inclusion of children's literature as a component. Only one program, *4Rs*, specifies the use of stories and book talks in its description ("4Rs: Reading, Writing, Respect, Resolution," n.d.). With so many amazing books available in which characters model prosocial solutions to real-world problems, this seems like a missed opportunity. The classroom is the perfect place to connect kids, books, and social emotional learning. That is the aim of *this* book.

Defining and Refining Social Emotional Learning

My favorite CASEL resource, with widespread appeal, is its definition of social emotional learning and its framework that breaks SEL down into five competencies and multiple focus areas within each competency. There are many ways we could carve up this field, but I like the five competencies identified by CASEL. Taken together, they cover a broad range of social emotional expectations and are well-suited to the classroom. A second reason for going with the CASEL framework is that many schools and districts already use it for SEL (sometimes with minor tweaks). This makes it easy to integrate new initiatives—such as the instruction I propose in this book—into other district efforts. Let's begin with CASEL's definition of social emotional learning.

The Collaborative for Academic, Social, and Emotional Learning (CASEL) defines social emotional learning as "the process through which children and adults understand and manage emotions, set and achieve positive goals, feel and show empathy for others, establish and maintain positive relationships, and make responsible decisions" (CASEL, n.d.). CASEL unpacks this definition into five general competencies (which it also calls skills):

- Self-Awareness
- Self-Management
- Social Awareness
- Relationship Skills
- Responsible Decision-Making

You can tell from this breakdown that the first two competencies relate to *emotional* learning, while the next two reflect *social* competencies. The final category, responsible decision-making, typically calls for both emotional and social skills.

For clarity, CASEL defines each competency and divides it into different focus areas. Chart 1.1 shows this breakdown. CASEL does not, however, define each focus area, leaving these labels open to interpretation. Chapters 3–7 explore each of the competencies and focus areas in depth. I've reordered the focus areas within a couple of competencies for a better instructional flow, in case teachers wish to progress through them sequentially. I've also tweaked "responsible decision-making" by synthesizing analysis and evaluation into a single focus area. From a practical standpoint, these are always connected in literature: First, a character gathers evidence to analyze, then evaluates it to find a solution.

My only other modification is that I chose a specific lens for "reflecting." There is no category among CASEL's focus areas that features *heritage* as a component of children's identity. Of course, students can reflect on all sorts of things, and there are numerous profiled titles in Chapters 3–7 that feature diverse characters in multicultural settings. But I wanted an opportunity for children to reflect more intentionally on the positive role their ancestry and ethnicity play in the way they relate to the world. It seemed a fitting way to end this book.

CHART 1.1: CASEL COMPETENCIES AND FOCUS AREAS

SEL COMPETENCY	DEFINITION	FOCUS AREAS
SELF-AWARENESS	The ability to accurately recognize one's own emotions, thoughts, and values and how they influence behavior. The ability to accurately assess one's strengths and limitations, with a well-grounded sense of confidence, optimism, and a "growth mindset."	• Identifying emotions • Accurate self-perception • Recognizing strengths • Self-Confidence • Self-Efficacy
SELF-MANAGEMENT	The ability to successfully regulate one's emotions, thoughts, and behaviors in different situations—effectively managing stress, controlling impulses, and motivating oneself. The ability to set and work toward personal and academic goals.	• Impulse control • Stress management • Self-Discipline • Self-Motivation • Goal-Setting • Organizational skills
SOCIAL AWARENESS	The ability to take the perspective of and empathize with others, including those from diverse backgrounds and cultures. The ability to understand social and ethical norms for behavior and to recognize family, school, and community resources and supports.	• Perspective-Taking • Empathy • Appreciating diversity • Respect for others
RELATIONSHIP SKILLS	The ability to establish and maintain healthy and rewarding relationships with diverse individuals and groups. The ability to communicate clearly, listen well, cooperate with others, resist inappropriate social pressure, negotiate conflict constructively, and seek and offer help when needed.	• Communication • Social engagement • Relationship-Building • Teamwork
RESPONSIBLE DECISION-MAKING	The ability to make constructive choices about personal behavior and social interactions based on ethical standards, safety concerns, and social norms. The realistic evaluation of consequences of various actions, and a consideration of the well-being of oneself and others.	• Identifying problems • Analyzing situations • Solving problems • Evaluating • Reflecting • Ethical responsibility

As we refine our pursuit of social emotional learning, there's a final point to keep in mind. In his *Ed Leadership* article "The Emotional Intelligence We Owe Students and Educators," Marc Brackett reminds us that competencies and focus areas are not personality traits: "It's certainly good to be warm, kind, and friendly, but these qualities don't necessarily pertain to whether a person uses emotions wisely; they fall into the category of personality traits." We can develop emotion-management skills even though a trait may not come naturally to us (Brackett, 2018).

This is good news for us all. While patience is not my strong suit, I can "manage" this quality when needed (well, most of the time). This whole book is about the emotions and social skills we want our students (and ourselves) to manage. Story characters will do the heavy lifting for us by showing strong social and emotional management skills in action. Then we'll follow up with opportunities for students to talk about these characters, their problems, and the way they managed them—connecting character actions to student actions going forward: How would *you* handle this situation?

Teacher Skills that Support SEL

There is much we can do to teach social and emotional management, through literature as this book suggests, or through other programs and initiatives. Since great literature should always be a part of your curriculum, reading and discussing the books profiled here would pair well with anything else you do to promote SEL. The intent is for students to grow socially and emotionally through experiences that also support academic achievement. But succeeding on this journey requires a mosaic of teacher skills that contribute to a positive classroom culture, which must be cultivated before we can expect students to thrive emotionally and socially.

There are many teacher skills essential to a healthy classroom climate, and when you look closely, they reflect many of the same social emotional skills we seek to develop in our students. Here are five important ones, and five others, briefly mentioned.

- **Good classroom management**

  Poor classroom management can bring down the best of intentions. Most classrooms I visit are well-run, with organized materials and orderly spaces. There may be a buzz of activity, but the overall feeling is not one of disorder. When I enter a chaotic room, however, the bedlam tends to prevail instead of the lesson, regardless of how good the lesson may be. You can't think when you can't get past the commotion.

- **High expectations for all students**

  Most teachers expect reasonable rigor from all their students, and think of them as academically capable—but not *all* teachers. In a recent grade level seminar, one teacher announced that she doubted her students could handle the task we were discussing: "They're really not very smart, you know." I (and her colleagues) were horrified that she'd make such a comment, but of greater concern to me was how she might be conveying that attitude in her classroom. She may not be saying it out loud, but kids just *know* when you don't believe in them.

- **Teacher language**

  They say that communication is 7% verbal and 93% non-verbal (tone and body language). So yes, our words matter. A compliment can lift a child up. Criticism has the opposite effect. This does not mean that we should never say anything negative to a student. But when we do, our tone and manner should still show warmth, compassion, and encouragement. This is the way *we* show respect. We can't expect our students to be respectful if we don't model this in our communication with them.

- **Motivation**

  I love to walk into a classroom in which the teacher is enthusiastic and there's a spring in his step. In these rooms, kids tune in to the lesson because the teacher makes it sound interesting. They don't want to miss anything. There are other classrooms I visit where, honestly, it's hard to stay awake. Kids equate flat affect with not caring—the opposite of what we want our SEL instruction to communicate.

- **Pace**

  Lesson pacing is a bigger deal than we sometimes recognize. We want to be thorough, but sometimes we get lost in the weeds. A lesson that could have been completed in 15 minutes drones on for twice that time. Why? We talk too much. Tangents take us off-track, or we try to include every detail that we find fascinating (or crucial). But a tight lesson that moves along briskly will be more likely to keep students focused.

- **Choice**

  If we want students to make responsible decisions, do we provide them with opportunities to make choices throughout the school day?

- **Reflection**

  If we want students to be reflective, do we give them opportunities to reflect regularly on their progress or behavior?

- **Teamwork**

  If we want students to build relationships and social skills, do we give them opportunities to work cooperatively with their peers?

- **Communication**

  If we want students to communicate well, do we provide them with opportunities for discourse?

- **Self-Discipline**

  If we want students to be self-directed, do we provide them with opportunities to set their own goals and work independently toward their achievement?

Even highly skilled teachers will not get perfect marks in all of these areas. But students should have the opportunity to *live* what we want them to *learn*. These 10 skills are organized on the following page into Worksheet 1.1: Reflecting on Teacher Skills that Promote SEL. Don't give yourself a score, but *do* be truthful about your strengths, and the areas where you'd like to grow. This is not intended to be a tool for administrative evaluation, only a means of self-reflection. Next, move to Chapter 2 to learn more about how this book will link social emotional learning to literacy.

WORKSHEET 1.1: REFLECTING ON TEACHER SKILLS THAT PROMOTE SEL

TEACHER SKILLS THAT SUPPORT SEL	HOW AM I DOING?
Good classroom management: Management issues don't get in the way of teaching and learning.	
High expectations for all students: My attitude, words, and learning opportunities reflect my belief that all children can achieve.	
Language: My words, tone, and body language convey support to students.	
Motivation: I am enthusiastic and animated in my delivery of instruction.	
Pace: My lessons move along without getting bogged down by too much detail. **Choice:** I provide my students with choices so that they can make some learning decisions for themselves.	
Reflection: I provide my students with regular opportunities to reflect on their learning.	
Teamwork: I give my students opportunities to work cooperatively with their peers.	
Communication: I give my students lots of opportunities for discourse.	
Self-Discipline: I give my students opportunities to set goals and to work through tasks independently	

CHAPTER 2
SOCIAL EMOTIONAL LEARNING THROUGH LITERACY

Planning for social emotional learning in the classroom should be like planning for any other explicit instruction, and the same key elements are important: learning goals, instructional implementation, and measurable outcomes. When the focus is literacy establish goals through English Language Arts (ELA) standards, use teaching practices that are matched to students' needs, and measure outcomes through Depth of Knowledge (DOK). Let's begin by examining the connection between SEL and ELA standards.

SEL and ELA Standards

Reading almost any story offers numerous opportunities for applying literacy standards. I code them here according to the Common Core, though they would be similar regardless of how they're organized, and applicable to any state's standards. Chart 2.1: Applying ELA Standards to SEL shows where to look for the application of individual standards within a text. However, there are differences between the way standards are applied in SEL lessons, and the way they will probably be applied to other lessons in the literacy curriculum.

When the literacy focus is comprehension, for example, the curriculum may specify one or sometimes a few standards to feature. When reading a fable, the focus might be *Standard 2: Determining central ideas and themes*, supported by *Standard 1: Citing evidence* and *Standard 4: Interpreting words and phrases*. The lesson would mainly examine points in the text that are matched to these standards. In other words, the standards drive the instruction. But this approach is not ideal when the goal is social emotional learning. For SEL, the content of the story should determine which standards you apply. This means that you will apply the standards as you arrive at places in the text where the standard fits best.

For instance, suppose you are reading aloud *The Tortoise and the Hare*. As students are introduced to the two characters and learn more about them as the story progresses, you would talk about characterization—that is, what each character is like. This is *Standard 3: How individuals, events, or ideas develop over a text.* As students question Hare's boastful attitude, you might consider the author's purpose, which

CHART 2.1: APPLYING ELA STANDARDS TO SEL

COMMON CORE STANDARD*	APPLICATION OF STANDARD TO SEL
CCRA.R.1 Read closely to determine what the text says explicitly and to make logical inferences from it; cite specific textual evidence when writing or speaking to support conclusions drawn from the text.	Citing evidence will always apply. Before students interpret any part of a text for SEL goals, make sure they can defend their reasoning with specific story details.
CCRA.R.2 Determine central ideas or themes of a text and analyze their development; summarize the key supporting details and ideas.	A key reason you are reading any book for SEL is for its message, so this will always come up at the end of a story. But focusing on the *development* of the central idea throughout the reading will make it even clearer to students.
CCRA.R.3 Analyze how and why individuals, events, or ideas develop and interact over the course of a text.	For any story, it's important to identify the plot elements. For SEL, be sure to focus on the setting as well as the problem and characters, as it may be significant to the message. Help students see how plot elements relate to each other (for example, how the time and place impact the problem).
CCRA.R.4 Interpret words and phrases as they are used in a text, including determining technical, connotative, and figurative meanings, and analyze how specific word choices shape meaning or tone.	For SEL lessons, think about the *tone* that words and phrases convey as well as their meaning. This will help students recognize the importance of word choice in crafting a text, and how words and phrases contribute to the overall message.

CCRA.R.5 Analyze the structure of texts, including how specific sentences, paragraphs, and larger portions of the text (e.g., a section, chapter, scene, or stanza) relate to each other and the whole.	Since most of the texts for SEL lessons will be stories with a problem-solution format, use this structure to help students identify story parts that will help with summarizing. Also be sure to address how parts of the story fit together.
CCRA.R.6 Assess how point of view or purpose shapes the content and style of a text.	For SEL, it will be important for students to consider who the narrator is, and how that affects the point of view. How would the story be different if told from another character's point of view?
CCRA.R.7 Integrate and evaluate content presented in diverse media and formats, including visually and quantitatively, as well as in words.	The illustrations in picture books provide meaning beyond what the words alone convey. For SEL, be sure to look for characters' facial expressions and body language, and also the colors the author uses to bring meaning to the page.
CCRA.R.8 Delineate and evaluate the argument and specific claims in a text, including the validity of the reasoning as well as the relevance and sufficiency of the evidence.	Common Core does not apply this standard to literary texts. However, evaluating the validity of reasoning is always a good skill. In SEL lessons, decide if the author has provided evidence that is relevant and sufficient enough to be convincing. What is the *kind* of evidence?
CCRA.R.9 Analyze how two or more texts address similar themes or topics in order to build knowledge or to compare the approaches the authors take.	Making connections between texts always enhances learning. For SEL, also consider text-to-world connections and personal connections that allow students to relate the author's message to their own lives.
CCRA.R.10 Read and comprehend complex literary and informational texts independently and proficiently.	The Common Core typically measures text complexity by Lexile. But for SEL, focus more on the complexity of the message. More complex themes are realistic and evolve from characters and problems that are multi-dimensional.

*There are many Common Core Reading Standards. These are the 10 College and Career Readiness Anchor Standards for Reading (National Governors Association Center for Best Practices, Council of Chief State School Officers, 2010).

relates to *Standard 6: Assessing point of view*. At the end of the story, you'll discuss the lesson, *Standard 2: Determining central ideas and themes*. A student might even remind you that the lesson in the story was like the one from another story you read last week: *Standard 9: Analyze how different texts address a similar theme*. When the intent is social emotional learning, applying standards should grow organically from the class's interactions with the book.

Building Good Literacy Habits

It's not just the *ability* to read that is aligned with success but also students' *willingness* to read. The Common Core overlooked this in its identification of College and Career Readiness Standards for Reading, which is a significant oversight. (National Governors Association Center for Best Practices, Council of Chief State School Officers, 2010).

Costa and Kallick (2000) identified 16 habits of mind necessary for working through real-world problems. Here are five habits that connect strongly to students' social emotional well-being as well as to their reading skills. Bottom line: we care about these habits not just because they're good for kids' reading, but because they're good for kids, period.

1. **The habit is accuracy; the SEL connection is analyzing and evaluating a situation**
   Above all, the new standards emphasize the importance of gathering precise evidence, which is the foundation of deeper thinking. Students cannot analyze or evaluate something in a social emotional context if they don't have their facts straight. If students develop precision and accuracy, they will, for example, take the time to reread a passage so that they can be sure to use the information correctly when making inferences.

2. **The habit is persistence; the SEL connection is self-discipline**
   Good readers stay focused on a task until completion. This is especially important for standards-based reading because the expectations for some standards are different from what students may have encountered in the past. Currently, there is a greater emphasis on the internal structure of a text—how parts are connected to each other. They also require more critical thinking. Even young students must now determine the relevance and sufficiency of evidence in informational passages. If students aren't willing to persist, they will not succeed in meeting these challenges.

3. **The habit is flexible thinking; the SEL connection is perspective taking**

   Students should be able to examine alternatives and consider different perspectives. According to the new standards, students are expected to make more connections between texts. This is not just so that they learn to synthesize information, but also to encourage them to examine ideas from different points of view. The classroom implication for SEL as well as for reading in general is the inclusion of more text-to-text lessons, providing students with opportunities to draw conclusions about similarities and differences between characters, problems, themes, the author's purpose, and more.

4. **The habit is communicating with clarity and precision; the SEL connection is motivation**

   Communicating with clarity is critical to writing. Students must learn to write pieces (be they narrative or analytical) that are not only well structured, but also well crafted. This means taking care to choose the best words, fully develop paragraphs, and link ideas together. Students who are motivated to invest themselves in the art of writing are more likely to meet these challenging writing standards. Writing is seldom easy, but good writers are motivated to keep going because they anticipate pride in a job well done.

5. **The habit is creating, imagining, and innovating; the SEL connection is problem solving**

   The highest level of standards-based performance is the now-legendary "performance task." The intent is for students to demonstrate their ability to design a unique written product by thinking both critically and creatively about a problem. The disposition to work systematically through all problem-solving steps yields the best results: identify the problem, gather your data, weigh the evidence, find a solution.

   What we see from these five indicators—something that many teachers see every day—is that students' success (or lack thereof) in meeting literacy standards is as dependent on their habits of mind as it is on their cognitive capacity. They may have great literacy skills, but without the right mindset, the results can be dismal. If we want students to meet current literacy standards (Common Core or otherwise), we need to attend to their social emotional learning as well as their literacy learning. We can begin by reimagining the instructional methods most likely to produce the outcomes we wish to achieve in both areas.

SEL Through Close Reading
and the Interactive Read-Aloud

When it comes to advancing literacy standards, we must acknowledge the power of close reading. Since the inception of the Common Core, close reading has been credited with improving students' reading performance. As the Partnership for Assessment of Reading for College and Careers (PARCC) noted:

> A significant body of research links the close reading of complex text—whether the student is a struggling reader or advanced—to significant gains in reading proficiency and finds close reading to be a key component of college and career readiness. (2012, p. 7)

Remember that standards do not prescribe methods, so linking standards to close reading as the Common Cards suggests is noteworthy. For any book to be useful for SEL, students must first gather observations about its content and consider how those observations contribute to the overall message. That makes close reading a two-step process when applied to social emotional learning. An initial close reading should focus on general understanding. Then students should return to the text for a follow-up lesson, during which they dig into a particular SEL focus area. Here's how it works.

SEL THROUGH CLOSE READING

Because it's so important for students to build a strong initial understanding of a text before moving on to discussing its deeper meaning, whether related to SEL or not, let's look at a few practices that support close reading before, during, and after the text has been read for the first time (Boyles, 2014).

Before reading

The goal of close reading is for students to get meaning from the text, not the teacher, so try to minimize frontloading. This means keeping the pre-reading part of the lesson short. Eliminate predictions (which are often random guesses) before students have more to infer from the story itself. Also, try to avoid those superficial personal connections that detract from meaning more than enhancing it. If you can address vocabulary needs through context as you read, rather than ahead of the story, that is also preferable. Finally, be selective about the background knowledge you share. Only offer information that the author does *not* clarify within the text. These tweaks to pre-reading will make *close* reading imperative for comprehension.

During reading

The key to reading closely *during* reading is engagement. Much of the time, when we say that students didn't understand a text, it's not that they *couldn't* read it or understand it. It's that they didn't focus enough to get the meaning. This has no failsafe solution, but for a first read, we teachers sometimes overemphasize text-dependent questions at the expense of holding students accountable for retrieving meaning themselves.

When we ask things like, *What problem did the main character face?* we are doing most of the work for our students, zeroing in on the details we want them to find. Instead, if we ask, *What details did you notice on this page?* Or, *What surprised you in this paragraph?* students need to figure out not only what the problem is, but also that the author is describing the problem rather than some other element of the story. Pausing frequently to ask this "noticing" question will keep kids focused and their comprehension on track. You'll know that they comprehended the basics when you follow up with a monitoring task after reading.

After reading

Since you will return to the same text another day for deeper thinking, in this case related to the relevant SEL focus area, your goal after reading is to confirm general understanding. When the text is a story, simply ask students to (orally) summarize it. This should include the characters, problem, setting, attempts to solve the problem, and the solution. If the text is a biography or personal narrative without the traditional problem-solution format, ask for a sequence of events. The conversation may drift to the theme or what the character learned. That's fine, however you'll be talking about those ideas in your SEL follow-up lesson, so try to save that discussion for then when you'll have more time.

SEL CLOSE READING FOLLOW-UP LESSON WITH QUESTIONS FOR SEVEN THINKING BOXES

In an ideal world, you'll have time in your schedule to teach two lessons related to the texts suggested in Part II of this book. In this case, you'll return to the book after an initial close read, this time using the questions from Seven Thinking Boxes for your story. If you've chosen one of the 24 featured titles, the questions have been prepared for you. If you choose another listed book, or a book from your own classroom library, you can create your own Thinking Box questions using Worksheet 2.1: *Questions to Ask about Any Book* for your focus area.

But before you get to the questions, clarify the SEL focus and introduce the lesson by asking your students what they know about the importance of the story's theme—

self-confidence, building relationships, reflecting on heritage, or whatever it may be. For example, you could say: *Self-confidence is important in this story. What is self-confidence? Why might it be important for a person to have self-confidence?* If you have read the story closely with your students, you probably won't need to reread it on the second day, though you may want to review it quickly. Then it's time to ask the Thinking Box questions.

The Seven Thinking Boxes comprise a comprehension strategy I developed several years ago. It's undergone a few transformations and name changes over time, but the basic concept remains intact. My goal was to provide students with kid-friendly visual representations of ways to think about a text. I stumbled on the idea of different types of boxes and since then, many students have engaged in "plain cardboard box thinking" and "puzzle box thinking"—among others. Some teachers have even constructed "real" boxes to match the seven categories. They pull questions from the boxes for discussion. In some classes, students add their own questions to each box once they understand what the boxes represent. Chart 2.2: Seven Thinking Boxes— Explained for SEL identifies each kind of thinking. A blank template follows for you to develop your own box questions.

CHART 2.2: SEVEN THINKING BOXES—EXPLAINED FOR SEL

PLAIN CARDBOARD BOX	BASIC THINKING
	Basic Thinking draws on evidence in a general way. Questions in this area might be "right there" questions, with the evidence directly stated in the text. Or, the questions might be inferential, where students *use* evidence to draw a conclusion. For SEL, these questions might introduce the focus area, or they might just monitor basic comprehension to pave the way for deeper SEL questions that follow.
PUZZLE BOX	PUZZLING DETAILS
	All stories contain some really great details to puzzle over. What are the lines that are the most significant for the SEL focus area? Can students identify these lines, sentences, and paragraphs? Can they explain the detail's connection to the story?

HEART BOX	**FEELINGS**
	Feelings play a big part in our interpretation of any text—both our own feelings toward different characters, and the characters' feelings about themselves and other characters. How do these feelings impact the SEL focus area of the story? Do these feelings change or remain the same throughout the story? What SEL concept is impacted?
UNUSUAL BOX	**CREATIVE THINKING**
	Creative thinking is at work on many different levels in all literature. Did a character find a unique way to solve a problem? How would *you* (the reader) have approached a similar problem if you had been that character? Why might your solution have been a better one? Try to relate creative thinking to the SEL focus area.
BROKEN BOX	**PROBLEMS AND ISSUES**
	Almost all stories have a *problem*, but sometimes the problem isn't what it seems to be on the surface. What was the issue that initiated the action? How does the problem relate to the SEL focus area? Look carefully at the way the author sets up the story and also at the characters' motivations.
TREASURE BOX	**SOMETHING TO TREASURE**
	We should finish all stories with a take-away to *treasure*. Sometimes this is determined by the author's message, or a lesson that a character learns. Other times the take-away might be more personal, another idea from the text that may not inspire everyone but speaks directly to *you*. Try to relate the message/lesson/theme to the SEL focus area. Also ask students to consider how the message will make a difference in their lives going forward.
TOOL BOX	**AUTHOR'S TOOLS**
	Authors use many different *tools* to tell a story. The tools show us *how* the author made the story interesting or lively. In any story, try to identify a few of these tools. They may or may not relate to the SEL focus area, but they will build a deeper understanding of the story, and can also be applied to students' own writing.

Text _____

SEL Competency: _____ Focus area: _____

PLAIN CARDBOARD BOX	**BASIC THINKING**
PUZZLE BOX	**PUZZLING DETAILS**
HEART BOX	**FEELINGS**
UNUSUAL BOX	**CREATIVE THINKING**
BROKEN BOX	**PROBLEMS AND ISSUES**
TREASURE BOX	**SOMETHING TO TREASURE**
TOOL BOX	**AUTHOR'S TOOLS**

There are many ways you can use the Thinking Box questions. If you have about 30 minutes for the lesson, you may be able to use all seven, or as many as you wish (even after your brief introduction). I like to open the conversation with one or two questions for the whole class, then ask students to work in pairs or small groups to respond to a question of their choice. I cut the Box questions into strips, read the questions aloud, and invite each partnership or group to select one they'd like. That way, the class considers the story from several angles.

I often give the same question to two groups because it's interesting to hear similarities and differences in their thinking. About 10 minutes should be plenty of time for the small group discussions. I circulate and insert a thought or two where it might be helpful. I also make sure the book is available so students can check evidence as needed. Then I bring everyone back together for 10 minutes to share. This exchange of ideas is useful feedback and helps me determine next SEL steps: Will I choose another picture book related to the same focus area, but with a different message? Will I choose a book that reinforces the same message? Or, will I move to a whole new focus area?

INTERACTIVE READ ALOUD WITH A SEL FOCUS

I prefer to teach a book over two close reading lessons as described previously. But sometimes that isn't possible. In such cases, approach the book as an interactive read aloud instead. An interactive read aloud is an opportunity for students to listen to a story and talk about it at the same time. When the focus is social emotional learning, the conversation will center on self-confidence, managing stress, solving problems, or whatever theme is featured. I've used this strategy many times because when I model lessons in classrooms, I'm not able to come back the next day.

In this case, I do frontload the focus and ask a couple of guiding questions before reading. To move the lesson along, I ask just enough monitoring questions to keep students engaged in the story. Then I finish with SEL questions that I've prioritized from the Seven Thinking Boxes for the story. For an interactive read aloud, you'll probably have time for two or three questions. Asking students to turn and talk to a partner about one of them will encourage more interaction. Aim to complete the whole lesson in about 30 minutes: 20 minutes for reading, 10 minutes for discussing.

Regardless of how you deliver your SEL lesson—as a follow-up to a close reading lesson or as an interactive read aloud—you'll want to listen carefully to students' answers to the Box questions as an indicator of their Depth of Knowledge.

SEL and Depth of Knowledge

Depth of Knowledge (DOK) refers to the level of thinking students demonstrate on a task, and the kind of thinking the task calls for (Webb, 2009). In this case, it will relate to SEL focus areas, although DOK can apply to any focus, not just social emotional learning. Different tasks demand different depths of knowledge. Chart 2.3: Depth of Knowledge in Social Emotional Learning explains each DOK level and, for clarification, applies it to the SEL focus "identifying problems" and the fairy tale "Goldilocks and the Three Bears."

CHART 2.3: DEPTH OF KNOWLEDGE IN SOCIAL EMOTIONAL LEARNING

DOK LEVEL	EXPLANATION	SAMPLE SEL QUESTION
1. EVIDENCE	DOK 1 questions ask for basic evidence related to the SEL focus that is stated directly in the text; no inferences are required. Look for accuracy.	What is the evidence that Goldilocks created a problem when she entered the bears' house?
2. APPLYING SKILLS AND CONCEPTS	DOK 2 questions ask students to apply a skill like "identify the main idea" or a concept like "discrimination." For SEL, this will mostly refer to concepts. Look for independent application.	Was Goldilocks trespassing when she entered the bears' house? How would you explain trespassing to someone who didn't understand the word?
3. STRATEGIC THINKING AND REASONING	DOK 3 questions ask for inferences about the SEL focus; there may be more than one viable answer based on defense of the evidence. Look for insight.	What do you think the author's purpose was for giving us so much evidence of the problem caused by Goldilocks?
4. EXTENDED THINKING	DOK 4 questions ask students to synthesize information about the SEL focus, often from multiple sources, to generate a unique product. Look for creativity and a unique voice.	Compare the problem caused by Goldilocks to the problem caused by Little Red Riding Hood. Which do you consider the more serious problem? Why?

Book _____ SEL focus area: _____

DEPTH OF KNOWLEDGE	PROFICIENT	DEVELOPING	FLEDGLING
1. Basic Evidence	Cites accurate, specific, and complete evidence	Cites accurate evidence, but may be too general or incomplete	Difficulty citing any accurate evidence
2. Application of skills and concepts	Understands key concepts related to the SEL focus area and can apply them independently	Generally understands related SEL concepts, but has difficulty paraphrasing them and applying them without support	Weak understanding of related concepts or labels for concepts. Needs lots of support to apply these concepts to the SEL book
3. Strategic Thinking and Reasoning	Inferences are insightful and show deep understanding of the SEL focus	Inferences are accurate but lack deep thinking about the SEL focus	Unable to make inferences or the inference about the SEL focus is illogical
4. Extended thinking	Product is complete, showing creativity, with a unique way of integrating SEL content through multiple resources	Product is complete but may be predictable in its presentation of SEL content with only superficial integration of multiple sources	Product may be incomplete or shows difficulty integrating SEL content from multiple sources

Areas and evidence of strength: _____

_____

_____

Areas and evidence of need: _____

_____

_____

Next steps: _____

_____

_____

Questions for Depths of Knowledge 1–3 are provided in the Seven Thinking Boxes for each featured title. Generic questions for *any* text within a focus area are included in a separate template so you can design your own questions for books that are profiled or listed, but not featured. Or, choose another book you love that matches the focus.

There are no DOK 4 questions in this book because there are no text-to-text lessons. I'll leave it up to you to decide how and when to connect texts. I'll also let you decide whether to have students answer any of these questions in writing. While I wholeheartedly recommend discussion of these questions *first*, there might be value in some cases in asking students to follow up with a written response. But be selective! Under no circumstances should students answer every Box question in writing, like it's a worksheet. Any SEL gains you make through reading and discussing a book would surely be lost in the drudgery of all that written response.

While we should not draw too many conclusions about students' SEL thinking based on their responses to a single text, Worksheet 2.2: Rubric for Estimating Students' Depth of Knowledge could be useful as a general gauge to plan next instructional steps. This might be better to use as a whole-class "big picture" measure rather than an assessment of individual students.

Note that plain cardboard box questions generally measures basic content knowledge, DOK 1. There are also questions attached to various boxes that address DOK 2 to solidify understanding of concepts like empathy and efficacy. However, most Box questions are inferential, addressing DOK 3—for a couple of reasons. First, when the focus is social and emotional learning, what we care about most is students' inferential thinking, their reasoning. Additionally, DOK 3 is often neglected in comprehension instruction. Try to include more of these questions in your literacy instruction—with or without a focus on SEL. For clarification, see Chart 2.4: Explanation of DOK 3 Questions. This chart provides a rationale for the alignment to both the standard and DOK for three sample questions. It also notes what to look for at each Depth of Knowledge level.

We've examined the link between literacy and social emotional learning through three lenses:

- Standards, the foundation of our curricular goals
- Instruction, the close reading and interactive read aloud processes through which we'll address social emotional issues
- Depth of Knowledge, how we'll measure what students are able to *do* with their SEL knowledge.

What we have not yet considered are the resources that will bring social emotional learning to life in the classroom, the books that engage the heart and the mind.

CHART 2.4: EXPLANATION OF DOK 3 QUESTIONS

DOK 3 QUESTION	RATIONALE
How does the message of *Weslandia* relate to self-efficacy (being the best you that you can be)? Support your response with evidence from the beginning, middle, and end of the story. How might this message make a difference to you in your life?	This is a DOK 3 "treasure box" question for the area of self-efficacy because it emphasizes inferential thinking about the theme. It also provides the opportunity for a *meaningful* personal connection, related to the central message. The Common Core anchor standard is CCRA 2: Identifying central ideas and their development in a text.
In *Muskrat Will be Swimming,* Grampa tells Jeannie that he experienced a similar problem with name calling when he was a child. Why do you think he tells her this? What is he trying to show her about the problems she's experiencing because of her Native American roots?	This is a DOK 3 question for appreciating diversity. It is listed under the "broken box" (problem) category and focuses on the author's purpose aligned to Common Core anchor standard CCRA 6: Determining author's purpose and point of view.
In your opinion, what do you consider the <u>best</u> quote in *The Empty Pot* showing the importance of ethical decision making? Why did you choose this quote?	This is a DOK 3 "Puzzle Box" question for ethical decision-making. I consider this a Common Core question for anchor standard CCRA 1: Identifying key evidence. Although some would argue that Standard 1 is too basic to qualify as DOK 3, the intent here is to use evidence *selectively*. This pushes the task to a deeper thinking level, something for students to puzzle over.

Books that Engage the Heart

Hands down, the best part of writing a book is the time I get to spend immersed in the children's literature I will integrate into the book's content. At the core of professional books about education is the *what* of teaching. But it's what we teach *with* that makes practices leap off the page and into our classroom. That's why I choose texts so carefully. The books I've selected in the past were chosen to help big ideas find their way into children's minds—to improve their literacy performance. But this time, the books I feature have been selected to help big ideas find their way into children's *hearts*—to help them see new possibilities for transforming their lives through literacy. It seems an even taller order, a greater responsibility. I embrace it here unequivocally, knowing that with the right story at the right time, we hold in our hands not just a book, but the power to help children envision their "best self"—the "me" they wish to be.

In choosing titles for this book, I searched for picture books with clearly written, well-developed storylines, beautiful illustrations that support the narrative, important messages, and characters that represent a range of diversities, free of stereotypes. While I appreciate the current emphasis on more informational sources across the curriculum, the texts featured in this book are almost entirely narrative. It's the *stories* of our lives that remain with us for continued contemplation. Some of these are true accounts about real people, like Sonia Sotomayor and Nelson Mandela, whose biographies inspire and guide. But most are fictional stories featuring characters who seem so real they could be one of our kindergarteners or fourth graders (although they may be little mice or koala bears). And they just happen to face the kinds of dilemmas our students face, too.

Because I want students to see themselves in the characters they encounter and the problems they face, I tried to select stories with a modern feel, about topics kids care about right now—although the story may be set in the past. Likewise, I mostly stayed away from fables and fairy tales in which the message may be on-point, but the characters are one dimensional—all good or all bad—because they fail to represent the complex personalities that make up our classrooms.

I like books where the central idea evolves from the unraveling of a robust plot that may reinforce several themes along the way. By contrast, some books exist to promote a single, simplistic message: Work hard. Be nice to your little brother. The dentist is your friend. Stories such as these are not generally featured in this book. But full disclosure: There are a few "self-help" books that are just so much fun that I couldn't resist them. *My Mouth is a Volcano* by Julia Cook, is "all about" the perils of impulsive talking, but shares its message in a manner that is more powerful because it amuses as it informs.

Choosing the most powerful books also means we can no longer address today's realities with yesterday's expectations for diversity. Instead, aim for inclusivity. Where once it was enough to show characters of different races, families from different parts of the world, and a sprinkling of children with "disabilities," we now need to move past tolerance of differences to a celebration of what makes us each unique. What about gender identity? What about kids with two moms or two dads? What about the newcomers streaming into our classrooms from around the globe? Do we choose to describe autism as a "disability" or as a "neurological difference?" What books best deliver on the promise of equity?

Some of the books featured in the following chapters are tried and true, beloved for decades, while others are hot-off-the-press. Sometimes an old friend like *Tacky the Penguin* (by Helen Lester) is exactly who we need to help us navigate a sticky situation. But don't be afraid to take a chance on a book that is brand new, or a title you haven't seen before. You'll never know how fabulous Rescue and Jessica can be (from *Rescue and Jessica* by Jessica Kensky and Robert Downes) as role models if you don't know their story, based on the 2013 Boston Marathon bombing. All books beg not only to be read, but to be discussed.

A few final notes about book selection: Whenever I share book titles in a workshop or in a professional book, some teachers feel compelled to race out and buy those exact titles. If you already own these books or can find them on the shelves of your school library, that's great. But remember that the titles I suggest and describe are examples of the *kinds* of books that will work. Lots of books address the same theme and often communicate a similar message about that theme. See what's already on your shelf before buying anything new.

The best advice? Look anew at the picture books you've used in the past. This time, think about how they might be applied to social emotional learning: What SEL competency is the best fit? Which focus area within the competency will it support? What is the author's message about that focus area? Then find some new titles to add dimension to SEL areas where your library may be lean.

You and I may look at the same book and I might see amazing potential for addressing self-perception. You may see instead the perfect opportunity for exploring self-discipline. We can both be right. Any of the books discussed here can be useful for multiple focus areas. The same will be true for the suggested grade-range for each book. While I am more inclined to choose some of these books for instruction in the primary grades (K–2, 3), and others for the intermediate grades (3, 4–6), remember that these parameters are only guidelines. Just because I've noted that a book works at the primary level won't always mean it's great for kindergarten.

On the other hand, books identified for primary grades could also support older readers. Sometimes a book that appeals to second graders, for example, because of its "cute" storyline delivers a message sophisticated enough for older students. Also, recognize that third grade is that gray area where children often toggle between the concrete thinking of little kids and the abstract reasoning of more mature readers.

One more point: Apologies for the books I've left out. I am already imagining your disbelief that I failed to include your absolute *favorite* title: How could she have missed *that* one? Know that I made some hard choices here. A book about books could be endless, and I hereby pass the baton to you. Described within the pages that follow are more than 200 books to get you started. The next 200? I am confident you have lots of worthy contenders.

And finally: a disclaimer. I'm suspicious of programs, strategies, and instructional resources that promise the moon: Just use this approach and "research shows" your students' performance will improve. I'm making no promises here. I believe with all my heart that I've chosen books worthy of the time you will spend reading them. But what happens next is up to you. If you use these books as catalysts for conversations about social emotional issues you may have overlooked in the past, they will serve their purpose. These stories will not singlehandedly change any child's social emotional behavior, but they can provide a start.

At last, here it is: the *full* list of 120 SEL books profiled in Part II—and just for good measure, a list of another 120 books too good to miss.

CURATED LIST OF BOOKS ALIGNED TO SEL SKILLS AND FOCUS AREAS

FOCUS AREA	PROFILED BOOKS	ADDITIONAL BOOKS
IDENTIFYING EMOTIONS	*When Sophie Gets Angry—Really, Really Angry* by Molly Bang	*The Memory String* by Eve Bunting
	Thunder Cake by Patricia Polacco	*Good-bye, 382 Shin Dang Dong* by Frances Park and Ginger Park
	Lou Gehrig: The Luckiest Man by David A. Adler	*Grandfather Gandhi* by Arun Gandhi and Bethany Hegedus
	The Rabbit Listened by Cori Doerrfeld	*There Might Be Lobsters* by Carolyn Crimi
	Mercedes and the Chocolate Pilot: A True Story of the Berlin Airlift and the Candy that Dropped from the Sky by Margot Theis Raven	*The Dark* by Lemony Snicket
ACCURATE SELF-PERCEPTION	*A Frog Thing* by Eric Drachman	*A Bad Case of Stripes* by David Shannon
	Suki's Kimono by Chieri Uegaki	*Chrysanthemum* by Kevin Henkes
	The Name Jar by Yangsook Choi	*I Am Enough* by Grace Byers
	Crown: An Ode to the Fresh Cut by Derrick Barnes	*Firenze's Light* by Jessica Collaço
	Last Stop on Market Street by Matt de la Peña	*The Invisible Boy* by Trudy Ludwig
RECOGNIZING STRENGTHS	*Home Run: The Story of Babe Ruth* by Robert Burleigh	*Mr. George Baker* by Amy Hest
	Koala Lou by Mem Fox	*Mango Moon* by Diane de Anda
	Tacky the Penguin by Helen Lester	*When Marian Sang* by Pam Muñoz Ryan
	Something Beautiful by Sharon Dennis Wyeth	*The Bat Boy and His Violin* by Gavin Curtis
	Melissa Parkington's Beautiful, Beautiful Hair by Pat Brisson	*Rosa* by Nikki Giovanni

FOCUS AREA	PROFILED BOOKS	ADDITIONAL BOOKS
SELF-CONFIDENCE	*Stand Tall, Molly Lou Melon* by Patty Lovell	*The Paper Bag Princess* by Robert Munsch
	The Little Engine That Could by Watty Piper	*Night Flight: Amelia Earhart Crosses the Atlantic* by Robert Burleigh
	Blizzard by John Rocco (Primary)	*Mirette on the High Wire* by Emily Arnold McCully
	Rosie Revere, Engineer by Andrea Beaty	*Brave Irene* by William Steig
	Little Star by A. J. Cosmo	*Wilma Unlimited: How Wilma Rudolph Became the World's Fastest Woman* by Kathleen Krull
SELF-EFFICACY	*Leo the Late Bloomer* by Robert Kraus	*Tomás and the Library Lady* by Pat Mora
	Peppe the Lamplighter by Elisa Bartone	*The Wednesday Surprise* by Eve Bunting
	The Wretched Stone by Chris Van Allsburg	*Amazing Grace* by Mary Hoffman
	Giraffes Can't Dance by Giles Andreae	*The Man Who Walked Between the Towers* by Mordicai Gerstein
	Weslandia by Paul Fleischman	*Hidden Figures: The True Story of Four Black Women and the Space Race* by Margot Lee Shetterly

FOCUS AREA	PROFILED BOOKS	ADDITIONAL BOOKS
IMPULSE CONTROL	*My Mouth Is a Volcano* by Julia Cook	*We Don't Eat Our Classmates* by Ryan T. Higgins
	Puppy Mind by Andrew Jordan Nance	*Lilly's Purple Plastic Purse* by Kevin Henkes
	The Snurtch by Sean Ferrell	*Interrupting Chicken* by David Ezra Stein
	Millie Fierce by Jane Manning	*No, David!* By David Shannon
	Testing the Ice: A True Story About Jackie Robinson by Sharon Robinson	*Wordy Birdy* by Tammi Sauer
STRESS MANAGEMENT	*Windows* by Julia Denos	*Weeds in Nana's Garden: A heartfelt story of love that helps explain Alzheimer's disease and other dementias* by Kathryn Harrison
	The Kissing Hand by Audrey Penn	*Frederick* by Leo Lionni
	A Quiet Place by Douglas Wood	*Nonni's Moon* by Julia Inserro
	Find Your Happy: A Kids Self Love Book by Patricia May	*The Story of Ferdinand* by Munro Leaf
	The Story of Ruby Bridges by Robert Coles	*My Very Own Space* by Pippa Goodhart
SETTING GOALS	*Nelson Mandela* by Kadir Nelson	*Ruby's Wish* by Shirin Yim Bridges
	Uncle Jed's Barbershop by Margaree King Mitchell	*Sixteen Years in Sixteen Seconds: The Sammy Lee Story* by Paula Yoo
	My Rows and Piles of Coins by Tolowa M. Mollel	*Dream: A Tale of Wonder, Wisdom & Wishes* by Susan V. Bosak
	Degas and the Little Dancer: A Story About Edgar Degas by Laurence Anholt	*On a Beam of Light: A Story of Albert Einstein* by Jennifer Berne
	Minty: A Story of Young Harriet Tubman by Alan Schroeder	*Grandma Gatewood Hikes the Appalachian Trail* by Jennifer Thermes

FOCUS AREA	PROFILED BOOKS	ADDITIONAL BOOKS
PLANNING AND ORGANIZATION	*Super-Completely and Totally the Messiest* by Judith Viorst	*Ten Rules of the Birthday Wish* by Beth Ferry and Tom Lichtenheld
	Galimoto by Karen Lynn Williams	*Dreamers* by Yuyi Morales
	The Librarian of Basra: A True Story from Iraq by Jeannette Winter	*Everything You Need for a Treehouse* by Carter Higgins
	As Good as Anybody: Martin Luther King, Jr. and Abraham Joshua Heschel's Amazing March toward Freedom by Richard Michelson	*The Little Red Fort* by Brenda Maier
	Down the Road by Alice Schertle	*Brick by Brick* by Giuliano Ferri
SELF-MOTIVATION	*More Than Anything Else* by Marie Bradby	*Me . . . Jane* by Patrick McDonnell
	The Boy Who Harnessed the Wind by William Kamkwamba and Bryan Mealer	*Virgie Goes to School with Us Boys* by Elizabeth Fitzgerald Howard
	Salt in His Shoes: Michael Jordan in Pursuit of a Dream by Deloris Jordan with Roslyn M. Jordan	*Miss Rumphius* by Barbara Cooney
	Snowflake Bentley by Jacqueline Briggs Martin	*Sit-In: How Four Friends Stood Up by Sitting Down* by Andrea Davis Pinkney
	After the Fall: How Humpty Dumpty Got Back Up Again by Dan Santat	*The Girl Who Never Made Mistakes* by Mark Pett and Gary Rubinstein
SELF-DISCIPLINE	*The Most Magnificent Thing* by Ashley Spires	*Drum Dream Girl: How One Girl's Courage Changed Music* by Margarita Engle
	The Bear and the Piano by David Litchfield	*The Girl and the Bicycle* by Mark Pett
	Emmanuel's Dream: The True Story of Emmanuel Ofosu Yeboah by Laurie Ann Thompson	*Brave Girl: Clara and the Shirtwaist Makers' Strike of 1909* by Michelle Markel
	Sonia Sotomayor: A Judge Grows in the Bronx by Jonah Winter	*Sojourner Truth's Step-Stomp Stride* by Andrea Davis Pinkney
	How Many Days to America? A Thanksgiving Story by Eve Bunting	*She Persisted: 13 American Women Who Changed the World* by Chelsea Clinton

FOCUS AREA	PROFILED BOOKS	ADDITIONAL BOOKS
PERSPECTIVE-TAKING	*Reflections* by Ann Jonas	*The True Story of the Three Little Pigs* by Jon Scieszka
	The Weird! Series by Erin Frankel (3-book series)	*Once Upon a Cool Motorcycle Dude* by Kevin O'Malley
	Squanto's Journey: The Story of the First Thanksgiving by Joseph Bruchac	*Voices in the Park* by Anthony Browne
	Encounter by Jane Yolen	*Masai and I* by Virginia Kroll
	Going Home by Eve Bunting	*Memoirs of a Goldfish* by Devin Scillian
EMPATHY	*Each Kindness* by Jacqueline Woodson	*Ordinary Mary's Extraordinary Deed* by Emily Pearson
	Four Feet, Two Sandals by Karen Lynn Williams and Khadra Mohammed	*The Invisible String* by Patrice Karst
	Ivan: The Remarkable True Story of the Shopping Mall Gorilla by Katherine Applegate	*Boxes for Katje* by Candace Fleming
	14 Cows for America by Carmen Agra Deedy	*Come With Me* by Holly M. McGhee
	The Journey by Francesca Sanna	*Be Kind* by Pat Zietlow Miller

FOCUS AREA	PROFILED BOOKS	ADDITIONAL BOOKS
APPRECIATING DIVERSITY	*The Other Side* by Jacqueline Woodson	*Freedom Summer* by Deborah Wiles
	One Green Apple by Eve Bunting	*The Crayon Box that Talked* by Shane DeRolf
	Heroes by Ken Mochizuki	*Lovely* by Jess Hong
	Separate Is Never Equal: Sylvia Mendez and Her Family's Fight for Desegregation by Duncan Tonatiuh	*The Big Umbrella* by Amy June Bates and Juniper Bates
	Muskrat Will Be Swimming by Cheryl Savageau	*Let the Children March* by Monica Clark-Robinson
RESPECT FOR OTHERS	*We're All Wonders* by R. J. Palacio	*Not All Princesses Dress in Pink* by Jane Yolen and Heidi E.Y. Stemple
	Julián is a Mermaid by Jessica Love	*Noah Chases the Wind* by Michelle Worthington
	Stella Brings the Family by Miriam B. Schiffer	*A handful of buttons: Picture book about family diversity* by Carmen Parets Luque
	Uniquely Wired: A Story about Autism and Its Gifts by Julia Cook	*Eggbert, the Slightly Cracked Egg* by Tom Ross
	The Summer My Father Was Ten by Pat Brisson	*America the Beautiful: Together We Stand* by Katharine Lee Bates

FOCUS AREA	PROFILED BOOKS	ADDITIONAL BOOKS
SOCIAL ENGAGEMENT	*The Relatives Came* by Cynthia Rylant	*A Sick Day for Amos McGee* by Philip C. Stead
	Mama Panya's Pancakes: A Village Tale from Kenya by Mary and Rich Chamberlin	*When I Was Young in the Mountains* by Cynthia Rylant
	Rescue and Jessica: A Life-Changing Friendship by Jessica Kensky and Patrick Downes	*Bigmama's* by Donald Crews
	Fox by Margaret Wild	*Saturdays and Teacakes* by Lester L. Laminack
	Meet Danitra Brown by Nikki Grimes	*Lubna and Pebble* by Wendy Meddour
RELATIONSHIP BUILDING	*The Recess Queen* by Alexis O'Neill	*Two Bobbies: A True Story of Hurricane Katrina, Friendship, and Survival* by Kirby Larson and Mary Nethery
	My Rotten Redheaded Older Brother by Patricia Polacco	*Boundless Grace* by Mary Hoffman
	Crow Call by Lois Lowry (intermediate)	*Pink and Say* by Patricia Polacco
	Sitti's Secrets by Naomi Shihab Nye	*Stick and Stone* by Beth Ferry
	The Raft by Jim LaMarche	*I'm New Here* by Anne Sibley O'Brien

FOCUS AREA	PROFILED BOOKS	ADDITIONAL BOOKS
TEAMWORK	*Goal!* by Mina Javaherbin	*Turtle, Turtle, Watch Out!* by April Pulley Sayre
	Brothers at Bat: The True Story of an All-Brother Baseball Team by Audrey Vernick	*Teammates* by Peter Golenbock
	A Chair for My Mother by Vera B. Williams	*Pop's Bridge* by Eve Bunting
	Swimmy by Leo Lionni	*Stone Soup* by Heather Forest
	Baseball Saved Us by Ken Mochizuki	*Roxaboxen* by Alice McLerran
COMMUNICATION	*The Sandwich Swap* by Her Majesty Queen Rania of Jordan Al Abdullah	*Happy Like Soccer* by Maribeth Boelts
	The Honest-to-Goodness Truth by Patricia C. McKissack	*Earrings!* by Judith Viorst
	My Name is Sangoel by Karen Lynn Williams and Khadra Mohammed	*The Word Collector* by Peter H. Reynolds
	Marianthe's Story: Painted Words and Spoken Memories by Aliki	*Seeds and Trees: A Children's Book about the Power of Words* by Brandon Walden
	The Day You Begin by Jacqueline Woodson	*A Boy and a Jaguar* by Alan Rabinowitz

FOCUS AREA	PROFILED BOOKS	ADDITIONAL BOOKS
IDENTIFYING PROBLEMS	*Beautiful Oops!* by Barney Saltzberg	*White Socks Only* by Evelyn Coleman
	Enemy Pie by Derek Munson	*The Pink Refrigerator* by Tim Egan
	A Thirst for Home: A Story of Water Across the World by Christine Ieronimo	*Shaking Things Up: 14 Young Women Who Changed the World* by Susan Hood
	Marisol McDonald Doesn't Match/ Marisol McDonald no combina by Monica Brown	*Lost and Found Cat: The True Story of Kunkush's Incredible Journey* by Doug Kuntz and Amy Shrodes
	Thank You, Mr. Falker by Patricia Polacco	*Ira Sleeps Over* by Bernard Waber
ANALYZING AND EVALUATING SITUATIONS	*Too Many Tamales* by Gary Soto	*Just a Dream* by Chris Van Allsburg
	Those Shoes by Maribeth Boelts	*Unspoken: A Story from the Underground Railroad* by Henry Cole
	Freedom School, Yes! by Amy Littlesugar	*Knuffle Bunny Free: An Unexpected Diversion* by Mo Willems
	The Yellow Star: The Legend of King Christian X of Denmark by Carmen Agra Deedy	*The Perfect Pet* by Margie Palatini
	The Three Questions: Based on a story by Leo Tolstoy by Jon J. Muth	*Fly Away Home* by Eve Bunting
SOLVING PROBLEMS	*Charlie Anderson* by Barbara Abercrombie	*Flowers for Sarajevo* by John McCutcheon
	Drawn Together by Minh Lê	*Beatrice's Goat* by Page McBrier
	Maddi's Fridge by Lois Brandt	*Ada's Violin: The Story of the Recycled Orchestra of Paraguay* by Susan Hood
	Dave the Potter: Artist, Poet, Slave by Laban Carrick Hill	*Steamboat School* by Deborah Hopkinson
	The Promise by Nicola Davies	*Harvesting Hope: The Story of Cesar Chavez* by Kathleen Krull

FOCUS AREA	PROFILED BOOKS	ADDITIONAL BOOKS
ETHICAL RESPONSIBILITY	*Fireflies* by Julie Brinckloe	*Hey, Little Ant* by Phillip and Hannah Hoose
	The Can Man by Laura E. Williams	*Mama Miti: Wangari Maathai and the Trees of Kenya* by Donna Jo Napoli
	Up the Learning Tree by Marcia Vaughan	*Good People Everywhere* by Lynea Gillen
	A Bike Like Sergio's by Maribeth Boelts	*Passage to Freedom: The Sugihara Story* by Ken Mochizuki
	The Empty Pot by Demi	*The Sad Little Fact* by Jonah Winter
REFLECTING	*The Lotus Seed* by Sherry Garland	*This Is the Rope: A Story From the Great Migration* by Jacqueline Woodson
	The Matchbox Diary by Paul Fleischman	*Tea with Milk* by Allen Say
	The Dress and the Girl by Camille Andros	*Alma and How She Got Her Name* by Juana Martinez-Neal
	The Fish House Door by Robert F. Baldwin	*Islandborn* by Junot Díaz
	A Different Pond by Bao Phi	*Thunder Boy Jr.* by Sherman Alexie

Moving Forward with Action Steps

Chapters 1 and 2 build a foundation for understanding the information in Part II, so it makes sense to read these chapters sequentially. However, the same is not true for Chapters 3–7. Each of the following chapters addresses a stand-alone SEL competency. You'll want to begin where your students need the most support. Where would be the best place for *you* to begin? Consider both the competency and the focus area. To help make that decision, this section concludes with Chart 2.5: Action Steps for SEL Competencies and Focus Areas.

2.5: ACTION STEPS FOR SEL COMPETENCIES AND FOCUS AREAS

SEL COMPETENCY: SELF-AWARENESS

The ability to accurately recognize one's own emotions, thoughts, and values and how they influence behavior. The ability to accurately assess one's strengths and limitations, with a well-grounded sense of confidence, optimism, and a "growth mindset."

FOCUS AREA	REASON FOR PRIORITIZING	ACTION STEPS
Identifying Emotions		
Accurate Self-Perception		
Recognizing Strengths		
Self-Confidence		
Self-Efficacy		

SEL COMPETENCY: SELF-MANAGEMENT

The ability to successfully regulate one's emotions, thoughts, and behaviors in different situations — effectively managing stress, controlling impulses, and motivating oneself. The ability to set and work toward personal and academic goals.

FOCUS AREA	REASON FOR PRIORITIZING	ACTION STEPS
Impulse Control		
Stress Management		
Setting Goals		
Planning and Organization		
Self-Motivation		
Self-Discipline		

SEL COMPETENCY: SOCIAL AWARENESS

The ability to take the perspective of and empathize with others, including those from diverse backgrounds and cultures. The ability to understand social and ethical norms for behavior and to recognize family, school, and community resources and supports.

FOCUS AREA	REASON FOR PRIORITIZING	ACTION STEPS
Perspective-Taking		
Empathy		
Appreciating Diversity		
Respect for Others		

SEL COMPETENCY: RELATIONSHIP SKILLS

The ability to establish and maintain healthy and rewarding relationships with diverse individuals and groups. The ability to communicate clearly, listen well, cooperate with others, resist inappropriate social pressure, negotiate conflict constructively, and seek and offer help when needed.

FOCUS AREA	REASON FOR PRIORITIZING	ACTION STEPS
Social Engagement		
Relationship-Building		
Teamwork		
Communication		

SEL COMPETENCY: RESPONSIBLE DECISION-MAKING

The ability to make constructive choices about personal behavior and social interactions based on ethical standards, safety concerns, and social norms. The realistic evaluation of consequences of various actions, and a consideration of the well-being of oneself and others.

FOCUS AREA	REASON FOR PRIORITIZING	ACTION STEPS
Identifying Problems		
Analyzing and Evaluating Situations		
Solving Problems		
Ethical Responsibility		
Reflecting		

PART II
UNDERSTANDING SOCIAL EMOTIONAL LEARNING THROUGH PICTURE BOOKS

CHAPTER 3

SELF-AWARENESS: A PLACE TO BEGIN FOR SOCIAL EMOTIONAL LEARNING

In life, social emotional learning has no real beginning or end. It's more of a circle that expands indefinitely. As you learn more about yourself and how to manage your emotions, you begin to interact differently with others, build stronger relationships, and make more responsible decisions—which gives you more insight into yourself and what's important to you. And so, the cycle continues. Self-awareness is a good place to begin because without an understanding of who we are individually, we have little to bring to our relationships with others.

CASEL defines self-awareness, the first competency of social emotional learning, as

"The ability to accurately recognize one's own emotions, thoughts, and values, and how they influence behavior. The ability to accurately assess one's strengths and limitations, with a well-grounded sense of confidence, optimism, and a 'growth' mindset" ("Core SEL Competencies," n.d.).

This competency is divided into five focus areas.

- Identifying emotions
- Accurate self-perception
- Recognizing strengths
- Self-Confidence
- Self-Efficacy

The most important consideration for the focus areas within this competency, as with all competencies and focus areas, is that there are many ways of looking at each one, and many messages to share. The first focus area within self-awareness, identifying emotions, is a perfect example: While identifying feelings appears basic, once we begin to probe below the surface, we see its intricacies.

Identifying Emotions

We often use the terms *feelings* and *emotions* interchangeably, but technically, they are not the same. Emotions are a physical response or reaction to something we experience. We cry, we laugh, our heart may begin to beat faster. For example, if you are in a plane and the air suddenly becomes turbulent, your heart rate may quicken. Labeling this as fear is the *feeling* generated by the emotion. Some travelers might label this as *thrilling*, but I wouldn't be one of them. Feelings are subjective. It's our capacity to use language to name these feelings that makes us human (Hampton, 2015). Technicality aside, CASEL and other organizations use these terms synonymously as they apply to instruction; I shall do the same.

WHAT WE HOPE TO SEE IN THE CLASSROOM REGARDING IDENTIFYING EMOTIONS, AND WHAT WE SOMETIMES SEE INSTEAD

It makes sense that identifying emotions (or feelings) is the first focus area within the first SEL competency, for if students can't name their feelings, how can we help them understand them and build on this foundation for either personal or social growth? In classrooms, I see two issues that commonly stand in the way. First, elementary students are often stuck in a rut when it comes to identifying a feeling, either their own or that of a character in a book. They are happy, sad, mad, or something else that is very general. There are seldom shades of difference: cheerful, pleased, thrilled, ecstatic. And they sometimes miss the mark entirely. They will claim that a character is sad when really she is worried, or frightened, or desperate. So, one thing we can do is encourage more precise labels for feelings. Lists of feeling words are easy to find through a quick Internet search. Some of these lists also include emojis or other visual references.

The second issue is that students sometimes *stop* with the identification of the feeling, whereas this should instead be a place to *start*: What caused you (or a character) to feel so frightened? What could you do next to feel less frightened? To get that conversation started, consider the following questions.

ENHANCING CLASSROOM CULTURE: QUESTIONS FOR TEACHERS TO ASK THEMSELVES ABOUT IDENTIFYING EMOTIONS

1. How can I help my students develop more precise labels for their feelings?

2. What feeling or emotion would be especially useful for my students to understand more deeply? What leads me to think this?

3. What kinds of feelings-problems should students try to solve independently? How can I help them recognize that *they* are capable of resolving them?

4. What kinds of feelings-problems usually require a helper to resolve? How can I help my students understand the difference between problems they can solve alone and ones that require a helper?

5. When is being a good listener the best support for a feelings-problem?

6. When is *hope* important? How can I communicate the power of hope in a person's life?

WHAT TO LOOK FOR IN BOOKS ABOUT IDENTIFYING EMOTIONS

There are several qualities I look for in books about feelings. In nearly all stories, characters experience feelings of one kind or another, so on the surface, finding a book for this focus area seems simple. But it can be challenging to find just the right book. What feeling are you targeting? What message about that feeling or ways of handling that feeling do you want to impart? For most of us, we experience a range of feelings, often in quick succession. So, I look for this in books, too—a character who may be feeling one way at the outset of the story, but then differently by the end, with some variation in between.

I mostly look for books that address *how* characters come to terms with their feelings—through their own problem-solving strategies, or someone else's support. For young children, I look for negative feelings to be resolved. For students at all grade levels, *how* the feelings-problem is resolved is what sets each book apart. Chart 3.1: Books Aligned to Identifying Emotions lists books that do the job well.

CHART 3.1: BOOKS ALIGNED TO IDENTIFYING EMOTIONS

THE MESSAGE	THE BOOK
Sometimes you can resolve feelings-problems on your own	*When Sophie Gets Angry—Really, Really Angry* by Molly Bang (primary)
Sometimes you need help solving a feelings-problem	*Thunder Cake* by Patricia Polacco (primary)
Sometimes just "being there" for a friend is the best comfort	*The Rabbit Listened* by Cori Doerrfeld (primary and intermediate)
Try to stay positive when times are tough	*Lou Gehrig: The Luckiest Man* by David A. Adler (intermediate)
Hope is the most important feeling of all	*Mercedes and the Chocolate Pilot: A True Story of the Berlin Airlift and the Candy that Dropped from the Sky* by Margot Theis Raven (intermediate)

Sometimes you can resolve feelings-problems on your own

There are plenty of serious situations in classrooms that teachers need to get involved in, but there are other "he said/she said" skirmishes that I try to let students work out on their own. "No, I didn't see which one of you was in line first, but I'm pretty sure you can solve this on your own," I told the two guilty-looking parties standing in front of me. "We've talked about things you can do when you're angry: Walk away from the problem, offer to compromise, and agree to cool down before continuing to discuss it." To help students solve anger problems independently, read **When Sophie Gets Angry—Really, Really Angry**.

At the start of the story, Sophie gets into a tussle with her younger brother about a toy. Much to her dismay, her brother is the victor, and Sophie becomes furious. She *explodes*, with a full-out temper tantrum. She heads for the woods. But there, surrounded by the quiet, she begins to calm down. By the time she returns home, all of her anger is gone, and Sophie is her happy self once again.

I like that this book affirms that anger happens—the tricky part is how to resolve it. But the real strength of this book is that it shows a character taming her own feelings. She walks away from a bad situation and gives herself some breathing space. This is the best-case scenario; we want students to see that they, too, can gain control over their emotions by taking charge of the way they respond. Sometimes they can solve their feelings-problems themselves.

Sometimes you need help to solve a feelings-problem

Other times, characters (and children) can't manage their feelings alone. That's when a helper (a teacher, parent, or friend) needs to step in for support. In the classroom, and in life, there are many incidents where this is the case.

In *Thunder Cake,* Tricia's grandmother recognizes the girl's fear of thunderstorms, and suggests that together they bake a "thunder cake." As the storm rolls in, the girl is distracted by gathering the ingredients, mixing them, and pouring the batter into pans. By the time the storm crashes overhead, the cake is ready, and grandmother and granddaughter are enjoying it too much to worry about the storm outside.

Sometimes, just "being there" for a friend is the best comfort

It's okay to admit when you're scared or worried, or experiencing some other feeling that's getting in the way of your most positive self. In fact, just talking about that feeling with someone you trust can be a useful step toward feeling better. But sometimes students don't feel like talking. This can be difficult for teachers because we pride ourselves on our capacity to comfort, and that typically involves the wisdom of our words. But maybe it's not our words that matter most.

In *The Rabbit Listened*, Rabbit lends us a bit of *his* wisdom. Taylor builds a glorious block tower, but in a single whoosh, it crashes to the floor. Several nursery animals arrive to suggest "cures": The chicken wants to talk about it (cluck, cluck). The bear wants to shout about it (grrrr). The elephant wants to remember exactly how the tower looked and rebuild it. Other animals come too, but when Taylor doesn't feel like heeding any of their suggestions, they leave. Then Rabbit appears, ever so quietly, and sits right next to Taylor. For a while they are just quiet together until Taylor is ready to talk. Rabbit listens while Taylor talks and shouts and remembers. At last, Taylor explains his plan to rebuild the tower, excited, by the possibility.

Sometimes the best way to help is simply by being present and showing you care— good advice for both adults and children. Talk with students about times when a friend might not feel like talking right away, but would welcome the comfort they bring by just being nearby.

Try to stay positive when times are tough

Some difficult situations students face at home spill over into the classroom, affecting their social emotional well-being. Parents lose their jobs. They get divorced. Someone gets sick or passes away. Our heart breaks for kids who get caught in a tangle of adult problems that they are helpless to solve. I'll never forget the conversation I had with one fifth grader I'll call Dana: "No homework *again*?" I sighed. This was the third time in as many days that Dana had not completed her math homework, and I was losing patience. "No," she said, "I don't have it," and then her eyes filled with tears, "because if I go out bowling with my mother at night, then she won't go drinking before she comes home."

While every difficult situation is different, we can try to help students stay strong in the face of adversity through examples of people (or characters) who have responded to crises with grace and a positive outlook. A real-life hero who modeled great resilience was Lou Gehrig. In *Lou Gehrig, The Luckiest Man,* Gehrig speaks to his Yankees teammates at his farewell dinner following his ALS diagnosis. He assures them that he is, in fact the "luckiest man" because he had a loving family, the good fortune to spend his life engaged in the sport he loves, and is surrounded by people he respects and who admire him. Kids love this book, and its affirming point of view somehow dominates its ultimately sad ending. After reading this book, I like to talk to students about reflecting on something "lucky" in their life that might take the sting out of the not-so-good stuff.

FEATURED BOOK FOR IDENTIFYING EMOTIONS: *Mercedes and the Chocolate Pilot: A True Story of the Berlin Airlift and the Candy that Dropped Out of the Sky* by Margot Theis Raven

Hope is the most important feeling of all
While I generally think students' needs should guide our selection of books about feelings, I also believe there's one feeling we absolutely want to target. That feeling is hope. Even if the problem they are experiencing in the moment is so devastating that staying positive might not be realistic, we also want students to know that someday, somehow, life will get better. One of my favorite books for inspiring hope is *Mercedes and the Chocolate Pilot: A True Story of the Berlin Airlift and the Candy that Dropped Out of the Sky*.

This is the book I feature for identifying emotions, the one for which questions will be provided for Seven Thinking Boxes. Although the topic is handled sensitively, its focus on war and the background knowledge needed about World War II might make it better suited to intermediate grade students.

The story opens on a double page spread of bombed out Berlin. There are no words, but children immediately recognize the devastation of war. As the story itself begins, Mercedes' mom is reading her an article about a "Chocolate Pilot," who, in addition to dropping food from those big "silver birds" to Berliners who have been cut off by the Russian Blockade, is also dropping candy for nearby children. Mercedes is beyond excited and begs her mother to take her to Tempelhof Air Base, where the pilot is dropping the candy.

Unfortunately, the little girl's excitement doesn't last, for the hands of other children are always quicker than her own. She decides to write the pilot a letter explaining her plight, and before long, a small package arrives—candy of course, and with it a note from the pilot himself. Mercedes is elated, and the story ends with the famed plane flying west from Berlin, the airlift over. What a nice story, you think to yourself. But in fact, the best part is yet to come.

The epilogue at the end of the book provides an update. Fast forward nearly 30 years. It's 1972 and the little girl is grown, a mother and a pilot herself, stationed at Tempelhof. The Chocolate Pilot, Lt. Gail Halvorsen, is back in Germany where he now commands the Tempelhof base. Mercedes invites Halvorsen to dinner, and after the meal, hands him a note that she pulls from a drawer. It's the note he wrote to her so many years ago, and of course he is stunned.

Why did Halvorsen continue his candy mission? He explains to Mercedes that with the chocolate and a few sticks of gum, he saw in the children's eyes hope for a better tomorrow. Although I find it hard to read this book without becoming emotional at the end (no matter how many times I read it), it's worth the misty eyes because its message is such a powerful one. The questions that follow for Seven Thinking Boxes will help you and your students dig deeper into this book.

SEVEN THINKING BOXES

Questions to ask about *Mercedes and the Chocolate Pilot: A True Story of the Berlin Airlift and the Candy that Dropped from the Sky* by Margot Theis Raven
SEL Competency: Self-Awareness   Focus: Identifying Emotions

PLAIN CARDBOARD BOX	**BASIC THINKING** Identify at least two times in this story that Mercedes felt hopeful. Why did she feel hopeful?
PUZZLE BOX	**PUZZLING DETAILS** Find a quote in this book that you think shows Mercedes' <u>strongest</u> feeling. What is the feeling? Why did you choose this quote?
HEART BOX	**FEELINGS** This story is not just about Mercedes' feelings, but also about the Chocolate Pilot's feelings. What feelings does the pilot show throughout the story? Why do you think he continued to drop candy?
UNUSUAL BOX	**CREATIVE THINKING** How did Mercedes' creativity help her solve the candy problem?
BROKEN BOX	**PROBLEMS AND ISSUES** What do you think is the biggest problem faced by the characters in this story? How do feelings make a difference to the solution of this problem? Explain using details from the text.
TREASURE BOX	**SOMETHING TO TREASURE** Why do you think Mercedes treasured the note she received from the Chocolate Pilot and kept it forever?
TOOL BOX	**AUTHOR'S TOOLS** This story includes an <u>epilogue</u>. What is an epilogue and how is it different from the rest of a story? Why do you think the author wrote this part of the book as an epilogue, and not as a continuation of the story itself? How does the epilogue make the feelings of both Mercedes and the Chocolate Pilot clearer?

SEVEN THINKING BOXES

Questions to ask about any book for identifying emotions

PLAIN CARDBOARD BOX	**BASIC THINKING** • What feeling (or feelings) do you find in this book? Give some specific examples. • Is there one feeling that seems <u>most</u> important in this book? What is it? What evidence supports your opinion?
PUZZLE BOX	**PUZZLING DETAILS** • What detail in this book shows the main character's feelings most strongly? Why did you choose this detail? • If you could change one detail in this book to show a character's feelings even more strongly, what would you change? Why?
HEART BOX	**FEELINGS** • Did the feelings in this book change? Where? How did they change from the beginning to the end? • Would you have felt the same way as the character about the problem in this book? Why or why not?
UNUSUAL BOX	**CREATIVE THINKING** • How did creative thinking help to solve a feelings problem in this book? • How else could the character have solved a feelings problem in this story? Why would this have been a good solution?
BROKEN BOX	**PROBLEMS AND ISSUES** • Give an example of a character who was able to solve a feelings problem by herself or himself. Why was this character able to solve the problem independently? • Give an example of a character who needed help to solve a feelings problem? Who helped? How? Why did this problem need someone's help?
TREASURE BOX	**SOMETHING TO TREASURE** • What message about feelings do you think the author wants us to treasure from this book? What details in the story show this? • What do you think the main character treasured the most in this story? What details show this?
TOOL BOX	**AUTHOR'S TOOLS** • What tools did the author use to show different feelings in this book? (Some examples might be: dialogue, similes, personification, strong verbs, descriptive words, or something else) • What illustration do you think does the best job of showing a feeling in this book? What is the feeling? What does the illustrator do to show this feeling so strongly?

Accurate Self-Perception

If we believe that perception is the way we think about or understand something or someone (Merriam-Webster Definition of "perception") then *self*-perception is the way we think about or understand ourselves. The challenge is that there are so many factors that impact the way we see ourselves. Students need help answering the very basic question: Who am I? And then they need some help sorting out the factors that enhance or impede their self-view—those that are pushing them to soar or pulling them down.

WHAT WE HOPE TO SEE IN THE CLASSROOM REGARDING ACCURATE SELF-PERCEPTION, AND WHAT WE SOMETIMES SEE INSTEAD

When all is going well, we see students who view themselves as lovable and capable, and are at the same time, humble and modest. These kids typically embrace new things with a can-do attitude and engage socially with their peers in a spirit of easy give-and-take. They hold themselves to high standards, but not so high that they make themselves miserable, always reaching for something just beyond their grasp. They smile a lot. Even an outsider can quickly spot them as happy members of our classroom.

We wish we had more of these happy, can-do kids. Other children in our room may be equally capable, perhaps even smarter. But they struggle with feelings of inadequacy: *I'm not good enough at sports (or math or writing). I'm too fat (or skinny or short). I'm not pretty. I can't learn this new thing.* For these students, *can't* dominates their self-view—and it doesn't matter how much we try to convince them otherwise. Then there are the issues outside our classroom that compound the situation: bullying, shaming, poverty, a chaotic home life, and so much more. How does our classroom culture matter to our students' self-perception, and how can we help strengthen it? To start, reflect on the questions below.

ENHANCING CLASSROOM CULTURE: QUESTIONS FOR TEACHERS TO ASK THEMSELVES ABOUT ACCURATE SELF-PERCEPTION

1. How can I more effectively recognize students whose behavior is driven by negative self-perception, and the factors that might be causing that perception?

2. How can I be a better role model of compassion and other attributes that I want my students to emulate?

3. What books appropriate to my grade level show characters displaying or achieving a healthy view of self? How can I use these books to generate discussions about self-perception in my classroom?

4. How can I help my students build relationships that heighten rather than diminish their sense of self-worth?

5. How can I help my students become stewards of their classmates' sense of self-worth in their day-to-day interactions with each other?

6. As a teacher, how can I help students develop a positive self-image?

WHAT TO LOOK FOR IN BOOKS ABOUT ACCURATE SELF-PERCEPTION

Low self-esteem often seems a bigger beast than we can tame. However, books are excellent conversation starters. While it's sometimes awkward and feels too personal to broach topics of self-worth with students directly, story characters are the perfect catalysts for discussion. Bottom line: I want students to recognize through the literature I choose that low self-esteem need not be a permanent affliction. They can (and should) feel good about themselves. And most importantly, *they* can make it happen! Hence, I select books that propose *realistic* self-perception, no exaggerated superpowers. I look for books about being honest with one's self, and why that matters. I look for books that feature a character's pride in their name, and stories about small moments that matter. There are wonderful books that meet all of these needs, listed in Chart 3.2: Books Aligned to Accurate Self-Perception.

CHART 3.2: BOOKS ALIGNED TO ACCURATE SELF-PERCEPTION

THE MESSAGE	THE BOOK
Be YOUR best self	*A Frog Thing* by Eric Drachman (primary)
Have the courage to be yourself	*Suki's Kimono* by Chieri Uegaki (primary and Intermediate)
Be proud of your name	*The Name Jar* by Yangsook Choi (primary and intermediate)
The little things in life can make a big difference to how we feel about ourselves	*Crown: An Ode to the Fresh Cut* by Derrick Barnes (intermediate)
How you feel about yourself depends on your life choices	*Last Stop on Market Street* by Matt de la Peña (primary and intermediate)

Be YOUR best self (No super-powers needed)

We focus a lot on children who have expectations for themselves that are too low. Those who don't want to take a risk, even a small one, because they think they'll fail. But other times children need to be reined in because they imagine abilities beyond what is realistic. "Here's what I'm going to do in reading workshop today," a third grader once told me. "I'm going to finish reading *Harry Potter*. Then I'm going to write a play about the book." Less than an hour remained in the reading block that day. The student had 100 pages to go in her book. And adapting the entire novel to a play might take a wee bit longer than even several weeks of reading workshop. This little girl needed some help establishing more attainable long- and short-term goals for herself.

I love the book **A Frog Thing** as a place to begin when talking about accurate self-perception. In this story, froggie Frank's greatest wish is to fly. After all, his parents once told him that if he tries hard enough, he can do *anything*. He does try hard, but the results are dismal. He looks to his parents for support, but they tell him as gently as possible that when they told him he could do anything he wanted, they meant any *frog* thing: "See, flying is a . . . BIRD THING . . ." In the end, Frankie recognizes that *swimming* is a frog thing—and his ability to swim saves the day! He rescues a little bird that falls into his pond. He decides to focus on being the best swimmer ever.

Even primary students can set *realistic* expectations about what they can accomplish. Although I often use this book with young children, the beauty of books used for SEL is that these stories often have a message that is sophisticated enough for older students, too.

Have the courage to be yourself

In every class I've taught, there are one or two kids that other students perceive as "cool." The criteria that elevates them to this status isn't always clear, but somehow, everyone just *knows*. This leads to lots of little clones with the same hairstyle, name brand sweatshirt, and trendy sneakers. But alongside those students who long to blend in, there are also children who are oblivious of trendsetters, preferring to march to their own beat. My daughter was one of these do-your-own-thing kind of kids. Everyone else came to kindergarten in jeans, but Caitlin regularly showed up in party dresses and patent leather shoes. She was a lot like Suki in **Suki's Kimono**. Perhaps Suki can help your students find the courage to be their own person instead of following the crowd.

Suki is a girl of deep convictions. She insists on wearing her new blue kimono on the first day of school, undeterred by the admonitions of her mother and sisters that the other children in her class will think her a bit odd. But this isn't a case of obstinance or rebellion. Suki chooses to wear her kimono because it was a gift from her grandmother, and wearing it reminds her of all the fun they had together the previous summer. Suki demonstrates the courage to be true to herself. Talk about this with students.

What is important enough to them that they would choose to follow their heart rather than follow the crowd?

Be proud of your name

We can't forget that our identity, our sense of self, is closely linked to our name. This can make it tough for kids who are targets of bullying due to a name that's convenient for teasing: Fat Pat, Jolly Roger. Other times, students—often immigrants—want to shed names that, to them, don't sound "American" enough. There are lots of picture books with various messages about names. *Chrysanthemum* by Kevin Henkes is a perennial favorite related to name bullying. Here I profile **The Name Jar** for its messages about both name bullying and names of ethnic origin.

Unhei is teased on the bus on her very first day in an American school. Kids can't pronounce her Korean name and make a show of mispronouncing it. When she arrives in her classroom, she tells her teacher she has not yet chosen her new American name. She doesn't want to be different, she explains to her surprised mom that evening. But what new name should she choose? A large jar is on her desk in the morning, and over the next few days, her classmates fill it with names they think Unhei might like. Some are appealing. But her Korean name reminds her of her grandmother, now so far away. And then a cashier at the Korean grocery reminds her of its meaning: grace. All Korean names have a special meaning. In the end, Unhei keeps her name. Even better, she stands before her class and explains why. It's part of who she is. What are the stories behind your students' names? How did they get their nicknames? How are their names part of who *they* are?

The little things in life can make a big difference in how we feel about ourselves

One of my most vivid memories of the impact that the little things have on a student's self-perception is the conversation I had with Anaya, a fourth grader, who nearly knocked down several classmates one morning to reach my desk before her peers arrived. "The best thing happened last night," she whispered, about three inches from my face. "I got an email from Stephanie and she invited me to her birthday party." What was it I saw reflected in that child's face—joy, pride, relief? "That's great," I replied. "You'll have fun." But what I was really thinking was, *What if she hadn't gotten this email?* I never would have known. But what I knew then was that in that brief moment, Anaya felt good about herself. It was a small victory for a child who didn't get many party invitations.

One of my favorite books about self-image is **Crown: An Ode to a Fresh Cut**. Just looking at the cover of this feel-good story makes me smile. What this book offers most is a reminder that it's sometimes life's small details that move a child's personal mood meter from "Feeling Okay" to "Feeling AMAZING"—like they can conquer the world. This is the case for the young boy in the story. He goes to the barber and gets a new haircut. It's "just" a haircut. But when he looks in the mirror, reflected back is not just his new 'do, but a "brilliant, blazing star." Among other wondrous feats, he's sure he can easily rearrange the principal's honor roll. It's a small thing, but for that short moment his self-esteem soars. How can we unleash this pride in our students? Do we know each of them well enough to imagine a small thing that could make a big difference?

FEATURED BOOK FOR SELF-PERCEPTION: *Last Stop on Market Street*
by Matt de la Peña

How you feel about yourself depends on your life choices
I fear there are many students who believe their self-perception is fixed. Good or bad, it is who they are, and nothing is about to change. This makes it even harder to reach students who need a self-perception adjustment. I walked into a sixth-grade social studies classroom recently and as I began the close reading lesson I was teaching, I noticed Jax slouched over his desk, head mostly disappeared into the hood of his sweatshirt. I asked him to sit up, which he did, though there was no mistaking his body language that screamed, *leave me alone.*

As students completed the task that followed the lesson, I stopped by Jax's desk. "What evidence did you find, Jax?" No comment, but he did pass me his paper. To my surprise he had answered the question, and his response was good: "This is great, Jax. Would it be okay if I call on you to read this when we share our work?" He didn't say no. "Let's hear from Jax," I invited, when I pulled the group back together. And then he spoke, quietly, to be sure. But he read his answer as if he did it every day.

"How did you get that kid to participate?" the classroom teacher asked later. "I've barely heard his voice all year." Truthfully, I have no idea. I think I just got lucky. I do know that we can't give up on the students in our classroom who seem perpetually tuned out. This may be the day that a tiny step forward opens the door to the next step, and the one after that.

My final title in the area of self-perception, and the one featured with accompanying Thinking Box questions, is **Last Stop on Market Street**. On the surface, this story doesn't even seem to focus on self-perception, and perhaps appears better-suited to discussions of empathy. But look more closely. As the story opens, CJ is getting onto a bus with his nana, complaining loudly that they must make this trip in a bus, not a car. (All his friends have cars.) Nana responds that *they* are the lucky ones because they get to ride in this "fire breather." Despite his grumpiness, Nana perseveres, reminding CJ to greet other passengers with a smile. CJ and Nana finally arrive at the soup kitchen where they will help serve lunch to a roomful of people, who are obviously happy to see them. In the end, CJ tells Nana that he is so glad they came.

I think **Last Stop on Market Street** is a fable for teachers as much as children. It reminds us that self-perception isn't ready-made, but shaped—and we can help shape it. Early in the story, CJ longs for the material wares of his friends. All the while, Nana leads by example, showing kindness, and expecting CJ to follow suit. By the last page, CJ "gets it." As teachers, we need to be like Nana, modeling the compassion we hope to see in our students and helping them see that a kind, thoughtful person *is* the type of person they wish to be. The questions that follow for Seven Thinking Boxes will help your students think more seriously about CJ's self-perception, and their own.

SEVEN THINKING BOXES

Questions for *Last Stop on Market Street* by Matt de la Peña
SEL Competency: Self-Awareness   Focus: Accurate Self-Perception

PLAIN CARDBOARD BOX	**BASIC THINKING** What were some of the things CJ complained about at the beginning of the story? Name at least three things. What does this show about CJ at the beginning of the story?
PUZZLE BOX	**PUZZLING DETAILS** CJ changed a lot by the end of the story. Do you think he said anything earlier in the book that he later regretted? Explain.
HEART BOX	**FEELINGS** At the beginning of this story Nana was the one who showed compassion. But by the end, CJ shows compassion, too. What do you think led to this change of feelings?
UNUSUAL BOX	**CREATIVE THINKING** Nana showed creative thinking several times in this story when CJ asked for something that he could not have. Give two examples that show this. How did this creative thinking help? What might have happened if Nana had just told CJ "no?"
BROKEN BOX	**PROBLEMS AND ISSUES** How does the problem in this story relate to self-perception? How does this problem get solved?
TREASURE BOX	**SOMETHING TO TREASURE** What does CJ learn about himself in this story? How does he learn it? Can you learn anything from CJ and Nana?
TOOL BOX	**AUTHOR'S TOOLS** This book won two awards: The Newbery and the Caldecott. The Newbery is awarded each year to the book considered to be the best <u>literature</u> for children. The Caldecott is awarded to the illustrator of the best <u>picture book</u> each year. Why do you think this book won both these awards?

SEVEN THINKING BOXES

Questions for teachers to ask about *any* book for accurate self-perception

PLAIN CARDBOARD BOX 	**BASIC THINKING** • What details in the story show how the main character (or another character) was feeling about himself/herself? • What details in the story show a <u>change</u> in how the main character (or another character) felt about himself/herself?
PUZZLE BOX 	**PUZZLING DETAILS** • Find a detail in the book that you think <u>best</u> shows how the main character (or another character) felt about himself. • Find something a character said in this story that was probably hurtful to another character's feeling about herself or himself. Why were these words so troubling?
HEART BOX 	**FEELINGS** • How did the main character (or other character) *feel* about himself or herself based on his/her sense of self? • How did the main character (or other character) make *other* people feel based on his/her sense of self?
UNUSUAL BOX 	**CREATIVE THINKING** • Did creative thinking play a part in changing anyone's self-perception in this story? Explain. • Can you think of another way a character might have handled a situation to have a more positive effect on someone's sense of self-worth?
BROKEN BOX 	**PROBLEMS AND ISSUES** • How is the main problem in the story connected to someone's feelings about themselves? • Did the solution to the problem in this story lead to anyone's improved self-perception? Explain using details from the book.
TREASURE BOX 	**SOMETHING TO TREASURE** • What would the main character treasure most by gaining a more positive feeling about himself or herself? What details in the story show this? • What new understanding about self-perception did you find most valuable from reading this book?
TOOL BOX 	**AUTHOR'S TOOLS** • How did the author <u>show</u> how a character was feeling about himself or herself without <u>telling</u> you directly about the feeling? • How does the author make the characters in this story seem <u>real</u>, so you can see how they feel about themselves? (Think about words, actions, inside thoughts, and body language)

Recognizing Strengths

Let's agree that *strengths* are the things we do in our everyday lives that we are good at, though the reverse isn't always true. The things we're not as good at aren't necessarily *weaknesses* or areas of *need*. Rather, they may be areas we haven't explored sufficiently, or that we've barely been exposed to. People might have artistic or athletic strengths. They could demonstrate exceptional leadership or critical thinking skills. They may excel at math or writing. I like to think that there are as many strengths as there are people in the world. One of the finest tributes to any teacher I ever heard was shared by a parent at my mother's retirement party: "In Mrs. Naumann's class, every student feels gifted." My mother, an elementary school teacher for many years, could find the strengths in any child. She brought out the best in them. She found gifts they didn't know they had.

WHAT WE HOPE TO SEE IN THE CLASSROOM REGARDING RECOGNIZING STRENGTHS, AND WHAT WE SOMETIMES SEE INSTEAD

We have tons of data about students' guided reading levels, their proficiency with constructed responses, and the skills and strategies they apply to decoding words. But how much do we know about the kinds of books they like to read? Do we know who's great at drawing, at playing the piano, at playing basketball? Before we can celebrate and nurture our students' strengths, we need to know what they are—or help them discover new passions and possibilities for themselves. For this we need to provide them with opportunities to broaden their horizons. How can we be that one teacher students will reflect on when they're 20 or 40 or 60 years old and think to themselves: *If it hadn't been for Mr. _____ , I never would have* ... How much do you know about *your* students' individual strengths? These questions will get you started.

ENHANCING CLASSROOM CULTURE: QUESTIONS FOR TEACHERS TO ASK THEMSELVES ABOUT RECOGNIZING STRENGTHS

1. Can I identify a strength of each of student in my classroom? Can I identify a strength of each student that they demonstrate outside of school?

2. What experiences can I provide to my students that will help them discover new areas of interest that might evolve into strengths?

3. Is there anything about my classroom or school that might be standing in the way of students recognizing or pursuing areas of strength? How could I make a difference?

4. Have I ever had a conversation with my students about the importance of recognizing and pursuing areas of strength? If not, what could I include in this conversation?

5. How can I help my students connect with mentors who can support specific areas of strength?

6. What would it look like if I taught to students' *strengths* instead of to their weaknesses? What does it mean to teach to a student's *strength*?

WHAT TO LOOK FOR IN BOOKS ABOUT RECOGNIZING STRENGTHS

What do we want kids to understand about recognizing strengths? First, it's not about physical strength; it's about having a mindset that finds joy in something that they're good at. We want students to gain a better grasp of their own strengths and the strengths of others, and know how to nurture these gifts. We want them to recognize what can get in the way of developing their strengths, how they can be empowered by feeling strong, and that they are loved not for what they're good at, but for the person they are inside. I look for these qualities in books about recognizing strengths. Five books are profiled here in Chart 3.3: Books Aligned to Recognizing Strengths.

CHART 3.3 BOOKS ALIGNED TO RECOGNIZING STRENGTHS

THE MESSAGE	THE BOOK
Nurture your gifts	*Home Run: The Story of Babe Ruth* by Robert Burleigh (intermediate)
You are loved with or without your strengths	*Koala Lou* by Mem Fox (primary)
Appreciate the unique strengths of others	*Tacky the Penguin* by Helen Lester (primary)
Recognizing your strengths is empowering	*Something Beautiful* by Sharon Dennis Wyeth (primary and intermediate)
Compassion is a strength	*Melissa Parkington's Beautiful, Beautiful Hair* by Pat Brisson (primary)

Nurture your gifts

When I taught third grade, I was amused by the number of my students who stated quite matter-of-factly that when they grew up, they were going to play baseball for a major league team, football for the NFL, or hockey for the NHL. The exact team changed from year to year, depending on the standings and their popularity at the time. Other students were headed to Broadway or the Olympics. Of course, these dreams *do* come true for some children, especially those who recognize that it's not just the dream that leads to greatness, but hard work as well. There are as many role models as there are dreams to dream. Babe Ruth is one example.

We'd all like to score a few figurative "home runs" to impress the world with our excellence, but Babe Ruth scored 714 *real* home runs. The Babe was a legend in his own time, a sports superstar. Although there are many books about Babe Ruth, I especially like **Home Run: The Story of Babe Ruth** because the writing is more poetry than prose and the author (Robert Burleigh) captures not just Ruth's skill, but the exquisiteness of his art. As the ball cracks off the bat, the author states, "Babe already knows. The perfectness. The feeling. The boy-fire inside the body of a man." As students build an understanding of their own strengths, an icon of unquestionable merit is surely worth reading about. What's more, this icon demonstrated that greatness is not just a gift, but the product of hard work, a labor of love.

You are loved, with or without your gifts

One memory of my years in the classroom that makes me sad every time I think about it is the children who were always stressed because they believed their parents would be disappointed if they didn't excel. Sometimes parental expectations are unrealistically high. But more often, I've found that it's the child's view of the situation that is the basis of the problem. I once spoke to Sarah's mom about her daughter's distress over meeting these perceived lofty standards. "I know," she sighed, "and I don't know what to do about it." This mom was a successful and well-respected professional in the community. We want mothers to be good role models for their daughters, but having a super-star for a parent can be intimidating.

Likewise, in the book **Koala Lou,** the main character falls short of perfection, and sees herself as a grim failure. Seeking her mother's approval, Lou decides to enter the Bush Olympics where she will practice hard to win first place in the gum tree climbing event. She dreams that her mom will fling her arms around her and proclaim her love and admiration. But in this case, practice does not make perfect and Koala Klaws wins instead. Oh, the disappointment! But Mom is waiting at home nonetheless, with the biggest hug, and just the right words: "Koala Lou, I DO love you! I always have, and I always will." It's not our achievements that inspire the love of others, but our "inside selves." Some students need frequent reminders of this.

Appreciate the unique gifts of others

Oliver was quirky. It wasn't that his fourth-grade peers disliked or bullied him. It was more that he had a brain full of random facts, and an uncommonly huge vocabulary for a nine-year-old. You never knew when a word or phrase would pop out that you weren't quite expecting. When another child's mom showed up unannounced with cupcakes one afternoon, Oliver's observation was, "Oh, great, some spontaneous frivolity." Generally, Oliver wasn't a popular guy, except when it was Quiz Bowl time. Then kids clamored to be on his team.

Tacky in *Tacky the Penguin* wasn't so fortunate (at first), and was more openly ostracized. His penguin companions, quite proper birds with names like Perfect and Goodly, were taken aback by Tacky's nonconformist behavior. He'd greet them with a hearty slap on the back, and rather than dive gracefully as they did, he preferred splashy cannonballs. He sang with a grating, screechy voice. But one day hunters arrived, and the perfect little penguins gained new respect for Tacky. While they cowered behind a block of ice, Tacky stood alone. He soaked the hunters with his splashy cannonball and hurt their ears with his screechy singing. The hunters ran away. Sometimes, it's our eccentricities that are our greatest strengths.

Recognizing your strengths is empowering

What does it take for students to feel empowered? I remember teaching the Langston Hughes poem "As I Grew Older" to a group of sixth graders. The narrator describes the way his world was shattered as a wall rose up between him and his dreams. But then his dark hands break through the wall to let through glimpses of the sun. "That's it!" exclaimed one student. "When I make something with my hands, I feel like I have something real." Other students weighed in; they were empowered by writing or drawing or playing the drums—creating beauty in their own way.

In the book *Something Beautiful,* the young narrator is saddened by the graffiti scrawled on her front door; the homeless woman, barefoot and wrapped in plastic, asleep on her street; and the trash in an alley behind her home. Her teacher writes the word *BEAUTIFUL* on the chalkboard and it gets the girl thinking: What is beautiful in *her* world? Her quest takes her to the local diner where the owner says her fish sandwiches sure are something beautiful. Her friends proclaim their jump rope game similarly beautiful, and an elderly gentleman says he finds beauty in the lucky stone he's always kept in his pocket. The girl feels stronger, and with a bucket of sudsy water, scrubs her doorway until the graffiti is gone. It's a small step, but by her own hand, *BEAUTIFUL* now has more meaning. What might be your students' "something beautiful?" What could they do, or what could they create, to make their world a more beautiful place?

Compassion is a strength

The importance of compassion is an important focus in many schools. It's a means of fighting back against bullying and disrespect, and we welcome role models strong enough to think of others' needs before their own.

Melissa Parkington from **Melissa Parkington's Beautiful, Beautiful Hair** exemplifies compassion in action. In this story, featured with questions for Seven Thinking Boxes, the main character is well-known for her "spectacular" flowing dark hair, but wants to be recognized for something more. She tries art and sports, but the results are decidedly unspectacular. She is, however, a notably compassionate little girl. One day as she walks by a beauty salon in the mall, she sees a sign: "Share your hair." So she decides to cut her hair short and donate it. Her dad always mentions Melissa's beautiful, long hair as he tucks her into bed at night. But this night, those words no longer work. She tells him it's okay—her hair is still beautiful, but on someone else. His new message: "Good night, my Melissa of the beautiful, beautiful *heart*." A beautiful heart—surely the greatest strength of all.

SEVEN THINKING BOXES

Questions for *Melissa Parkington's Beautiful, Beautiful Hair* by Pat Brisson
SEL Competency: Self-Awareness   Focus: Recognizing Strengths

PLAIN CARDBOARD BOX	**BASIC THINKING** Before Melissa cut her hair, what were some of the other ways she showed kindness?
PUZZLE BOX	**PUZZLING DETAILS** In your opinion, what line in this story best shows Melissa's strength as a kind person?
HEART BOX	**FEELINGS** Reread the end of this story: How do you think Melissa's father felt about her haircut? Explain your thinking.
UNUSUAL BOX	**CREATIVE THINKING** Think of some different ways Melissa could have shown kindness that would have helped other people, too.
BROKEN BOX	**PROBLEMS AND ISSUES** Do you think that there is really a "problem" in this story? Why or why not?
TREASURE BOX	**SOMETHING TO TREASURE** What kind of strength did Melissa show? Explain how could *you* demonstrate this same strength.
TOOL BOX	**AUTHOR'S TOOLS** The author uses a lot of synonyms to describe how beautiful Melissa's hair is. What are these descriptive words? Think of three other words that would also describe her hair.

SEVEN THINKING BOXES

Questions to ask about *any* book for recognizing strengths

PLAIN CARDBOARD BOX	**BASIC THINKING**
	• What is one <u>strength</u> you recognized in this story? What details show this strength?
	• Which character do you view as the best example of this strength? Explain your thinking with details from the story.
PUZZLE BOX	**PUZZLING DETAILS**
	• In your opinion, which sentence or paragraph <u>best</u> shows the strength that this author is describing?
	• Is there anyone in this story who does not appreciate the main character's strength? Who is it? What sentence shows this most clearly?
HEART BOX	**FEELINGS**
	• How did the main character's strength make a difference to another character's feelings?
	• Although strength is often connected to happy, positive feelings, were there any sad or negative feelings in this story? Who experienced them?
UNUSUAL BOX	**CREATIVE THINKING**
	• How did creative thinking help characters' strengths to shine through in this story?
	• What else could the character have tried to show his or her strength?
BROKEN BOX	**PROBLEMS AND ISSUES**
	• Did strength or lack of strength cause a problem in this story? How?
	• Did the main character have to overcome any problems in order to make the best use of his or her strength? Explain.
TREASURE BOX	**SOMETHING TO TREASURE**
	• What strength is featured in this story? Do you consider this an <u>important</u> strength? Would it be important to you? Explain.
	• Does the main character recognize his or her strength right away? If not, when do they first see it? How does it make a difference?
TOOL BOX	**AUTHOR'S TOOLS**
	• How does the author use descriptive words to help you visualize the main character's strength in this story?
	• How does the author use dialogue to show characters' strength?

Self-Confidence

Self-confidence is a general feeling of trust in our ability to achieve what we want to achieve: *I've got this. I can handle just about anything.* By contrast, lack of self-confidence results in insecurity and self-doubt. *I will probably fail . . . I can't.* While some people's level of confidence makes them appear boastful or arrogant, self-confidence is typically viewed as a positive quality, one we want our students to demonstrate in the classroom.

WHAT WE HOPE TO SEE IN THE CLASSROOM REGARDING SELF-CONFIDENCE, AND WHAT WE SOMETIMES SEE INSTEAD

Self-confidence is a challenge in the classroom because some children come to us with a healthy can-do attitude, while others, despite equal measures of intelligence or other personal strengths, exhibit pervasive self-doubt. We are pleased when students raise their hands to volunteer answers, and when they are eager for new experiences. These students are risk-takers, undaunted by uncertain outcomes. But other students are too timid to take such risks, cowering behind their bolder, more assertive classmates.

This is a paradox, because one becomes more confident by achieving success. But if you don't give something a try, you never get to be successful. It's a cycle we see repeatedly. The students who never raise their hand because they're afraid to be wrong will never get to be right. Or, the same student who just provided a brilliant oral response may be reluctant to pick up her pencil and commit the same answer to paper—publishing your thinking is just too scary!

We try to provide low-risk opportunities that allow *all* students to succeed, in classrooms that are accepting of individual differences and where kindness prevails. But how often do we address this head-on, *naming* self-confidence as a concept? Consider the questions below as you make self-confidence a priority in your classroom.

ENHANCING CLASSROOM CULTURE: QUESTIONS FOR TEACHERS TO ASK THEMSELVES ABOUT SELF-CONFIDENCE

1. Have I ever had a conversation with my students about what self-confidence is and why it is important? How could I talk with my class about this?

2. Can I identify the students in my class who are appropriately self-confident, and those who need some support in this area?

3. Feeling confident in any area is at least partly dependent on one's skill in that area. Which of my students lack confidence in reading because of a lack of reading skills? What would be a good next step in addressing this?

4. Since feeling confident is ultimately a personal decision, how can I motivate my students to give something a try?

5. How can I help my students support each other in learning to take responsible risks?

6. How can I help parents and caregivers better understand the importance of their student's self-confidence, and become partners in supporting confidence at home?

WHAT TO LOOK FOR IN BOOKS ABOUT SELF-CONFIDENCE

Stories with messages about self-confidence sometimes illustrate the boldness and bravery that children often associate with self-confidence. But they can also demonstrate that confidence is just as often *not* big and bold, more of a whisper than a roar. When I choose books about self-confidence, I look for ones in which characters exemplify healthy levels of this trait. I also seek stories in which a character's self-confidence needs a boost. I want students to be able to answer the questions: What contributes to a person's self-confidence? How can *I* learn from storybook characters to enhance my own self-confidence? The books identified below in Chart 3.4: Books Aligned to Self-Confidence meet these criteria.

CHART 3.4: BOOKS ALIGNED TO SELF-CONFIDENCE

THE MESSAGE	THE BOOK
Self-confidence helps you face down a bully	*Stand Tall, Molly Lou Melon* by Patty Lovell (primary)
Sometimes self-confidence is NOT big and bold	*The Little Engine that Could* by Watty Piper (primary)
Being prepared increases your self-confidence	*Blizzard* by John Rocco (primary)
Don't let failure destroy your self-confidence	*Rosie Revere, Engineer* by Andrea Beaty (primary)
You need to find confidence within yourself	*Little Star* by A. J. Cosmo (primary and intermediate)

Self-confidence helps you face down a bully

There are countless situations in which self-confidence is helpful. But when the situation is bullying, self-confidence is essential. Bullies prey on people who lack the self-confidence to stand up to them. People who don't fight back are easier targets. When a bully strikes, it's too late to think about *building* self-confidence. Students need to be ready. The question is: How can we help children acquire the emotional resources they'll need for these tough times?

The book *Stand Tall, Molly Lou Melon* is exactly what we need to model both how to respond to a bully, and how to develop resilience. Molly Lou has an amazing grandmother who uses every opportunity to build the little girl's sense of self-worth. Although Molly Lou is the shortest kid in class, Grandma tells her to "stand tall" and the world will look up to her. Never mind those buck teeth! Smile big and the world will smile, too. With all her imperfections, Grandma makes it clear that Molly Lou is just perfect and needs to face the world with that attitude.

Then Molly Lou moves away. How will she survive without Grandma? To make it worse, her new classmate Ronald Durkin is a terrible bully. Ronald calls Molly Lou Shrimpo because of her diminutive stature, Bucky-Tooth Beaver for her buckteeth, and criticizes her croaky singing voice, like that of a frog. But Molly never lets Ronald get her down, every time standing up to his unwelcome remarks: She can balance pennies on those buck teeth. Can he do that? Eventually, Ronald stops bullying Molly Lou. He realizes he can't intimidate her and *he's* the one who looks silly.

We can learn from Molly Lou in this story, but we can also learn from Grandma. Having a personal cheerleader in your corner to reassure and celebrate you can be empowering. How can we be that cheerleader for our students? How can we help them to cheerlead for each other?

Sometimes self-confidence is NOT big and bold

Molly Lou Melon is a paragon of self-confidence, and a great role model to introduce to students because we'd love to see such assertiveness from them. But often, that's not the way self-confidence works. I remember watching the finalists in the fifth-grade spelling bee one year. It was Ella's turn and her word was *disastrous*. She closed her eyes, took a deep breath, and ever so slowly spoke each letter. Correct! Her skill as a speller gave her just enough confidence to confront this tricky word.

For life's everyday challenges, could there be a better role model than the little blue engine in the beloved classic, *The Little Engine that Could*? Remember that it was the bigger engines that were first approached about carrying toys over the mountain, but they refused. They were too tired or important or cool for such a mission. But when the little blue engine was asked, she hesitated a moment, never having been over the mountain before. And then a bit timidly agreed to give it a try. The little train chugged and puffed, and puffed and chugged, but in the end, made it to the village on the other side of the mountain. Children need to know that scrabbling up a mountain you haven't climbed before is the way most of us initially get to the top. To get started, all you need is enough confidence to "think you can."

Being prepared increases your self-confidence

Preparation has always been my first defense against low self-confidence. A few lifetimes ago, after I'd written a book or two and had worked with teachers on school-based professional development, I began to get requests to do large district workshops. Who, me? Public speaking had about as much personal appeal as getting a root canal, but I was determined to try. I reasoned that if I was super-prepared, what could go wrong? Turns out you can never totally predict the reliability of the technology you're using and about a hundred other things. But I could at least make sure that my visuals were ship-shape, that I had good content, and had anticipated potential questions teachers might ask. Good preparation reduces last-minute panic.

For a spot-on example of the value of preparation, meet the narrator in the book *Blizzard*. This narrator (and author) recounts his experience as a child during the Blizzard of 1978, which dumped feet of snow on New England. It was exciting for a while (no school for days), until his family and neighbors began to run out of food. The boy researched the design of makeshift tennis-racket snowshoes, drew a map to guide him through the snow, hitched up his sled, and made his way through shoulder-high drifts to the local store. He had canvased his neighbors ahead of time and had a list of everyone's grocery needs in hand. There are a couple of worthy messages here: First, like the little blue engine, it's sometimes easier to step up to a task when other people need your help. Also, this boy did his homework. Before setting out, he learned how to make snowshoes, figured out his route, and organized his shopping list. This preparation made it easier for him to carry out his task.

I think the first step in building students' confidence to accomplish a task is to ask what worries them. Then ask them to think about the steps needed to solve that problem. If they can anticipate what *might* go wrong, they can be proactive about finding a solution.

Don't let failure destroy your self-confidence

Self-confidence is fragile for lots of children. They want so badly to explore and create, but when they don't succeed right away, they get discouraged. They give up. Don't quit, we tell them. Don't let mistakes destroy your self-confidence.

In *Rosie Revere, Engineer*, Rosie secretly picks through the trash to retrieve treasures for inventions that she likes to design and build. She builds things in places hidden away, where no one can see, desperate to avoid the mocking laughter of friends and family. Truthfully, her inventions always somehow fall short of her expectations—her hotdog dispenser with helium pants, for example. Then one day her great-great-aunt

Rose shows up, a kindred spirit. Great-Great-Aunt Rose has only one wish: to fly—and Rosie wants to make it happen. She makes one last valiant attempt, engineering a helio-cheese-copter, and it's quite spectacular. But it crashes. Rosie is devastated. However, Great-Great-Aunt Rose sees the situation differently and cheers her on: "Your brilliant first flop was a raging success!" Don't quit. Learn from your mistakes. Move on.

FEATURED BOOK FOR SELF-CONFIDENCE: *Little Star* by A. J. Cosmo

You need to find confidence within yourself

Many of the scenarios and books highlighting self-confidence suggest that others—teachers, friends, parents—can give students confidence. It is certainly true that others can provide needed support. But in the end, the student must take up the challenge and believe in him or herself.

For this message, I share the featured book for self-confidence, **Little Star**. The author is A. J. Cosmo, which I mention because there are several books with this same title, and it's the Cosmo book you want. And yes, you really do want it. You could just gaze at the gorgeous photographs taken by the Hubble Space Telescope, with whimsical pictures of book characters painted onto them. But then you'd miss the delightful story and its message.

Little Star didn't believe he could shine brightly, and looked to his friends in the galaxy for validation. Another star confirms that he can indeed shine, but Jupiter is doubtful: if he hasn't been able to shine yet, it probably isn't meant to be. His family, of course, supports him, but Little Star continues to be skeptical. Finally, he approaches wise Mr. Moon, who replies that no matter what, there will always be believers and nonbelievers. Only *you* can truly believe in you. Somehow, we need to communicate this important message to our students—that having self-confidence is a decision they ultimately must make for themselves. The questions that follow for Seven Thinking Boxes will get your students thinking about their role in building their own self-confidence.

SEVEN THINKING BOXES

Questions for *Little Star* by A. J. Cosmo
SEL Competency: Self-Awareness   Focus: Self-Confidence

PLAIN CARDBOARD BOX	**BASIC THINKING** • Who did Little Star ask for advice about shining? What did each one tell him?
PUZZLE BOX 	**PUZZLING DETAILS** • Choose a quote from this book that you consider the <u>most</u> important. Why did you select this quote?
HEART BOX	**FEELINGS** • What feelings do you think Little Star was experiencing as he asked each of his friends about shining?
UNUSUAL BOX	**CREATIVE THINKING** • If Little Star had asked *you* whether he could shine, what advice would you have given him?
BROKEN BOX	**PROBLEMS AND ISSUES** • On the surface, it looks like the problem in this story is that Little Star doesn't shine. But look deeper: What is the *real* problem?
TREASURE BOX	**SOMETHING TO TREASURE** • What big idea does the author want us to think about through this story? What can *you* learn from this story?
TOOL BOX	**AUTHOR'S TOOLS** The illustrations in this story are very interesting. Each page has a photograph taken by the Hubble Space Telescope. Then the author has painted the characters on top of the photos. How do the photographs make the story more meaningful? How do the painted characters make the story more meaningful?

SEVEN THINKING BOXES

Questions to ask about *any* book for self-confidence

PLAIN CARDBOARD BOX	**BASIC THINKING** • What is one situation in this story that occurred because someone was <u>not</u> confident? • What is one situation in this story that occurred because someone <u>was</u> confident?
PUZZLE BOX	**PUZZLING DETAILS** • What details in this story most clearly show confidence (or a lack of confidence)? • What details in this story show that the problem was solved? How did confidence play a part in the solution?
HEART BOX	**FEELINGS** • When [Character] was not feeling confident, what *other* feelings did this lead to as well? • In this story, what other character could have helped the main character to feel more confident? What could this person have said?
UNUSUAL BOX	**CREATIVE THINKING** • Did creative thinking play a part in solving the problem of confidence in this story? How? • What *other* solution(s) could have solved this character's problem with confidence?
BROKEN BOX	**PROBLEMS AND ISSUES** • Was lack of self-confidence a problem for anyone in this story? Explain. • What scene from this story <u>best</u> shows how the problem with confidence got started?
TREASURE BOX	**SOMETHING TO TREASURE** • What is the author's message in this story about self-confidence? How could this message apply to you in the future? • If you had the opportunity to speak to the main character in this story about confidence, what would you say?
TOOL BOX	**AUTHOR'S TOOLS** • How did the author *show* lack of confidence? (It might have been through dialogue, descriptive words, or something else) • How did the illustrations in this book show the characters' confidence or lack of confidence?

Self-Efficacy

Of all the SEL focus areas, this one is perhaps the most unclear. When I ask teachers what they think self-efficacy might be, many aren't even willing to hazard a guess. Albert Bandura is the psychologist credited with defining it: "Self-efficacy refers to an individual's belief in his or her capacity to execute behaviors necessary to produce specific performance attainments" (Bandura, 1977).

Still confused? Think of it this way: Self-efficacy is a lot like self-confidence, except it's more specific. Self-confidence means having a pervasive can-do attitude. You might characterize a person as generally self-confident or not self-confident. But self-efficacy means you feel you have the ability to live up to your potential in a *particular situation*, or on a *particular task*. You believe you can get a perfect score on today's math test or bake the cake that will win the gold ribbon at the school fair.

WHAT WE HOPE TO SEE IN THE CLASSROOM REGARDING SELF-EFFICACY, AND WHAT WE SOMETIMES SEE INSTEAD

Although the term and its definition may seem abstract, self-efficacy (or lack thereof) is very real in our classroom. We have students who try so hard, motivated by some internal drive to produce the best possible piece of writing, drawing, test score, or other demonstration of their skill. They work with painstaking precision and deliver a top-of-the-line performance. But we also have students whose main goal is not excellence, but compliance. Just get the job done. Close is good enough. Settle for average!

These students frustrate us because we know they could be so much more than average: "Don't guess. Go back and reread that paragraph. The answer's right there." "You just gave me a great oral answer to this question. Where are all those details in your written response?" Reading stories about people who strive for excellence probably won't change the game for students who are content with mediocrity. But using stories to start a conversation on the topic could be a good place to begin.

One consideration, however: As you strive to make self-efficacy real to kids, skip the label *efficacy*. Go with a simpler phrase like "setting high standards for yourself" or "living up to your potential."

ENHANCING CLASSROOM CULTURE: QUESTIONS FOR TEACHERS TO ASK THEMSELVES ABOUT SELF-EFFICACY

1. How can I talk about self-efficacy with my students, without using the term itself?

2. Do I know one thing that is so important to each of my students that they would be willing to work hard for it—regardless of potential challenges?

3. Is lack of self-efficacy impacting my students? How?

4. What challenges in the classroom might be making it harder for my students to pursue an important goal? How can I help?

5. How can I help my students think about a goal that is important to them, and then find the courage to reach for it?

6. What real-life role models (people they might know from the community or the news) could I discuss with students to help them see self-efficacy in action?

WHAT TO LOOK FOR IN BOOKS ABOUT SELF-EFFICACY

For this focus area, I've chosen some titles because the characters demonstrate precisely the kinds attitudes and behaviors that contribute to setting high standards and achieving goals. These are our role models. Other books show obstacles or challenges that can get in the way of self-efficacy—parents who are disappointed by their children's goals or performance, for example. There are also characters represented who need to set higher goals for themselves, or look for new ways to reach their goals. Chart 3.5: Books Aligned to Self-Efficacy, lists these titles.

CHART 3.5 BOOKS ALIGNED TO SELF-EFFICACY

THE MESSAGE	THE BOOK
We all bloom in our own time	*Leo the Late Bloomer* by Robert Kraus (primary)
Do your best, even when others don't support you	*Peppe the Lamplighter* by Elisa Bartone (primary and intermediate)
Living up to your potential means using your gifts	*The Wretched Stone* by Chris Van Allsburg (intermediate)
Sometimes you need to look for a different way to achieve your dream	*Giraffes Can't Dance* by Giles Andreae (primary)
Be resourceful to be successful	*Weslandia* by Paul Fleischman (intermediate)

We all bloom in our own time

How vividly I remember a conversation I had with the parent of one of my first grad-ers at our November parent-teacher conference. I explained that Vincent was doing fine. But his mom saw only the "S" for satisfactory next to the grade for Reading on his report card. "Oh," she sighed. "Do you think this will keep him out of Yale?" The child was two months into first grade! It might have been a little early to predict his academic future. I wish I could say this was the only parent of a six-year-old with whom I had to discuss Ivy League aspirations.

Leo, I feel your pain! Young Leo the lion in **Leo the Late Bloomer** was not "bloom-ing" according to the timeline his father had in mind. He couldn't read, write, or draw, and he was a very sloppy eater. His mother, by contrast, urged patience. And what do you know: in good time, Leo could do all the things his father had fretted about. Sometimes the best gift we can give children is time—time to mature into the skill proficiency we wish they would show right now. This might be a good book to read to children who feel pressure to succeed at something for which they're not quite ready: Even if you can't ride that two-wheel bike today, you'll try it again when your legs are a little longer.

Do your best, even if others don't support you

We talk a lot in schools about the importance of supporting students' dreams, and I expect we all do our best to give them the tools they need to reach their goals. But out-side of school, some students may not feel supported. The impact can be demoralizing. This was the case for Peppe in **Peppe the Lamplighter**.

This turn-of-the-20th-century story takes place in New York City. Peppe is part of a large immigrant family with many sisters. His mom has died, and his father is too ill to work. Peppe seeks a job to ease his family's financial strain and is proud to announce to his dad and sisters that he has been hired as a lamplighter. But while his sisters are pleased, his father is not: "Did I come to America so my son could light the street lamps?" Though saddened by his father's response, he is undeterred at first, making a small wish for each member of his family as he lights each lamp—a special hope for their future.

But Father continues his tirade, shaming Peppe, telling him he will "one day belong to the streets." Eventually, completely disheartened, Peppe quits. The streets are dark, and one night his littlest sister cannot find her way home. At last, Peppe's father recog-nizes the importance of Peppe's work, and as the story ends, Father tells Peppe that it's a *good* job, and that he is proud.

There are multiple messages here: We should feel pride in any job done well. But the biggest take-away, I think, is the importance of respecting and nurturing someone else's dream. In this story, it wasn't that Peppe had *no* support, because his sisters did believe in him. But he didn't have support from the person whose approval meant the most—his father. It is especially hard for children when someone they love rails against a personal goal borne of deep convictions. How can we help students stay strong in the face of such criticism?

Living up to your potential means using your gifts

One of the bigger frustrations faced by a parent or teacher is a child who chooses not to live up to their potential. "You've had two weeks to work on this report. This is what you're handing in?" It was hockey season, and from the scant two pages he had written, Patrick's mind was not focused on history, his best subject.

Perhaps if we could help children see self-efficacy (living up to their potential) from its flip side, it would help. What happens when you abandon your goals and ignore the talents that help you reach them? For that answer, read *The Wretched Stone*. Told from the point of view of a ship's captain as a series of journal entries, this story describes the perilous journey of the ship, the Rita Anne.

At the outset of the voyage, the captain praises his crew, who are always on top of their game—singing, dancing, and reading whenever they have a free minute. But alas, the men discover a huge "rock" which emits an alluring glow. They forego creativity, transfixed by the magnetism of the strange object, and stare at it endlessly. The captain plans to throw the "wretched stone" overboard, but doesn't get the chance before a fierce storm rolls in and scuttles the Rita Anne. Miraculously, the crew survives, and the men gradually resume more intellectual engagement. Television? Video games? Computers? The culprit here is technology, though of course there are many rogue forces capable of scuttling our dreams. A question for our students: What might get in the way of you becoming your best self?

Sometimes you need to look for a different way to achieve your dream

One of the most endearing moments I witnessed in a school recently occurred in a first grade classroom, where students were partner-reading. The first partner was struggling over the word *stone*. His buddy looked at him: "What strategy are you trying?" Said the reader, "I found a little word in the big word—*on*." His friend looked again: "I think you need a different strategy this time. Try magic *e*."

Sometimes finding a solution to a problem is just a matter of approaching it differently. Much to the delight of the giraffe in *Giraffes Can't Dance*, he really *could* dance. But it turned out that he'd been swaying to the wrong music, a kind that just didn't work for his long legs and neck. But when someone convinced him to change the tune, his long legs and neck were a perfect match for the new tempo. All it took was the keen eye of a friend to help him see the problem in a new way—just like our first-grade friend. We can be that careful observer for our students, ready with a suggestion to try Plan B when Plan A misses its mark.

Be resourceful to be successful

"Use your imagination," I implored my fourth graders. Our school was participating in the state's Invention Convention for the first time, and a few students stood before me with the sad news that there wasn't one thing left in the world to invent. "You all face problems every day that beg for solutions. What is something that could make your life a little easier or more fun? Maybe it's a way to keep crayons from breaking. Maybe you need something to keep your jewelry from getting tangled. Think about the little inconveniences you face every day."

Wesley, the main character in **Weslandia,** would have loved this project. He's a guy who refuses to follow the crowd—which is one of the big ideas that emerges from the book. Even bigger is the message that it's one's resourcefulness that can lead to the greatest success. School is out for the summer, and before the first day is over, Wesley is already bored. His parents wish he'd be more like other kids: someone who loves pizza and trendy haircuts, or a football fanatic. But Wesley doesn't love any of those things and is furthermore undaunted by his peers teasing him for being different. What he really wants is to create his own civilization.

Brick-by-brick, his new world, Weslandia, takes shape. The seeds Wesley plants aren't the usual fare, and grow into a blend of peach, strawberry, pumpkin pie, and other entrancing flavors. He fashions the plant's bark into a sun hat and its oil into mosquito repellent. He invents his own language, counting system, and games. Along the way, Wesley's former tormenters become curious, and then even admirers. With tongue-in-cheek humor best appreciated by intermediate grade students, this author illuminates the path to becoming the best you can be: begin with a clear goal, use your resourcefulness along the way, and never mind the crowd! This book is featured for self-efficacy with questions for Seven Thinking Boxes.

SEVEN THINKING BOXES

Questions for *Weslandia* by Paul Fleischman
SEL Competency: Self-Awareness   Focus: Self-Efficacy

PLAIN CARDBOARD BOX	**BASIC THINKING**
	• Name five things Wesley invented to achieve his goal of creating a civilization.
PUZZLE BOX	**PUZZLING DETAILS**
	• Choose a line that you think shows something that was important to Wesley as he worked toward his goal. What is the line? What does it show?
HEART BOX	**FEELINGS**
	• By the end of the story, Wesley's peers changed their feelings about him. Why do you think they formed a different opinion? How does this relate to self-efficacy (being the best you can be)?
UNUSUAL BOX	**CREATIVE THINKING**
	• There were many examples of creative thinking in this book. Which example impressed you the most? Do you think you need to be a creative person to be the best you can be? Explain.
BROKEN BOX	**PROBLEMS AND ISSUES**
	• Why do you think Wesley had tormentors at school? Do you think he should have changed to be more like them? Why or why not?
TREASURE BOX	**SOMETHING TO TREASURE**
	• How does the message of *Weslandia* relate to self-efficacy (being the best you that you can be)? Support your response with evidence from the beginning, middle, and end of the story. How might this message make a difference to you in your life?
TOOL BOX	**AUTHOR'S TOOLS**
	• The author of this book uses <u>humor</u> in telling the story. Identify at least two lines that are intended to be funny. What makes them funny? Are the lines just funny, or are they intended to send a stronger message?

SEVEN THINKING BOXES

Questions to ask about *any* book for self-efficacy

PLAIN CARDBOARD BOX	**BASIC THINKING**
	• What was most important to this character in achieving his goal? • Who helped this character achieve her goal? How did this person help?
PUZZLE BOX	**PUZZLING DETAILS**
	• What was the turning point for this character in moving forward with this goal? Did anyone in this story provide good advice to this character? What words in the story show this?
HEART BOX	**FEELINGS**
	• How could you tell that this character felt strongly about what s/he wanted to achieve? • What feelings does the character experience when someone or something stands in the way of what s/he would like to accomplish? Explain.
UNUSUAL BOX	**CREATIVE THINKING**
	• Was resourcefulness important to this character in achieving his goal? How? • How else could this character have moved forward to achieve her goal? Would the result have been the same or different? Explain.
BROKEN BOX	**PROBLEMS AND ISSUES**
	• Who or what stood in the way of this character achieving his goal? What happened because of this? • What might have been the result if this character had <u>not</u> achieved her goal?
TREASURE BOX	**SOMETHING TO TREASURE**
	• Why do you think achieving this goal was so important to this character? • In what ways are you <u>like</u> or <u>unlike</u> this character in your efforts to achieve something important to you?
TOOL BOX	**AUTHOR'S TOOLS**
	• How did the author make the situation this character faced seem real? • Identify three words the author used to show the importance of this goal to this character? Why do you think the author chose each of these words?

CHAPTER 4
SELF-MANAGEMENT: PRESENTING YOUR BEST SELF TO THE WORLD

The idea that we "manage" ourselves will be new for lots of students. They're familiar with the idea of self-control, mostly as it relates to impulsive behavior. But they probably don't see the bigger picture—that self-management isn't just about their in-the-moment response, but something that contributes to both long- and short-term success.

Let's define self-management as "the ability to successfully regulate one's emotions, thoughts, and behaviors in different situations—effectively managing stress, controlling impulses, and motivating oneself. The ability to set and work toward personal and academic goals" ("Core SEL Competencies," n.d.). This includes six focus areas:

- Impulse control
- Stress management
- Goal-Setting
- Self-Motivation
- Organizational skills
- Self-Discipline

While self-awareness may be the foundation of social emotional learning, it is often self-management that makes students' level of emotional health most visible in the classroom. How well do they control their impulses and manage stress? Do they set goals for themselves and organize for action? Are they motivated to get going and disciplined enough to see a task through to completion? Many teachers have expressed that it's their students' lack of self-management and regulation that is responsible for the lion's share of their own stress.

There is no quick cure for students' poor self-management, although there's value in being proactive rather than reactive. In the middle of a crisis, emotions run high and too often preclude logical thinking and sound solutions. But in calmer moments, when the issue feels less personal, matters can be addressed more objectively. You can open the door to these conversations with just the right book.

Impulse Control

Impulsivity is acting on a whim with behavior that shows little forethought or consideration of consequences. So, impulse *control* is the capacity to behave in a way that reflects logical thinking and recognition of the possible cost of one's actions. Teachers can recount almost limitless examples of lack of impulse control in the classroom—from the not-so-bad to the really ugly.

WHAT WE HOPE TO SEE IN THE CLASSROOM REGARDING IMPULSE CONTROL, AND WHAT WE SOMETIMES SEE INSTEAD

What we hope to see in the classroom regarding impulse control is students who resist sudden urges to jump up from their seat, blurt out answers, speak unkind words to classmates, use their fists to solve problems, and countless other behaviors that may be small infractions, but nonetheless deplete our energy. We are exhausted by students who cannot manage their impulses, and instead require us to do the managing for them:

"Josh, why are you walking around the classroom?" Josh has no answer. Or, "Catherine, it's Maya's turn. When you yell out the answer first, you are not helping her learn." I'd reminded her of this many times before.

Or, one of my all-time favorites from first grade:

Jasmine: "Mrs. Boyles, Mark called me a name."
Me: "What did he call you?"
Jasmine: "He called me a vegetarian."

I'm guessing that neither Mark nor Jasmine knew what a vegetarian was. However, Mark meant to insult—and he had succeeded. I then had to offer up lecture #999 on "no name calling." *And*, I got to explain vegetarianism.

ENHANCING CLASSROOM CULTURE: QUESTIONS FOR TEACHERS TO ASK THEMSELVES ABOUT IMPULSE CONTROL

1. What impulsive behaviors in my classroom have I been most successful at reducing? How have I achieved this?

2. What impulsive behaviors in my classroom have I been *least* successful at reducing? Why has this been such a struggle?

3. Which students are typically the most impulsive? What might be contributing to this?

4. What is the impact of impulsivity in my classroom? How does it affect me? How does it affect other children?

5. What is one impulsive behavior that I would *most* like to curtail? How could I be proactive in addressing this?

6. Which students in my classroom model good impulse control? What can I learn from these students that might help their more impulsive peers?

WHAT TO LOOK FOR IN BOOKS ABOUT IMPULSE CONTROL

For this focus area, I did not adhere as tightly to my criteria for selecting books—well-rounded characters, authentic problems, and a message that evolves as the story unfolds. Instead, most of the books described here address issues of impulse control in a very direct way. That is to say, the books listed in Chart 4.1: Books Aligned to Impulse Control are *about* interrupting, or talking too much, or inappropriate attention-seeking.

I looked for books that feature some of the most common kinds of classroom impulsivity. I also looked for characters who might make students laugh along the way. I hope while they giggle over the antics of these impulsive kids, they will see a bit of themselves reflected in their behavior—while also recognizing that although such behavior is undesirable, it is fixable. In several of these stories, the undesirable behavior has a name: *Volcano, Puppy Mind, Snurtch, Fierce*. I like the idea that the behavior has an identity separate from the child herself. This way, resolving the problem seems like less of a personal attack, and leaves the child with more dignity: It's not *you* who talks too much; it's that *volcano*—and we need to get control of it.

CHART 4.1: BOOKS ALIGNED TO IMPULSE CONTROL

THE MESSAGE	THE BOOK
Talking too much can be a problem	*My Mouth is a Volcano!* by Julia Cook (primary and intermediate)
Not focusing can be a problem	*Puppy Mind* by Andrew Jordan Nance (primary and intermediate)
Out-of-control behavior can be a problem	*The Snurtch* by Sean Ferrell (primary and intermediate)
Seeking attention in negative ways can be a problem	*Millie Fierce* by Jane Manning (primary and intermediate)
Losing your temper can be a problem	*Testing the Ice: A True Story About Jackie Robinson* by Sharon Robinson (primary and intermediate)

Talking too much can be a problem

My neighbor's daughter Marissa is four years old. She wasn't an early talker, and so I was quite surprised when shortly after her second birthday I arrived at her house and she announced to her mother, "Mrs. Boyles is here, and she brought Mr. Boyles. Mr. Boyles is bald." That day, and every day since, she's provided a running commentary on whatever pops into her mind. She recently changed preschools and I asked her how she likes her new one. "I like it a lot. I like my teacher. She says I talk a lot." Just in case, maybe I should gift Marissa's teacher a copy of **My Mouth is a Volcano!**

Like Marissa, many kids who talk a lot (or talk too much, depending on the circumstance) believe that their words have a life of their own. In this story, Louie explains that *his* words travel from his brain, sliding onto his tongue, and then explode through his teeth. It just happens. Additionally, he believes that every word is important, begging to be shared. But when classmates interrupt *him*, he begins to see this behavior as rude and vows to take charge of his volcano.

Not focusing can be a problem

When I began teaching, I remember being astounded that the kid with the raised hand during a social studies discussion sometimes wasn't eager to contribute to the conversation about Abraham Lincoln, but instead wanted to know, "How many more minutes until lunch?" Over the years I got better at aborting these off-topic inquiries, but it's harder to rein in little minds that wander away quietly.

For students who find it difficult to focus, I love the book ***Puppy Mind***. Puppies dart from one thing to the next—the squeaky toy one second, the rawhide bone the next—for no apparent reason. Children (as well as their teachers, if we're being honest here) are sometimes guilty of the same behavior. The author of this book suggests *breathing* as a solution: When your puppy mind begins to wriggle and squirm, breathe slowly three times to bring it back to the place it is intended to be.

Out-of-control behavior can be a problem

Students who talk a lot or who have trouble focusing may require redirecting from us to function optimally in our classroom, but they don't *exhaust* us. Some impulsive behavior, however, is exhausting! It tends to be more extreme and unpredictable: The child who reaches across to the next desk for no apparent reason, for example, and scribbles all over her classmate's carefully crafted story. The child who throws her math book across the room. The child who runs out the classroom door when his teacher asks him to sit down. How can teachers diffuse such out-of-control behavior?

Maybe ***The Snurtch*** can help. The author of this book suggests that the real culprit isn't a "bad kid," but that there's a *Snurtch* lurking about that sometimes takes control in wholly inappropriate ways. The Snurtch isn't who we really are, but we need to take back control, or people will get the wrong idea about us: "I think your Snurtch got the better of you when you scribbled on Adrianna's paper. What can you say to your Snurtch? What can you say to Adrianna?"

Seeking attention in negative ways can be a problem

For some students, negative behavior might be more intentional than impulsive. Is being recognized for bad behavior preferable to receiving no attention at all? Maybe! Millie in ***Millie Fierce*** was a quiet kid. Her classmates barely listened to her during show-and-tell. She didn't have the kind of cool clothes for which she got noticed. She felt invisible. But she discovered she could change all that by being loud, barging in front of people, and being generally obnoxious. "Just ignore her," people said. Then one day, Millie realized being fierce wasn't as satisfying as she'd hoped. Instead she tried being extra-kind. And what do you know....people noticed. I expect the questions we need to ask ourselves to change this attention-seeking behavior are: Why does this child feel invisible? What are some of this child's strengths that we can celebrate?

Losing your temper can be a problem

A specific but alarming aspect of impulsivity is uncontrolled temper. Anger is dangerous not just for its physical implications (a student who strikes out with his fists can cause great physical harm), but also because of the possible long-term implications for the perpetrator. Even when the response is not physical, an angry outburst can lead to loss of opportunities going forward.

For a real-life example of the importance of anger management, there's no better book than *Testing the Ice: A True Story about Jackie Robinson,* the book featured here for Seven Thinking Boxes. There are many important messages in this book, but I find the conversation between Jackie and the Dodgers' coach, Branch Rickey, to be especially powerful. As they contemplate Jackie's potential future as the first African American on a major league baseball team, Rickey tells Jackie that he'd welcome him aboard, but asks if he can control his temper: There will be name-calling and plenty of vocal protest to a black player elevated to the major leagues.

Jackie could be the one to break the color barrier. Or, he could succumb to the taunts and further derail efforts to integrate his sport. He accepts the challenge and succeeds. We often have to remind students to honor their long-term goals rather than give in to the urge to retaliate against an in-the-moment injustice: "If you strike back you will be equally at fault. There will be consequences."

FEATURED BOOK FOR IMPULSE CONTROL: *Testing the Ice: A True Story about Jackie Robinson* by Sharon Robinson

SEVEN THINKING BOXES

Questions to ask about *Testing the Ice: A True Story about Jackie Robinson* by Sharon Robinson
SEL Competency: Self-Management   Skill: Impulse Control

PLAIN CARDBOARD BOX	**BASIC THINKING** Name two positive character traits that Jackie Robinson demonstrated in this story that helped him control his emotions. Give examples from details in the text. How did each one help to make him the best he could be?
PUZZLE BOX	**PUZZLING DETAILS** What details does the author provide in this story to help you understand Jackie's strong emotions, and his ability to control those emotions?
HEART BOX	**FEELINGS** This story shows Jackie's feelings in different situations. One time he had to control his temper when people were yelling insults at him. Another time, he had to go out on the ice with his children although he could not swim. In which of these situations do you think Jackie did a better job of responding to his feelings in a positive way? Explain.
UNUSUAL BOX	**CREATIVE THINKING** Is there another way that Jackie could have solved his problem about going out onto the ice that might have been less stressful for him and for his children? Explain your thinking.
BROKEN BOX	**PROBLEMS AND ISSUES** Which problem do you think was more emotionally stressful for Jackie—signing on with the Brooklyn Dodgers, or testing the ice for his children? Why?
TREASURE BOX	**SOMETHING TO TREASURE** This story was written by Jackie Robinson's daughter. Why do you think she wrote it? What did she want us to know about her dad? What do you think she wanted us to think about for our own lives?
TOOL BOX	**AUTHOR'S TOOLS** The author includes a flashback in this story. How does the author show the flashback? How does this flashback make the story stronger? How does it give you more insight into Jackie's emotional control?

SEVEN THINKING BOXES

Questions to ask about *any* book for impulse control

PLAIN CARDBOARD BOX 	**BASIC THINKING** • What details in this story show either *good* impulse control or *not enough* impulse control? • What character in this story would have benefited from more impulse control? What is the evidence?
PUZZLE BOX	**PUZZLING DETAILS** • What details in this story *best* show the need for impulse control? • Choose a quote from this story that helps you better understand the need for impulse control. What can you learn from this quote?
HEART BOX	**FEELINGS** • Whose feelings were hurt because someone in this story had a hard time controlling their impulses? What were these feelings? • How do you think the character without impulse control *really* feels about his or her actions? Why do you think he or she continues to act this way?
UNUSUAL BOX	**CREATIVE THINKING** • What creative solution could have helped this character better control his or her emotions? • Who needed to think creatively in this story to help the character in need of more impulse control? How can *you* be a friend to someone who needs better impulse control?
BROKEN BOX	**PROBLEMS AND ISSUES** • Did poor impulse control lead to other problems in this story? Explain. • What was the <u>effect</u> of not enough impulse control in this story?
TREASURE BOX	**SOMETHING TO TREASURE** • Did one or more of the characters in this story learn anything about impulse control? Explain. • What do you think the author wanted readers to learn about impulse control from this story?
TOOL BOX	**AUTHOR'S TOOLS** • Did the illustrator of this story use cartoon characters to show the importance of impulse control? Why do you think the author used cartoon characters instead of "real" people? • Sometimes authors use names for impulsive behavior like "the Snurtch," or "Puppy Mind," or "Volcano." Why do you think they give names like this to impulsive behavior?

Stress Management

Mayo Clinic defines stress as "an automatic physical, mental and emotional response to a challenging event and a normal part of everyone's life" ("Stress Management," n.d.). Hence, stress *management* is the way we deal with stress and adversity in our lives. Approaches to stress management might include improving problem-solving skills and the capacity to prioritize, along with cultivating optimism and nurturing more positive personal relationships. Relaxation also helps reduce stress. Since many of these skills are explored in relation to other SEL competencies, we'll focus here on students' ability to relax.

WHAT WE HOPE TO SEE IN THE CLASSROOM REGARDING STRESS MANAGEMENT, AND WHAT WE SOMETIMES SEE INSTEAD

Students face many sources of stress during the school day that make it difficult for them to relax. Some relate to outside forces, like wondering if the school bully will leave them alone on the bus that afternoon. But there are plenty of causes of stress right in the classroom: *Will I finish my writing assignment on time? Will I understand the new math concept my teacher is introducing?* Then there's the stress that students acquire vicariously from their stressed-out teachers. Kids can tell when we are tense about an upcoming walkthrough from our principal, about running out of time during a lesson, or other anxiety-producing day-to-day classroom realities.

We all need to "just breathe." The widespread recognition that stress has invaded classrooms in tsunami-size proportions has led to mindfulness initiatives in many schools. I've seen this implemented effectively, with classroom teachers tuning into important cues from their students and responding accordingly. I've also seen some questionable practices. For example, I was visiting one school where an administrator boomed over the loudspeaker at pre-determined points during the day: "Everyone, this is a reminder that for the next five minutes we will all practice our breathing exercises." What if no one needed breathing exercises at that exact moment? I prefer to let the need for mindfulness dictate when and how we engage in mindful practices.

ENHANCING CLASSROOM CULTURE: QUESTIONS FOR TEACHERS TO ASK THEMSELVES ABOUT STRESS MANAGEMENT

1. To what extent do I think stress plays a role in my students' capacity to perform optimally—emotionally, socially, and academically?

2. What factors seem to cause the most stress in my classroom?

3. How am I contributing to my students' stress? What can I do so that *my* stress does not become *their* stress?

4. In the past, how have I helped my students "destress" when tensions are running high?

5. How could I discuss stress with my students to help them understand it and to help them manage their own stress a little better?

6. What else could I try to help my students alleviate stress?

WHAT TO LOOK FOR IN BOOKS ABOUT STRESS MANAGEMENT

While books about mindfulness are becoming more plentiful at all grade levels and can support stress management, I don't think we need the "mindfulness" label to help students manage their stress. There are many books available that tease out specific aspects of stress management—from the importance of feeling safe to finding a quiet, peaceful place. Other stories offer strategies for stress reduction, and there are books with worthy examples of characters who manage stress well. Most of these are stories, which can provide our students with insights from situations that characters (or real people) face. But this is also an area that lends itself to self-help books. A mix of such books are listed in Chart 4.2: Books Aligned to Stress Management.

CHART 4.2: BOOKS ALIGNED TO STRESS MANAGEMENT

THE MESSAGE	THE BOOK
It's important to feel safe	*Windows* by Julia Denos (primary and intermediate)
How to feel better when you miss someone	*The Kissing Hand* by Audrey Penn (primary)
Sometimes you just need a place to calm down	*A Quiet Place* by Douglas Wood (primary and intermediate)
Learn how to manage your stress	*Find Your Happy: A Kids Self Love Book* by Patricia May (primary and intermediate)
Learn from a role model to manage stress	*The Story of Ruby Bridges* by Robert Coles (primary and intermediate)

It's important to feel safe

There's a phrase that I've heard often as educators learn more about social emotional learning: You can't do Bloom until you do Maslow. It's a valid point, and the need for safety is very close to the bottom of this "needs" pyramid, right after physiological requirements like water, food, and shelter. It's not until you get further up that pyramid that self-actualization matters (Cherry, 2018). So, beginning with a book about feeling safe is a good place to start for stress management.

The main character in the book **Windows** finds solace in the windows he passes each night on his walk home. Sometimes it's the comfort of seeing the same windows he's passed a hundred other times. There's contentment in the familiarity of knowing what to expect. Sometimes this character's well-being comes from glimpsing what's happening on the other side of the window: People cooking dinner, watching television, or playing piano. There's safety in the predictable routines of every-day life. Most of all, the boy is reassured as he approaches the front window of his own home and sees his family within. What helps your students feel safe? What is familiar or predictable that adds to their security? *Who* helps them feel safe, and *how*?

How to feel better when you miss someone

Missing someone can be especially stressful. Students of all ages experience this, but you usually know right away with young children. They cry, or they become fixated on the door, awaiting someone's return. I'll never forget one occasion when my mother picked my daughter up from day care so that I could attend a meeting: "I drove up, and there was that little face, pressed against the window." Thanks for the guilt trip, Mom.

Maybe this is why I've always had such an affinity for Chester Raccoon in **The Kissing Hand**. He begs his mother to let him stay home from school because he thinks it will be scary to be there without her. But Mama Raccoon has an idea. She kisses his hand and tells him that whenever he is lonely and needs some affection from home, he can press his hand to his cheek to remind himself of how much he is loved. What a smart mom! And what a sweet strategy for helping a little one feel safe. What simple strategy might calm the fears of your students when they are missing a special someone?

Sometimes you just need a place to calm down

Sometimes in a classroom it seems like *all* the students need to calm down. The talking is loud and kids shout over each other to be heard. The teacher asks the students to come to the rug for a story and there is a wrestling match for everyone's favorite blue beanbag chair. Two girls are barreling down the hall at such speed that you fear the outcome if another student innocently rounds the corner at the wrong moment. At times like these, we all need a quiet place, a peaceful place, a place where we can gather our thoughts and simply *be*.

A Quiet Place is a book that offers readers this sense of serenity by describing a "time out" that is not a punishment, but an opportunity to reflect and reclaim a more peaceful state of mind. Ask your students: Where might you go to be quiet? Maybe, like the character in the story, they could go to their back yard. They could crawl under a bush and listen to the sounds of the world from afar. At a pond they might imagine themselves to be the world's greatest fisherman, calmly awaiting a nibble on the end of a line. On a hilltop they could see a long way and think long thoughts. They could go many places. But in the end, they all lead inside the quiet place inside *themselves*, where they can feel their own feelings and think their own thoughts. It's not only a quiet place, but a *happy* place. Do you have a special place in your classroom where students can feel calm? Where is their happy, calm place outside of school?

Learn how to manage your stress

What's in your bag of tricks for helping students relieve stress? From Chester Raccoon we learned that a hand can hold a kiss. We learned from other books that a special place can have a calming effect, and that what's familiar in our life can inspire peace. But sometimes hands-on is the best route when you want to engage students. I tried an activity I learned online with a class of third graders, and they loved it. The gist was to fill a jar with water, add about a tablespoon of glitter, and shake it up. (Did I mention that the jar needs to have a lid?) Ask students if they can see the glitter clearly. When they respond that they cannot, explain that this is similar to times when they are angry or upset and try to see their thoughts clearly; you just can't do it. Wait a few minutes and ask the same question again about the glitter, now that it has settled to the bottom of the jar. "That's amazing," said Randall before I had the chance to make the analogy myself. "When you calm down, you can see all your thoughts clear as day." Imagine that! (Ackerman, 2019).

For a nice repertoire of interactive activities suitable for the classroom, I suggest *Find Your Happy: A Kids Self Love Book*. This book is useful for all grades and includes mindful meditations, tools for positive thinking, confidence boosters, calming techniques and physical exercises. When students can *do* something to reduce the noise from the commotion around them, the result is harmony.

FEATURED BOOK FOR STRESS MANAGEMENT: *The Story of Ruby Bridges* by Robert Coles

---

Learning how to manage stress from a role model

I cannot think of a better role model for stress management than Ruby Bridges. There are many books about Ruby, but the one I like best is the picture book *The Story of Ruby Bridges* by Robert Coles. First published in 1995, this story was well known to a generation of children, many of whom also saw the made-for-TV "Ruby Bridges" movie, though fewer students today are familiar with it. The most obvious SEL application of this book (or movie) is its message about discrimination and its devastating personal costs. But I also want students to reflect on how this young child survived her incredibly stressful circumstances.

In 1960, Ruby was the only black child sent to William Frantz Elementary School as part of New Orleans' desegregation effort. She was entering first grade. As she climbed the school steps on her first day, a large crowd of protesters stood before her with "whites only" signs, shouting mean words and threatening to hurt her. The city and state police stood by but did nothing. Ruby continued to climb those steps that day, and for weeks and months to come, despite the relentless anger, and despite being the only child in her first-grade class—the white parents had decided to keep their children home rather than face integration. Ruby's teacher wondered how she did it, "How she went by those mobs and sat here all by herself and yet seemed so relaxed and comfortable." At one point, Ruby told her teacher that each morning she was praying for forgiveness for the people who hated her.

In Ruby's case, it was her faith that resolved her stress. In the public school classroom, we don't want to champion religion as the go-to stress remedy, but we do want to convey that each of us can look to someone, something, or someplace to restore our emotional well-being. For me, it's often an early morning walk on the beach where my steps are the first to make their mark on the new day. How can we make stress management visible to our students?

SEVEN THINKING BOXES

Questions for *The Story of Ruby Bridges* by Robert Coles
SEL Competency: Self-Management   Focus: Stress-Management

PLAIN CARDBOARD BOX	**BASIC THINKING** What was Ruby's difficult situation, and why would it be stressful for any child?
PUZZLE BOX	**PUZZLING DETAILS** Which detail in the story do you think *best* shows how well Ruby handled her stress? Explain your thinking.
HEART BOX	**FEELINGS** Ruby's teacher said she didn't seem upset by the ways people were trying to scare her. How do you think Ruby managed to handle her stress so well?
UNUSUAL BOX	**CREATIVE THINKING** Ruby stopped before going in to school to pray for the people saying terrible things to her. Do you think this was a creative solution for managing her stress? Why or why not?
BROKEN BOX	**PROBLEMS AND ISSUES** The problem that Ruby faced in this book was just one example of a much bigger problem in our country. What was it? If you had been Ruby would you have been willing to take the chances she took, or would it have been too stressful for you? Explain your thinking using details from the story.
TREASURE BOX	**SOMETHING TO TREASURE** Why do you think Ruby's parents were willing to put her through all of this stress? What was the benefit to Ruby? What was the benefit to other children?
TOOL BOX	**AUTHOR'S TOOLS** The author includes an "Afterward" at the end of this book. How does this add to your understanding of Ruby's story and the stress she encountered as a little girl?

SEVEN THINKING BOXES

Questions to ask about *any* book for stress management

PLAIN CARDBOARD BOX	**BASIC THINKING** • What is the stressful situation in this story? • Who is experiencing stress in this story? How?
PUZZLE BOX 	**PUZZLING DETAILS** • What sentence or statement in this story <u>best</u> shows how stress was handled well? • What sentence or statement in this story <u>best</u> shows the effect that stress had on the story characters?
HEART BOX	**FEELINGS** • What feelings did characters in this story experience because of stress? How did they show these feelings? • Who could help these characters feel less stressed? How could they help?
UNUSUAL BOX	**CREATIVE THINKING** • Did creative thinking play a part in reducing this character's stress? How? • How else might this character have reduced his or her stress? Would the outcome have been the same or different from what occurred in the story? Why?
BROKEN BOX	**PROBLEMS AND ISSUES** • What was the problem that led to the stress in this story? • Do you think this problem would have been as stressful to you as it was to the character in the story? Explain using details from the text.
TREASURE BOX	**SOMETHING TO TREASURE** • Why do you think this author wrote about characters experiencing stress? What can you learn from these characters? • Was managing stress the main message in this book? Was there something else? Explain.
TOOL BOX	**AUTHOR'S TOOLS** • How does the illustrator of this book add to your understanding of the characters' stress through their facial expressions or other kinds of body language? • What strong words does the author use to show the characters' stress?

Setting Goals

The remaining focus areas related to self-management and emotional regulation are so interconnected that it's difficult to talk about one without also considering the others. We typically begin with a *goal* and then use *organizational skills* to plan and work toward that goal. Along the way, *motivation* is important as well as the *self-discipline* to keep going. Almost any book cited for one focus area could support the others.

Simply stated, a goal is something a person wants to achieve. It could be something immediate and modest in scope, like finishing a book before dinner. Or, it could be a long-term goal with life-altering implications, like eventually going to medical school and becoming a doctor. We recognize the value of setting short- and long-term goals in school, and actively work toward both with students in the classroom.

WHAT WE HOPE TO SEE IN THE CLASSROOM REGARDING GOAL SETTING, AND WHAT WE SOMETIMES SEE INSTEAD

When students have a goal, they are purposeful learners. They have their eye on whatever it is they wish to accomplish, and often proceed systematically toward it. The best goals are those that students identify for themselves: I want to turn my report on George Washington's Battle of Trenton into a PowerPoint presentation and share my information that way. Alternately, a goal can be one we've established for them: You will write an essay comparing the development of the theme of courage in both sources. Some kids are the kind of worker-bees who embrace academic goals just because the teacher thinks something is important. But other times, these can be "fake goals." In this case, achievement is driven by *compliance*.

Unfortunately, I see a lot of compliance in classrooms. A quick classroom walkthrough could indicate that most students are engaged and on-task. But when you look more closely or ask a question like, "What are you working on?" the insights are disappointing. I saw this first-hand when I visited a classroom where students all had individual "power goals" for their new literacy program. "What's your power goal?" I asked one second grader. He wasn't sure but took me to a bulletin board where everyone's goal was posted: "It's *pronouncing multi-syllable words*," though he couldn't explain to me what "multi-syllable" words were. And when I looked through the book he was reading to meet his goal, I noted that it contained only two words that fit that criteria.

Having a goal is not all students need to *achieve* their goal, but it's a start. When a goal isn't accompanied by a plan, the motivation to achieve it, or the will to persist amid setbacks, it might be abandoned, or achieved at a less-than-ideal level. We'll save those conversations for later in this chapter.

ENHANCING CLASSROOM CULTURE: QUESTIONS FOR TEACHERS TO ASK THEMSELVES ABOUT GOAL SETTING

1. What could I include in a conversation with my students about goals? How could I help them understand the difference between short- and long-term goals?

2. What examples could I provide to my students to help them understand short- and long-term goals?

3. What role models (such as sports figures or other accomplished individuals) could I cite as examples of people with worthy goals?

4. How could I help my students establish a short-term goal for themselves that is both measurable and attainable?

5. How can I encourage my students to consider long-term goals for themselves?

6. How can I help my students invest in curriculum goals that are important, but may not be personal goals?

WHAT TO LOOK FOR IN BOOKS ABOUT SETTING GOALS

There are many stories about people who accomplish great things, although they may not have had that specific goal in mind at the outset. I've always wondered, for instance, how many Supreme Court justices would have said when they were a kid, "When I grow up, I want to be a Supreme Court justice." Was it their dream when they were awarded their law degree? At what point, if ever, did it become an objective? For this focus area, I don't choose stories about people who grow into their roles as their lives evolve. I look for real people and characters who have big dreams for the world, or something personal they'd like to achieve—either right then, as a child, or later as an adult. I look for books in which goals are not achieved in a predictable way, and where several attempts may precede the attainment of a goal. Examples of these books are listed in Chart 4.3: Books Aligned to Setting Goals.

CHART 4.3: BOOKS ALIGNED TO SETTING GOALS

THE MESSAGE	THE BOOK
You can set BIG goals	*Nelson Mandela* by Kadir Nelson (intermediate)
Set a long-term goal for yourself	*Uncle Jed's Barbershop* by Margaree King Mitchell (primary and intermediate)
Set an immediate short-term goal for yourself	*My Rows and Piles of Coins* by Tololwa M. Mollel (primary and intermediate)
Sometimes goals are achieved differently from how you planned	*Degas and the Little Dancer* by Laurence Anholt (intermediate)
Sometimes goals are not achieved right away	*Minty: A Story of Young Harriet Tubman* by Alan Schroeder (primary and intermediate)

You can set BIG goals

With students' heightened awareness of the need for global changes comes the inspiration to dream big: How can *you* be the change? But dreams can become starry-eyed fantasies without more understanding of what having a goal means.

Looking at a world leader like Nelson Mandela can provide this grounding, and the picture book **Nelson Mandela**—with both words and beautiful illustrations by Kadir Nelson—is the perfect resource. From a young age, Mandela's goal was to eliminate apartheid in South Africa, so that the country could be for *all* South Africans. But along with explaining his goal, this book also offers a glimpse into the factors that helped Mandela achieve it: relentless hard work, the ability to stand up for his beliefs, and the willingness to endure hardships (in this case imprisonment for more than 27 years). In *Nelson Mandela*, students see not just the goal, but the leadership qualities that helped him achieve it.

Set a long-term goal for yourself

My brother often jokes that I was born wanting to be a teacher, and I suppose it's true. I was so focused on this goal that I never even considered any other profession. I've loved my work, although my role within the field of education has changed in ways that I never anticipated or planned. Along the way, I had plenty of support, and no significant bumps in the road. Not everyone is so fortunate.

A favorite book about setting a long-term goal is **Uncle Jed's Barbershop**. Uncle Jed lives in the Depression-era south where, according to his niece (and the narrator of the story), his life-long goal is to own his own barbershop. No one believes he can make it happen, but Uncle Jed saves up his money anyway. Then his niece gets sick, and every saved-up cent goes toward doctor bills to cure her illness. Uncle Jed must start over. He's an old man when his shop finally opens, and he dies soon after. But he dies a happy man with a dream come true. In this story, students see not just a goal, but the willingness to pursue it even when others doubt you, even when the goal is delayed.

Set an immediate short-term goal for yourself

Students need to recognize that goals are not just for grown-ups. Satisfying in-the-moment needs (or wants) also qualify. The challenge is to help them identify worthy short-term needs or wants. "I *want* to be first in line," or "I *need* this video game," don't quite make the cut.

For a great book about a kid with a kid-sized goal, check out ***My Rows and Piles of Coins***. The story is set in Tanzania in the 1960s and centers on a little boy who dreams of owning a bike. He wants to help his mother take goods to the market and sees that a bike could help. While he is enticed by the toy trucks and marbles at the market, he holds tightly to his coins, remembering how much he wants the bike. His coin box gets heavier and he finally empties its contents into rows and piles, thinking himself the richest boy in the world.

But the bicycle salesman at the market just laughs when he shows him his pile of coins—it's not nearly enough for a bike. The boy confesses his disappointment to his mama on the way home. In the end, his father sells him his old bike, and the boy is thrilled. He realizes he did not need a shiny new bike after all; his dad's old one will be fine. Forego immediate gratification to achieve a larger goal! Satisfy a *need* rather than a *want*! These are the messages we want our students to recognize.

Sometimes goals are achieved differently from how you plan

If it isn't achieved in the way you anticipated, have you still achieved your goal? It's an interesting question, worthy of pondering, and ***Degas and the Little Dancer*** is a good catalyst for this discussion. Marie, the story's main character, dreams of only one thing: She wants to be a ballerina at the Paris Opera House. She is finally accepted at a competitive dance school and is in line for a leading part when her father becomes ill, and there's no money to continue her classes. Enter the great artist Dégas, who selects Marie to pose for him.

Dégas, as it turns out, is a very bad-tempered old man at this point with failing eyesight. He can no longer paint his iconic ballerinas and instead fashions a clay sculpture of Marie. She earns a few francs for being his model, but not enough to resume her classes. Her dreams of being a dancer are shattered. But then she receives an invitation to an art show. Works of Dégas are on display, and in a large glass box stands

The Little Dancer, a clay figure clad in real clothes. It's Marie, and she will now be "a little dancer" forever. Did she achieve her goal? Think of all the different perspectives students could consider when sorting out the answer to this question—truly the stuff of deeper depths of knowledge.

FEATURED BOOK FOR SETTING GOALS: *Minty: A Story of Young Harriet Tubman* **by Alan Schroeder**

Sometimes goals aren't achieved right away

Another "what if": What if you have a goal, but lack the courage to achieve it? To reflect on this question, I turn to *Minty: A Story of Young Harriet Tubman*. It's one of my favorite picture books, as it offers several important messages, mostly related to discrimination and the cruel treatment of slaves. But I also like it for the opportunity to reflect on setting and achieving goals for which the timing isn't quite right.

Following one especially brutal beating, young Harriet tries to run away, but she's caught and suffers harsh consequences. Her mama encourages her to obey in order to avoid further punishment, but her papa sees the seriousness of her goal and teaches her survival strategies for escape. Other attempts follow, but each time, Harriet loses her courage. As the story ends, Harriet still has not run away.

Many students are familiar with Harriet Tubman's contribution to the Underground Railroad, plotting not only her own escape, but also that of dozens more slaves. "She never forgot her goal," one fourth grader once observed, "but this just wasn't the right time." Students don't have the benefit of hindsight when projecting about how their own goals will turn out one day. But how comforting to see that a dream deferred is not a dream abandoned.

SEVEN THINKING BOXES

Questions to ask about *Minty: A Story of a Young Harriet Tubman* by Alan Schroeder
SEL Competency: Self-Management   Focus: Goal Setting

PLAIN CARDBOARD BOX	**BASIC THINKING**
	Minty let the muskrat go even though she knew she could get punished for doing this if she got caught. Why do you think she was willing to take this chance?
PUZZLE BOX	**PUZZLING DETAILS**
	What did Minty's mama, Old Rit mean when she said, "If your head is in the lion's mouth, it's best to pat him a little. Your head's in his mouth, Minty. . . Pat the lion, Minty. It ain't gonna kill you." Was Old Rit's goal for Minty the same as Minty's goal for herself? Explain.
HEART BOX	**FEELINGS**
	Which cruel event in this story do you think was *most* responsible for Minty's goal to run away? Why?
UNUSUAL BOX	**CREATIVE THINKING**
	Who was more creative in helping Minty achieve her goal of running away, her mother or her father? Explain your thinking.
BROKEN BOX	**PROBLEMS AND ISSUES**
	Although Minty had a goal (running away) she couldn't quite make herself take the steps to achieve her goal. What do you think was getting in the way? Explain.
TREASURE BOX	**SOMETHING TO TREASURE**
	At the end of the story Minty cried for a long time because she didn't achieve her goal when she had a chance. But then she realizes she *will* achieve her goal someday. What can you learn from this about setting and achieving your own goals?
TOOL BOX	**AUTHOR'S TOOLS**
	The author uses different <u>symbols</u> in this story to make the story more meaningful. Some of these symbols are the story of David, the lion's mouth, and the muskrat. What do each of these symbols stand for?

SEVEN THINKING BOXES

Questions to ask about *any* book for setting goals

PLAIN CARDBOARD BOX	**BASIC THINKING** • In this story, who set a goal? What was the goal? • When the story ended, had the character achieved his or her goal? What is the evidence?
PUZZLE BOX	**PUZZLING DETAILS** • What detail or quote in this story do you think <u>best</u> shows the importance of this goal? Why did you choose this detail? • What detail or quote in this story do you think <u>best</u> shows how this goal could change someone's life?
HEART BOX	**FEELINGS** • Did setting this goal affect anyone's feelings? Explain. • How did *you* feel about this character's goal? Was it important? Why?
UNUSUAL BOX	**CREATIVE THINKING** • Did achieving this goal require creative thinking? Explain using details from the text. • How might you have helped this character reach her goal differently?
BROKEN BOX	**PROBLEMS AND ISSUES** • Was this goal achieved easily, or were there problems along the way? What were the problems? • What problem led to setting this goal?
TREASURE BOX	**SOMETHING TO TREASURE** • What did the character in this story treasure that made him or her want to set this goal? • What can you learn from this story about setting goals and achieving them?
TOOL BOX	**AUTHOR'S TOOLS** • How does the author of this story <u>build suspense</u> after the character sets her or his goal? • How does the author of this story use <u>dialogue</u> to communicate the character's goal? Are any other crafts used to describe the goal? Explain.

Planning and Organization

If something is organized, it is arranged in an orderly way with a logical system. An organized *space* is typically neat without a lot of clutter and you can find what you need when you need it. Everything has a designated place. Organization also implies planning. It contributes to social emotional well-being because moving toward a goal requires having a system. A goal is *what* is to be done. The plan for achieving the goal describes *how* and *when* it will happen. The plan is all the decisions made between identifying the goal and achieving it, and most effective plans are generated *before* moving toward a goal. Sometimes the planning process is lengthy, requiring weeks, months, or even years. Other times plans are created quickly due to an urgent need.

WHAT WE HOPE TO SEE IN THE CLASSROOM REGARDING PLANNING AND ORGANIZATION, AND WHAT WE SOMETIMES SEE INSTEAD

The first thing one notices when walking into most classrooms is the space itself. Of course, some of this—organized or disorganized—is the domain of the teacher. But I consider students' desks to be their own small realms. Sometimes they are pristine, with clean, clear surfaces and carefully arranged contents. But others....I try to avoid even touching them. I attempted to extricate an assignment from one student's desk years ago, and in the process uncovered: three Shel Silverstein poetry books that had been missing from the classroom library for weeks, the stapler from my desk, a half-empty water bottle (at least the cap was on), too many pens and pencils to count, a bag of something that at some point might have been lunch, and jammed in, somehow, his math and social studies textbooks. The rest of the class just stared.

The kind of organization that involves planning is subtler, but often has a greater impact on the classroom than a messy desk. One of the biggest complaints I hear from teachers is that students cannot work independently. They need constant supervision to stay on task. They bounce out of their seat to get a drink of water, sharpen their pencil, or simply wander around the room. This explains why whole class instruction dominates many classrooms. Monitoring all of this off-task behavior is exhausting for teachers as they try to meet with small groups and find themselves continually distracted. However, by being at students' side all the time, we're enabling the kind of behavior we'd like to change. Students need to recognize the value of planning as they pursue a goal.

ENHANCING CLASSROOM CULTURE: QUESTIONS FOR TEACHERS TO ASK THEMSELVES ABOUT PLANNING AND ORGANIZATION

1. What can I do to set a better example of organization in my classroom? What needs to change?

2. Which students need help to better organize their personal space? How could I help them?

3. Which of my students are "planners?" What do they do that other students do not do?

4. How can I demonstrate to students the power of planning—how it can make a difference to them personally, and how it might help others?

5. What examples of good planning can I share with my students to help them better understand what planning is?

6. What could I ask my students to plan so that they can see first-hand the power of planning? How would I help them get started?

WHAT TO LOOK FOR IN BOOKS ABOUT PLANNING AND ORGANIZATION

While it's easy to identify books that focus on goals or persistence, it's not so easy to locate titles that emphasize planning. This section highlights titles in which the planning process is a significant part of the goal's ultimate success. I also selected books that describe plans created by children that enact a personal, kid-size need, and others where adults are the planners and the impact is far-reaching. Finally, I chose books where the plan may take a very long time to implement, and where things may not go as planned. With a little digging, there are many books that highlight the value of planning and being organized, five of which are listed below in Chart 4.4: Books Aligned to Planning and Organization. I'll begin with an amusing tale of a little girl who was "totally the messiest."

CHART 4.4: BOOKS ALIGNED TO PLANNING AND ORGANIZATION

THE MESSAGE	THE BOOK
Organize your space!	*Super-Completely and Totally the Messiest!* by Judith Viorst (primary)
You need to know *how* to plan	*Galimoto* by Karen Lynn Williams (primary)
Planning can save the day	*The Librarian of Basra: A True Story from Iraq* by Jeanette Winter (primary and intermediate)
Don't give up on a plan, even if it takes a long time to reach your goal	*As Good as Anybody: Martin Luther King, Jr. and Abraham Joshua Heschel's Amazing March Toward Freedom* by Richard Michelson (intermediate)
Sometimes plans go wrong—and it's okay	*Down the Road* by Alice Schertle (primary and intermediate)

Organize your space!

With Judith Viorst's characteristic kid-voice, she tells the story of Sophie, who is **Super-Completely and Totally the Messiest!,** as decreed by the book's title. The tale is told from the perspective of Sophie's older (and nearly perfect) sister, Olivia. And Olivia has a ton of evidence to defend her claim. There's so much stuff on Sophie's bed that you can only see the top of her head. An avalanche of toys and clothes tumbles out of her closet when she opens the door a wee crack. She can wipe out an entire village of sandcastles as she dashes down the beach with her towel flying behind her.

What I like about this book is that it catches kids' attention through its silliness. The perils of disorganization are demonstrated in a light-hearted manner (complete with comical illustrations) that send young students a clear message without being threatening. Observed one student: "If Sophie came to our classroom, we'd surely have to teach her a thing or two about getting organized."

You need to know *how* to plan

Lots of students fail to recognize the significance of planning in achieving a goal. I'm always reminded of the "Plan Ahead" poster, where the first few letters are super-sized, but then become smaller and smaller as the last few letters nearly run off the page—obviously the result of *not* planning ahead. Like this artist, some students dive into a project before thinking it through. Kondi is a worthy role model to demonstrate *how* to plan.

Kondi is the main character in **Galimoto,** the story of a young African boy who wishes to make a "galimoto"—though the author does not reveal what a galimoto is until the end of the story. For this he needs wire, which his older brother tells him he will not be able to get. But Kondi has a plan. First, he barters with his friend to trade his knife for a few lengths of wire. Next, he approaches a shopkeeper and asks for the wires that held some old packing boxes together. In a trash heap, he finds some broken spokes from a bicycle. There are other steps along the way, too, and soon Kondi has all the wire he needs to make his galimoto—a toy vehicle made of wires. Kondi thought about all the ways he could get wire, and systematically worked through his plan.

Planning can save the day

Galimoto shows students *how* to plan. **The Librarian of Basra: A True Story from Iraq** shows them *why* they should plan. In the book, the librarian Alia Muhammad Baker is worried that the thousands of books in her library could be destroyed when war threatens her country. She needs a plan to hide the books, and her friend who owns a nearby restaurant agrees to help—just in time, too. The library is soon bombed and burns to the ground. But even then, Alia must continue to plan for the safety of her books. She hires a truck to bring all 30,000 of them to her own house, and the houses of her friends. Throughout the war, Alia tries to stay one step ahead of the soldiers—and she succeeds. Why is this problem plan-worthy? What is so important to your students that they would stop whatever they were doing and create a plan to protect it? Imagine the conversation these questions might inspire in your classroom.

Don't give up on a plan, even if it takes a long time to reach your goal

Patience is seldom children's strong suit. They're into instant gratification. So, if you plan to save up for some new techno-toy starting today, you should be able to buy it tomorrow. However, the higher and more important the stakes, the longer it may take to get there. For this message I love the book **As Good as Anybody: Martin Luther King, Jr. and Abraham Joshua Heschel's Amazing March Toward Freedom.**

How could a Baptist preacher from Atlanta and a rabbi from Poland have much in common? They both fought for justice and equality, aiming to end the discrimination against black people in America and Jews in Europe that plagued their lives. Theirs was the kind of plan that required decades to execute—marches, sit-ins, speeches, so many forms of protest—all to show the world they're *as good as anybody.* Eventually their paths (and plans) crossed, and they marched together for the first time in Selma, Alabama in 1965. Three years later, Abraham Heschel spoke at King's funeral about King's sacred mission and long-term vision. It's a plan still seeking a just resolution.

FEATURED BOOK FOR PLANNING AND ORGANIZATION: *Down the Road* by Alice Schertle

Sometimes a plan goes wrong—and it's okay

Sometimes plans don't work out, and students are quick to judge: "You said if I studied hard for this test, I would get a good grade. Well, I studied really, really hard and I only got a *C*." How will we encourage students to respond when their plan falls short of expectations? I love the book ***Down the Road***, not just for its great example of a plan gone awry, and the response of the main character, but also for the response of the main character's parents.

In the story, nine-year-old Hetty lives in a rural community and is eager to show how responsible she is by walking to the general store by herself to purchase a dozen eggs. Mama is going to make eggs for breakfast. So she sets off on her mission with egg basket in hand, walking extra carefully, just as she plans to do when her basket is full of eggs. And after she's acquired the eggs, she *is* careful—at least until she spies some luscious apples hanging from a nearby tree. She knows how much her parents love apples and decides to get one for each of them. But as she reaches for Papa's apple, the egg basket tips. You can guess the outcome.

Hetty climbs the apple tree, thinking it's a good place to hide from her parents who are sure to be furious that her plan to be responsible fell woefully short. Papa comes along soon after and Hetty tearfully confesses. But Papa isn't mad. In fact, he climbs the tree to sit alongside Hetty as she thinks things over. Then Mama arrives and responds similarly. In the end, they all walk home with their basket full of apples and a new plan to have apple pie for breakfast. I often use this book at parent workshops. What a beautiful example of parenting that looks at children's shortcomings in a way that says, "It's okay." Maybe *this* plan didn't work out. But we can improvise, and tomorrow is a new day.

SEVEN THINKING BOXES

Questions for *Down the Road* by Alice Schertle

SEL Competency: Self-Management   Focus: Planning and Organization

PLAIN CARDBOARD BOX	**BASIC THINKING** Hetty had a plan to be very mature and responsible at the beginning of this story. What events in the story showed her effort to be responsible?
PUZZLE BOX	**PUZZLING DETAILS** There are several details in this story that show what happens when Hetty's plan doesn't work out. Choose one detail that best shows how even when a plan <u>doesn't</u> work out, it can be a good experience. Explain your thinking.
HEART BOX	**FEELINGS** Why do you think Hetty is so upset that her plan didn't work out? What is she mostly concerned about?
UNUSUAL BOX	**CREATIVE THINKING** In the end, Hetty's parents don't seem that upset about Hetty's failed plan. How did creative thinking make a difference in this situation?
BROKEN BOX	**PROBLEMS AND ISSUES** Although Hetty's dad realized that she did not make a good decision when she decided to pick the apples, he wasn't really angry. Why not? What does this show about the way this dad understands his daughter and her plan?
TREASURE BOX	**SOMETHING TO TREASURE** If Hetty becomes a mom when she is older, how do you think this experience with the eggs will make a difference to the way she helps her children plan? (What did she learn from this?)
TOOL BOX	**AUTHOR'S TOOLS** In this story the author uses a lot of <u>dialogue</u> to show us more about the characters. What do we learn about the three main characters: Hetty, her mom, and her dad through their own words? Which lines of dialogue show us the most about the way they plan?

SEVEN THINKING BOXES

Questions to ask about *any* book for planning and organization

PLAIN CARDBOARD BOX	**BASIC THINKING** • What is the <u>plan</u> in this story? What was the plan designed to achieve? • Was there someone in this story who needed to be better organized to achieve their plan? Who? Explain.
PUZZLE BOX 	**PUZZLING DETAILS** • What were the details of the plan? Did any details stand out? Explain. • What details <u>best</u> show poor organization?
HEART BOX	**FEELINGS** • What feelings led the character to become more organized or to plan? Explain. • How did the character feel when the plan worked out? Explain.
UNUSUAL BOX	**CREATIVE THINKING** • In what way did the plan require creative thinking? • How might you have changed the plan to solve this problem? What would you have done differently?
BROKEN BOX	**PROBLEMS AND ISSUES** • Why did the character's disorganization matter? Explain • What problem led to this plan? Who was affected by the problem and how will this plan make a difference?
TREASURE BOX	**SOMETHING TO TREASURE** • What did you learn from this story about organizing or planning well? Explain. • What do you think the character(s) learned about organizing or planning well? Explain.
TOOL BOX	**AUTHOR'S TOOLS** • What tools that the author uses <u>best</u> show why this plan was created? (It might be dialogue, description, body language, or something else.) • If the author uses illustrations to show poor organization, how did this add to your understanding of the problem?

Self-Motivation

If you are self-motivated, you are willing to do whatever is necessary to get a job done without the encouragement of someone else. Sometimes people are motivated because they expect success or conversely, because they fear failure. Motivated people pursue a goal even when it's challenging because they are invested in the outcome. The outcome might be the personal satisfaction one derives from, for example, learning a new skill. Personal satisfaction is considered an *intrinsic* reward. Or, the outcome might be receiving a good grade on a test, or some other outside acknowledgement of success, which is an *extrinsic* reward. Students are motivated both intrinsically and extrinsically.

WHAT WE HOPE TO SEE IN THE CLASSROOM REGARDING SELF-MOTIVATION, AND WHAT WE SOMETIMES SEE INSTEAD

A frequent complaint from teachers is that kids are not as motivated today as they were in the past. While it's true that there are some students who do not seem very interested in school, I see plenty of students who are very committed. They begin their work promptly and follow tasks to completion. They raise their hand to answer questions and are active members of the classroom community. They show us in many ways that they're in school to *learn*. But at the next desk might sit another student, seemingly less motivated. This child needs reminders from the teacher to get started on an assignment, and then more reminders to stay focused and get the job done.

We sometimes blame lack of motivation on a too-prescriptive, standards-based curriculum bound by rigid expectations: "If only students could choose their own goals, they would be more motivated." I'm not sure the curriculum is the culprit. I watch many teachers deliver lessons, and there are times when the teacher does almost all the talking. There are also times when the instruction is not clear. There are times when the follow-up task does not match the lesson just taught, or when the resource used for the activity is not a good match to the lesson objective. Before we label students "unmotivated" perhaps we should reflect on our own practice.

ENHANCING CLASSROOM CULTURE: QUESTIONS FOR TEACHERS TO ASK THEMSELVES ABOUT SELF-MOTIVATION

1. Which students in my class appear the most motivated? What do they do that shows this motivation? What is it that motivates each of these students?

2. Which students in my class appear the least motivated? How do they show their lack of motivation?

3. Is there anything I could do in my interactions with unmotivated students to increase their investment in learning?

4. Is there anything I could change in my instruction to better support unmotivated students and change their behavior?

5. What do I want my students to understand about the role of motivation in their learning, and how could I talk about this with them?

6. How could I show my students the power of motivation in contributing to achievement? Who are some possible role models?

WHAT TO LOOK FOR IN BOOKS THAT ADDRESS SELF-MOTIVATION

Books about self-motivation typically show characters with a goal, a plan, and persistence. But the books I feature here in Chart 4.5: Books Aligned to Self-Motivation strongly emphasize *what* motivates the character. The motivation might come from a personal need, passion for a hobby, a desire to excel, or from a need that reaches beyond themselves into their community or the world. I also include a book for students who may have fallen short of meeting a goal and need to motivate themselves to try again.

CHART 4.5: BOOKS ALIGNED TO SELF-MOTIVATION

THE MESSAGE	THE BOOK
Sometimes we are motivated by a personal goal	*More Than Anything Else* by Marie Bradby (primary or intermediate)
Sometimes we are motivated by others' needs	*The Boy Who Harnessed the Wind* by William Kamkwamba and Bryan Mealer (primary and intermediate)
Sometimes we are motivated to excel at a skill	*Salt in His Shoes: Michael Jordan in Pursuit of a Dream* by Deloris Jordan with Roslyn M. Jordan (primary and intermediate)
Sometimes we are motivated by a special hobby or passion	*Snowflake Bentley* by Jacqueline Briggs Martin (primary and intermediate)
Sometimes we are motivated by failure—and the need to try again	*After the Fall (How Humpty Dumpty Got Back Up Again)* by Dan Santat (primary and intermediate)

Sometimes we are motivated by a personal goal

The greatest motivator is *need*, with some needs taking precedence over others. Again, I summon Maslow and his hierarchy. Self-actualization is at the very top of this pyramid, and can only be pursued after other more basic needs have been met: physiological needs, safety, love, and esteem (Maslow, 1943). The desire to learn falls within this top tier, and explains why students who don't know where they'll be sleeping that night might not be that interested in mastering short vowel sounds.

But regardless of our perception of children's needs, *they* decide when they're ready for personal growth. ***More Than Anything Else*** by Marie Bradby is a wonderful example. It's the story of a young former slave and his desire to learn to read in the years following the Civil War. The boy works from sunup to sundown packing salt in barrels at the saltworks. With no shoes to protect his feet from the sharp salt crystals, it's a painful, backbreaking job. Then one evening after work he spots a man who looks a lot like him reading a newspaper to a gathering of people. He thinks, "I have found hope, and it is as brown as me." This is my favorite line in the book and I always pause to discuss it with students. What does the boy mean? "Oh," someone always exclaims, looking at the illustration.

As the story progresses, the boy perseveres even after long days at the salt mines, even after his early attempts to read fail. He wants to be *that* man. He can see himself reading to that same crowd, teaching others to read. Eventually he finds the newspaper man who helps him, and his joy at finally succeeding nearly leaps off the page. I don't tell my students until we finish that this is a *true* story. The young boy is Booker T. Washington, and his motivation to read "more than anything else" led to the achievement of his dreams. I leave it up to the kids to research exactly what Booker achieved as an adult.

Sometimes we are motivated by others' needs

Thanks to social media, the nightly news, and our own efforts in the classroom, many students are more globally aware than they were in the past. Some even envision themselves solving global problems. Kids *can* make a difference, and William Kamkwamba is just the kid to demonstrate this to our students.

William is the child featured in ***The Boy Who Harnessed the Wind***. He grew up in a village in Malawi, Africa, where people had no money for lights, and a drought had scorched the fields of maize that were the villagers' only source of income. Without enough food for his family to eat (or the $80 per year for tuition), William could no longer attend school. But he was determined to help. He visited his small village library and found a book with a picture of a tall machine with blades like a fan. He was able to translate the caption into his own language: "Windmills can produce electricity and pump water." William vowed to build "electric wind."

And he did—using discarded bits and pieces from the junkyard. His friends laughed at his efforts, but William kept bolting and banging. Though rough and rickety, William's windmill worked. It was the beginning of a wind project that would go on to feed his country. William graduated from Dartmouth College in 2014 and now works with a global agency on projects to improve the standard of living for those in need. His story is also told in a wonderful Netflix documentary (with the same title as the book), though a couple of violent scenes may make it unsuitable for younger students.

Sometimes we are motivated to excel at a skill

Lots of kids have big dreams. They want to be world-renowned superstars— artists, ballerinas, soccer players, or the like. Some of them (alone, or with their parents' encouragement) keep that dream alive with relentless hard work. But others—like Michael Jordan, as the story goes—seek something like "salt in their shoes" to turn their dream into reality.

Salt in His Shoes is a story about Michael Jordan when he was a boy, told by his mom and sister. Michael loved basketball, but he was *short,* hard though that is to believe. Michael thought the secret to winning was growing taller, and he begged his mother for a solution. She claimed that putting salt in his shoes every night before bedtime would get the job done. To his dismay, the salt didn't work, and for a while he stayed away from his neighborhood basketball court. That's when his dad stepped in. He said that being taller might help a little, but what he needed most was practice and determination. That was the day Michael finally shot the ball over the tall guy's head and made the winning basket. The message to our students is: Motivation to excel takes a lot more than a wish.

Sometimes we are motivated to excel at a special hobby or passion

There always seems to be some fad going around—here today, gone tomorrow. But while it prevails, it morphs into a near obsession, and students feel that they're somehow a little cooler if they're part of the frenzy. Think slime, unicorns, and fidget toys. On a personal note, I just disposed of several bins of Beanie Babies, a remnant of my daughter's childhood (and am hoping I didn't sacrifice the family fortune to the town's recycling center).

Some children, however, are less motivated to follow the crowd into the next mania, and instead focus on passions that their friends might find a bit unique, even odd. For students who need motivation to follow their heart, read *Snowflake Bentley.* Wilson Bentley was born in 1865 in northern Vermont, where there are more than 100 inches of snow every year. He liked nature of all kinds but loved snowflakes best. He was mesmerized by their intricate patterns and was astounded that no two snowflakes were alike. The camera he eventually acquired was hardly the stuff of today's technology, but was the tool he needed to photograph snow crystals. Even today, it's "Snowflake Bentley's" book *Snow Crystals* that is the starting point for snow scholars. A monument and museum now honor Wilson Bentley as a lasting tribute, but I'm guessing the joy he got from snowflakes during his lifetime was tribute enough.

FEATURED BOOK FOR SELF-MOTIVATION: *After the Fall (How Humpty Dumpty Got Back Up)* **by Dan Santat**

Sometimes we are motivated by failure—and the need to try again

The featured book for self-motivation, ***After the Fall (How Humpty Dumpty Got Back Up)*** is literally a story about falling down and getting back up. Students of all ages will enjoy the comical illustrations and amusing tale of the well-loved egg of nursery-rhyme fame. Although in this version, all the king's men *do* manage to put Humpty together again. Nonetheless, he's a long way from the top of his wall, and in the aftermath of his accident, he is now afraid of heights. What to do!

He watches the birds from afar, and longs to be up on the wall with them. At last he gathers every ounce of courage and begins the climb, terrified. He makes it and hopes he'll now be remembered not as the little egg who fell, but the one who got back up. It's a lovely fable for children who need an extra spark of motivation to attempt something again that might have ended badly at first but. Questions for Seven Thinking Boxes follow to get this conversation going in your classroom.

SEVEN THINKING BOXES

Questions for *After the Fall (How Humpty Dumpty Got Back Up)* by Dan Santat
SEL Competency: Self-Regulation   Focus: Self-Motivation

PLAIN CARDBOARD BOX	**BASIC THINKING** What motivated Humpty Dumpty? What details in the story show this?
PUZZLE BOX	**PUZZLING DETAILS** Some of the best details in this story are shown through the expression on Humpty Dumpty's face. Look closely at these illustrations. What do these images show about him?
HEART BOX	**FEELINGS** Humpty Dumpty was afraid of falling again but managed to climb the wall again anyway. What feelings motivated him to do this?
UNUSUAL BOX	**CREATIVE THINKING** How did Humpty Dumpty's creativity help to motivate him to try again?
BROKEN BOX	**PROBLEMS AND ISSUES** Which of Humpty Dumpty's problems in this story could be solved? Which problems could *not* be solved? Did the unsolved problems get in the way of his motivation? Explain.
TREASURE BOX	**SOMETHING TO TREASURE** Is this story just about a little egg who falls off a wall? Is there a bigger message about motivation? What is it? How might you apply this message to yourself?
TOOL BOX	**AUTHOR'S TOOLS** The author makes Humpty Dumpty sound like a kid. What are some examples of Humpty's words that make him sound like he's having a conversation with one of his friends? Why do you think the author chose to have Humpty tell the story using this kind of voice?

SEVEN THINKING BOXES

Questions to ask about *any* book for self-motivation

PLAIN CARDBOARD BOX	**BASIC THINKING**
	• Who needs to be motivated in this story, and what do they need to be motivated to do?
	• How does motivation change the outcome of this story? What would have happened if the character was <u>not</u> motivated?
PUZZLE BOX	**PUZZLING DETAILS**
	• What details in this story <u>best</u> show the character's motivation? Explain.
	• Did you find any of the details in this story troubling? Why?
HEART BOX	**FEELINGS**
	• How does the character feel <u>before</u> finding the motivation to move forward toward his or her goal? How did the character feel afterward? Explain.
	• Did you feel sorry for this character at any point? Why?
UNUSUAL BOX	**CREATIVE THINKING**
	• Does this character think creatively to motivate herself or himself to work toward a goal? Explain.
	• How could *you* have motivated this character to move forward toward his or her goal?
BROKEN BOX	**PROBLEMS AND ISSUES**
	• Is there a problem in the story that requires motivation to overcome? Explain.
	• What is standing in the way of this character's motivation to overcome this problem?
TREASURE BOX	**SOMETHING TO TREASURE**
	• Is this character motivated to achieve a goal that would make him or her a more fulfilled person? Or, is the character motivated to achieve a goal that would help improve the world? Explain.
	• Think about this character's motivation. Would he or she have been a good influence on you? Or, would you have been a good influence on this character? Why?
TOOL BOX	**AUTHOR'S TOOLS**
	• Authors don't <u>tell</u> you that a character is motivated, you need to <u>infer</u> it. How did this author <u>show</u> that the character was motivated?
	• Who is the narrator in this story? How does that matter to the way you understand the character's motivation?

Self-Discipline

Self-discipline refers to students' willingness to follow a task through to completion, whether or not they feel inspired to do so. Sometimes this means standing up to challenges or overcoming obstacles. In school it can mean powering through an assignment or lesson they find uninteresting or not particularly relevant. Unlike some SEL concepts, students in many classrooms are familiar with the meaning of self-discipline, though more common labels are perseverance, determination, or grit. Aside from the implications for their own self-management, self-discipline is a frequent theme in children's literature, and students are quick to identify characters they've met who demonstrate this quality.

WHAT WE HOPE TO SEE IN THE CLASSROOM FOR SELF-DISCIPLINE, AND WHAT WE SOMETIMES SEE INSTEAD

What we'd appreciate in the classroom are students who finish what they start in a timely manner, to a high standard, and with a smile on their face. Of course, we do see this with some students, perhaps many students. Disciplined students have those other self-management pieces in place: a goal, a plan, and motivation. Now they just need to get the job done. Self-disciple is one of those qualities that we are more aware of when it is *not* present than when it is.

Kids without self-discipline seem to come in two varieties. Some of them sigh a bored sigh before we even finish giving directions for an assignment. They lose interest in a close reading lesson before we reach the second paragraph. They're often passive learners without a clear goal, plan, or motivation, so they find it difficult to maintain the stamina needed to see a task through to completion. But other not-very-disciplined students present differently. We have high expectations for these students because they can be enthusiastic at the outset of a project. They come to us with grand ideas for accomplishing the task creatively and we think, "Wow, this kid is amazing!" For a while they are busy with whatever their creative process entails. But then. . . nothing much happens. Somewhere along the way they lose steam, or some other venture catches their interest. It's not clear exactly where their plan derailed.

However, I think, their "plan" (or lack thereof) often *is* the problem: They have a goal and plenty of motivation, but no real plan to get there. All that creative energy is never converted into actionable steps. As their teachers, we may not spot these creative underachievers in the first round. But afterwards, we should be more tuned in, and ready to guide them.

ENHANCING CLASSROOM CULTURE: QUESTIONS FOR TEACHERS TO ASK THEMSELVES ABOUT SELF-DISCIPLINE

1. How do I label self-discipline in my classroom? (It might be perseverance, determination, stamina, grit, or some other term.)

2. What books have I read to my students in which the character shows self-discipline? Have I discussed this trait with students, and its role in helping the character achieve their goal?

3. Which students in my class typically show self-discipline? What seems to be responsible for this stamina in completing a task?

4. Which students in my class typically do not show enough self-discipline? What seems to be responsible for this lack of stamina?

5. How can I better support the students in my class who need more self-discipline?

6. What real-world role models can demonstrate the importance of self-discipline? (Consider story characters and individuals who have persevered to overcome obstacles.)

WHAT TO LOOK FOR IN BOOKS ABOUT SELF-DISCIPLINE

On the surface, most books about self-discipline appear to communicate the same central idea: Work hard and you will reach your goal. And in fact, this message *is* conveyed frequently. But it's the underlying issues that I want students to recognize: What made this character *need* stamina, perseverance, grit, or determination? Our students may see themselves in some of these situations. Perhaps they, too, have tried, failed, and need to keep trying. Maybe there are hardships or biases to overcome, like poverty, race, or cultural factors. Maybe there's risk involved, or trade-offs that require sacrifice. The books listed below in Chart 4.6: Books Aligned to Self-Discipline address these issues.

CHART 4.6: BOOKS ALIGNED TO SELF-DISCIPLINE

THE MESSAGE	THE BOOK
Keep trying, even if at first you don't succeed	*The Most Magnificent Thing* by Ashley Spires (primary and intermediate)
Self-discipline can lead to surprising results	*The Bear and the Piano* by David Litchfield (primary and intermediate)
Don't let physical or other limitations get in the way of self-discipline	*Emmanuel's Dream: The True Story of Emmanuel Ofosu Yeboah* by Laurie Ann Thompson (primary and intermediate)
Don't let poverty get in the way of self-discipline	*Sonia Sotomayor: A Judge Grows in the Bronx* by Jonah Winter (intermediate)
Sometimes self-discipline involves risk	*How Many Days to America?: A Thanksgiving Story* by Eve Bunting (primary and intermediate)

Keep trying, even if at first you don't succeed

One of the reasons I encourage teachers to work with students in small groups for reading is not so they can vary the instructional level (all students need challenge), but for the social emotional benefits of working in a small group. I was working with one small group of students recently on a written response that involved identifying the author's message, then summarizing the evidence for their claim. "Is this enough? My hand hurts!" one child asked, handing me her paper, "You haven't provided enough evidence yet, but you're doing great. Keep going." It's much easier to be the cheerleader students need when there are only a few of them at a time who need your attention. Of course there are other SEL benefits to small group instruction too, like more student interaction.

The main character in **The Most Magnificent Thing** didn't have a teacher to support her, but she did have her dog. As the story begins, she has a vision for engineering "the most magnificent thing," though we don't yet know what it is. She is repeatedly perplexed by how not-magnificent her creations are and begins to lose patience. Things get worse when she hammers her thumb, and in an angry meltdown, she decides to take a break. Her not-magnificent products are strewn about the sidewalk, but she suddenly sees that though they miss the mark, there is something good about each one. She revises, refines, reimagines, and voila—the result is a magnificent little cart attached to her scooter so that her dog can ride along. In fact, the cart is more wobbly than magnificent. But it's exactly what she had in mind.

Many messages prevail in this book beyond "hard work pays off." There's acknowledgement of the disappointment, and even anger, you may feel when at first you don't succeed. There's the decision to take a brief break, and a demonstration of how this can change your perspective. There's the acceptance of imperfection as sufficiently magnificent. The main character in this book is a young child, but the author's many layers of meaning make it suitable for older students, too.

Self-discipline can lead to surprising results

"If you work hard on your writing this year, those skills will serve you well next year, and every year after that…" Getting students to understand that perseverance is worth the effort can be challenging, because their idea of the future can be as limited as what will happen after lunch. Nonetheless, this is an important message because the goal of teaching is *transfer*. If students can't apply their learning beyond that day's lesson, what have we really achieved? **The Bear and the Piano** can help students see that today's hard work can pay big dividends down the road.

There was once a little bear who found a piano in the forest. At first, he didn't know what it was, but after some unmusical plinks, he learned to make sounds that were quite beautiful. His bear friends came from afar and applauded his efforts, and the little bear tried even harder. Then a girl and her father happened along and told the bear he was so remarkable he could play his music in grand concert halls in big cities. The bear began to attract even larger audiences, and he loved it. Although he had never expected (or even hoped) to become a great pianist, it's where his hard work took him. Hard work can pay off in surprising ways.

Don't let physical or other personal limitations get in the way of self-discipline

Like the little bear taught us, it's all a matter of perspective: How do you see yourself? How do others see you? Sometimes students are reluctant to persevere because they don't believe in themselves, and perceive that others regard them as incapable as well. **Emmanuel's Dream** is the true story of Emmanuel Ofosu Yedboah, born in Ghana, West Africa. Emmanuel was born with a deformed leg, a physical limitation that caused most people to dismiss him.

But Emmanuel's mother was not "most people." She told her son he could do anything and didn't allow his weak leg to stop him. When he got too heavy for her to carry to school, she told him to hop—two miles each way. As he grew, he was more determined than ever to prove that "being disabled does not mean being *un*able." What he needed was a bike! He got one and trained hard, pedaling his way around his country. Along the way Emmanuel talked with many people, some with physical and other challenges and some without. He wanted everyone to hear his message: Don't give up!

Don't let poverty or bias get in the way of self-discipline

Like Emmanuel, Sonia Sotomayor was born into circumstances that would not have caused many people to foresee a bright future for her. Her picture book biography, *Sonia Sotomayor: A Judge Grows in the Bronx* explains that she was just a little girl growing up in the projects in the Bronx, New York City, where her world featured chain-link fences and abandoned buildings. But like Emmanuel, Sonia had a mom who believed in her, *and* she had determination to succeed. While Sonia's mom never made it beyond third grade in her native Puerto Rico, she worked multiple jobs so her children could attend private schools.

Sonia vowed to be unstoppable, and eventually graduated from Princeton. She became a judge, and unlike many others in her role, knew what prejudice was—what it was to be judged by your race and where you came from. Then came the chance of a lifetime: President Barack Obama nominated her to be a Supreme Court justice, the first Latin American to be appointed to this role. Indeed, Sonia Sotomayor was, and still is, unstoppable. What can our students learn from this strong woman? How can we help them to be unstoppable even in the face of poverty and prejudice?

Sometimes self-discipline involves risk

For this notion, there is no better book than *How Many Days to America?: A Thanksgiving Story*. A family faced with political tyranny in their Caribbean country makes the difficult decision to board a small boat in the dark of night with other asylum seekers to journey to America. It is not an easy trip. The boat is crowded. The motor stops working. Heavy winds and rolling waves make everyone sick. There are many occasions when turning back is a tempting option. But the travelers keep going; freedom in America will make the voyage worth the perils of getting there.

Especially for students who have failed at a goal in the past, expending new effort to pursue the same goal is risky business. They reason that if they don't try, they can't fail again. As their teachers, we see it differently: If they don't try, and lack the self-discipline to work toward a goal, they have no chance of succeeding. We just need to change the fixed mindsets that preclude productive struggle.

FEATURED BOOK FOR SELF-DISCIPLINE: *How Many Days to America? A Thanksgiving Story* by Eve Bunting

---

SEVEN THINKING BOXES

Questions for *How Many Days to America?: A Thanksgiving Story* by Eve Bunting
SEL Skill: Self-Management   Focus: Self-Discipline

PLAIN CARDBOARD BOX	**BASIC THINKING** Why did this family want to leave their country? What details show this?
PUZZLE BOX	**PUZZLING DETAILS** What details in this story show that this was a very risky journey? Find one or two quotes, and then put them into your own words.
HEART BOX	**FEELINGS** This journey to America led to many different feelings for members of this family. Identify two or three feelings. What details show these feelings? What was responsible for these feelings? Explain.
UNUSUAL BOX	**CREATIVE THINKING** How might you welcome travelers like this who came to America seeking safety?
BROKEN BOX	**PROBLEMS AND ISSUES** What problems requiring self-discipline might this family face now that they've arrived in America? Explain.
TREASURE BOX	**SOMETHING TO TREASURE** What do you treasure from this book? What do you think the author wanted us to realize about self-discipline?
TOOL BOX	**AUTHOR'S TOOLS** The author of this book chose the subtitle: *A Thanksgiving Story*. It's true that this family's boat arrives the day before Thanksgiving. But what other reason might the author have had for choosing this subtitle?

SEVEN THINKING BOXES

Questions to ask about *any* book for self-discipline

PLAIN CARDBOARD BOX 	**BASIC THINKING** • In this story, who needed self-discipline? Did they always have self-discipline or did they need to learn the importance of this throughout their life? Explain. • What life circumstances made things difficult for this character, and made self-discipline even more important?
PUZZLE BOX 	**PUZZLING DETAILS** • Find a quote that you think best shows this character's understanding of the importance of self-discipline. What else does this show about this character? • Who helped the main character in this story understand the importance of self-discipline? What details show this?
HEART BOX 	**FEELINGS** • What feelings do you think were getting in the way of this character's self-discipline? Explain. • Did this character eventually have more self-discipline? How did this make her feel?
UNUSUAL BOX 	**CREATIVE THINKING** • How would you have helped this character realize the importance of self-discipline? • Did this character's self-discipline lead to creativity? What evidence in the text shows this?
BROKEN BOX 	**PROBLEMS AND ISSUES** • What problem would self-discipline have solved in this story? Explain. • What was the problem in this story that needed someone's self-discipline?
TREASURE BOX 	**SOMETHING TO TREASURE** • What do you think this author wanted you to learn about self-discipline from this story? • Do you think you will remember this character? Will you remember him or her for their self-discipline, or for something else? Explain.
TOOL BOX	**AUTHOR'S TOOLS** • What new title could you give to this book that would show the importance of self-discipline? • Rewrite the ending of this story showing what might have happened if this character had not been self-disciplined.

CHAPTER 5

SOCIAL AWARENESS: BRIDGING THE DIVIDE BETWEEN SELF AND OTHERS

While both self-awareness and self-management often involve others in some way, the impact is more coincidental than intentional. Though it may not be planned, someone may get in the way of another's accurate self-perception or diminish their self-confidence. They might interfere with their personal goals or contribute to their stress. Social awareness, by contrast, means you're tuned in to the people around you and recognize that your actions make a difference to them, in addition to yourself. CASEL defines social awareness as "The ability to take the perspective of and empathize with others, including from diverse backgrounds and cultures. The ability to understand social and ethical norms for behavior and to recognize family, school, and community resources and supports" ("Core SEL Competencies," n.d.).

This includes four focus areas:

- Perspective-Taking
- Empathy
- Appreciating diversity
- Respect for others

Having social awareness means that you recognize that other people matter. It requires asking if there's another way to look at a situation. Ask: who's in control here? Who has the power to make changes? Why does this matter? It means imagining yourself as *that* person in *that* situation. How would you feel? What would be important to you? How could you respond with empathy? Would it require a deeper understanding of diverse races or experiences? Would it lead to greater respect for others? For social awareness, there are many questions we need to ask ourselves and our students. We are fortunate that this is an area with many wonderful books to help us find the answers.

Perspective-Taking

Perspective, point of view, and *opinion* are often confused with each other. *Perspective* means the angle from which you see something, the things you may know because of your experience or knowledge. Your *opinion* is how you feel about something. In literature, *point of view* relates to who is telling the story: Is it an outside narrator, or one of the characters?

I'll use my dog to illustrate all three of these terms. Chloe is an eight-pound Pomeranian, under a foot tall. When I'm preparing food at the counter and drop something onto the floor, she's there immediately. From her perspective, so close to the ground, and with her sharp nose, she's much more aware of what falls than I am. But whether she scarfs it down depends on what it is. Cheese or bacon? Inhaled in an instant. Diced onion? Nope. The girl has a definite opinion about what constitutes a worthy windfall.

I've also noticed that the Chloe stories we tell in our family depend on the teller: We both witness the same doggie behavior, but choose different details when describing it. A doorbell rings on TV and she races to the door barking incessantly. How annoying! (my opinion). My husband is actually amused: Why does the dog run to the door when we've never lived in a house with a doorbell?

From a more literary standpoint, think about the book ***The True Story of the 3 Little Pigs by A. Wolf.*** In this story you get the events of the fairy tale from the wolf's perspective, who, as the tale goes, has access to details about what happened that an outside narrator could not know. It's the shift in perspective that gives the story new life.

Sometimes we have a choice about the way we look at something, though we may not wish to acknowledge that. Our first job in the classroom is to show students how perspective matters: Just because you've always believed something to be true doesn't mean there's not another way to see it. An openness to different perspectives might even provide insights that will change your thinking.

WHAT WE HOPE TO SEE IN THE CLASSROOM REGARDING PERSPECTIVE-TAKING, AND WHAT WE SOMETIMES SEE INSTEAD

We love to see kids who are open to learning about things from perspectives that may be different from their own. This involves really listening to their peers during a discussion. Much of the time we don't see this at all. Instead we see kids waiting for a classmate to finish sharing an idea, hand waving frantically to get our attention.

Then you call on that student with the raised hand and she says exactly what she was going to say before the other student spoke. Did she even hear what her friend said? Is she building on that idea, agreeing or disagreeing based on the content of the comment? How are students linking ideas from varying perspectives? We should be able to watch our students' thinking evolve through classroom discourse. Asking ourselves some key questions can lead us—and our students—in the right direction.

ENHANCING CLASSROOM CULTURE: QUESTIONS FOR TEACHERS TO ASK THEMSELVES ABOUT PERSPECTIVE-TAKING

1. Do my students know the difference between a perspective, an opinion, and point of view? How could I clarify the meaning of these terms for them?

2. What books do my students know that are written from a first-person point of view? Can they explain how the story might be different if it was told from the point of view of another character in the story?

3. Which of my students appear open to varying perspectives and are willing to consider new information before rushing to judgment on a topic?

4. Which of my students seem especially close-minded, unwilling to consider perspectives other than their own? How can I help these children to be more open to different perspectives?

5. What topic could my students discuss that would help them see the possibility of another perspective?

6. How could I help my students listen more actively so that they build on the ideas of their peers during a group discussion?

WHAT TO LOOK FOR IN BOOKS ABOUT PERSPECTIVE-TAKING

There are many books available for teaching the importance of perspective-taking. Some are light and humorous, like *The True Story of the 3 Little Pigs by A. Wolf.* Others are more thought-provoking, and explore personal issues such as bullying or sensing what it feels like to walk in someone else's shoes. There are other books that examine historical events from perspectives that are different from the commonly held view. For social emotional learning, I have selected stories of a more serious nature, listed in Chart 5.1: Books Aligned to Perspective-Taking, though each is intriguing in its own way.

CHART 5.1: BOOKS ALIGNED TO PERSPECTIVE-TAKING

THE MESSAGE	THE BOOK
Looking at something differently can lead to a new view of the situation	*Reflections* by Ann Jonas (primary and intermediate)
There can be many sides to the same story	*The Weird! Series* by Erin Frankel (3 books) (primary and intermediate)
A commonly held belief may not be the only way of looking at something	*Squanto's Journey: The Story of the First Thanksgiving* by Joseph Bruchac (primary and intermediate)
Ignoring a different perspective might lead to unfortunate consequences	*Encounter* by Jane Yolen (Intermediate)
Try to see something through another person's eyes	*Going Home* by Eve Bunting (Primary and Intermediate)

Looking at something differently can lead to a new view of the situation

Ann Jonas has written and illustrated two books, **Round Trip** and **Reflections,** that show the importance of perspective in astonishing ways. Both are excellent. Here I focus on **Reflections.**

It was late on Friday afternoon when I recently visited a fourth-grade classroom to read this story. At the outset, no one seemed especially thrilled to be ending their week this way, and I had to ask them (more than once) to move closer to me so they wouldn't miss the details in the pictures. Keeping them engaged during the first half of the story was a challenge. A child wakes up in a small seaside town and throughout the day, encounters morning fishermen, the first ferry of the day, an approaching storm, a boat yard, a peach orchard, and a grove of trees. Until this point, it's a simple personal narrative, no high adventure here.

Then there's the trip back home—at which point, readers are prompted to turn the book around. The scary birch grove has now transformed into a pond with lily pads and frogs. The boat yard, turned upside down, is a campsite, the rowboats reimagined as tents. A family flying kites has taken the place of sailboats under gathering clouds. Students are mesmerized by these and other transformations, astounded that they could have missed this alternate view the first time around. Which is the whole point!

"You changed my life!" one boy announced after I'd read the last page. I doubt it, but I did help him and his classmates recognize that if they don't look hard for other possible perspectives, they will probably miss them. I often read this book before discussing a topic that begs for more of an open mind than I think will come easily to some students.

There can be many sides to the same story

If there's one issue that has the attention of all educators, it's bullying. We implore our students: Think about how *you'd* feel if you were the kid being bullied. Sometimes they heed our lectures, other times, not so much. The set of three books called the *Weird! Series* goes a step further. It tells the same bullying story from three different perspectives: the child being bullied, the bully, and the bystander. What I especially like is that it helps readers understand that all the players are victims in their own way.

I begin by reading **Weird**, which is the bullied-child's version of the story. Luisa gives up many of the things she loves because Sam, the bully, belittles her at every turn: her polka dot boots, the way she greets her father in Spanish, and greets her mom with a kiss. Sam says she's just *weird*, which prompts Luisa to be "unweird" by giving up the things that are important to her—until eventually, she barely recognizes herself. She tries ignoring Sam instead, and finds this is the best remedy. No longer able to intimidate Luisa, Sam gives up her bullying ways.

I then read **Tough,** the story from the bully's perspective. Sam wants to keep things "cool" at school, letting everyone know *she's* the one to make the rules. Her goal isn't to be mean so much as to make sure everyone knows she's tough. As the story proceeds, readers see what's behind her behavior: Sam is bullied at home by her big brother and at school, needs to feel like she's in control. Readers see how hard it can be to break the cycle, though eventually with the help of her teacher, Sam sees that being kind can also be cool.

Finally, there's **Dare,** the story of the bystander, Jayla. She was Sam's victim last year, and is so relieved that Luisa has taken her place that she won't stand up to Sam, even when Sam dares her to do hurtful things like tell Luisa her hair looks weird or that she can't sit at their table during lunch. Jayla doesn't like the person she's becoming, and eventually *dares* to tell Luisa how sorry she is for not standing up for her. Instead of being scared, she now feels prepared with strategies to respond to Sam's toughness. Gradually, Sam begins to leave Jayla *and* Luisa alone. There are many messages to extract from these three books, perhaps the most basic of which is that bullying and how to handle it is complicated.

A commonly held belief may not be the only way of looking at something

The Thanksgiving story we've typically shared with students is more of a fairytale than a verified account of history. There were no tall hats with buckles on them. It was a raucous party with drinking and gambling as opposed to a religious event. The partygoers ate deer, not turkey. It was most likely held in September or October, not

November. And the role of Native Americans was significantly different from the way it is often portrayed. ("6 Things Everyone Believes About Thanksgiving," n.d.)

We need a book with a different perspective to give students a more accurate view of the *real* Thanksgiving story. For this, **Squanto's Journey: The Story of the First Thanksgiving** is a great resource. Told in the first-person from Squanto's point of view, he explains how he was tricked by a white friend, taken to Europe, and enslaved. The myth of the great friendship between the Native Americans and pilgrims is dispelled by Squanto's stories of his people's generosity and the poor treatment they received in return at the hands of the white settlers. This story is a great conversation starter, with opportunities for some of that careful listening mentioned earlier.

Ignoring a different perspective might lead to unfortunate consequences

Sometimes failing to listen is not only limiting, as demonstrated by the many untrue beliefs about Thanksgiving, but also potentially dangerous, as it was in **Encounter**, an alternate version of the Columbus story. In this book, a young Taino boy runs to his chief to report "three great-sailed canoes" nearing their shore, and is fearful of what might happen next. But the chief will not heed the warning, telling the boy he is only a child.

From the boy's perspective, the strange creatures who arrive on the boats may not be human, because they hide their bodies in colors and hide their feet as well. There are bushes growing on their chins, and how could skin so pale come from the earth? Students are intrigued to see the world through this boy's eyes—the evil he recognizes in the silver spears of the strangers, and in the darts that thunder from their sticks. Still, his elders will not listen. Then the boy is captured, forced to sail away on one of the great canoes. The last page shows an old man in a suit jacket perched on a tree-stump many centuries later, reminiscing about his lands forever lost to the pale-faced strangers. How important is listening? How important is exploring a different perspective? This book invites such important conversations.

FEATURED BOOK FOR PERSPECTIVE-TAKING: *Going Home* by Eve Bunting

Try to see something through another person's eyes

Sometimes we ask students to understand another person's perspective just because it's the "right" thing to do, although they may not know much about the situation that calls for this response. Insight into the underlying issue is key to more genuine buy-in when it comes to perspective-taking. The book **Going Home** illustrates this. In the story, Carlos describes his family's visit to Mexico for Christmas. He and his sisters were born there, but came to America with their parents years earlier. The children can't fathom why their parents are so excited to make the trip, but that changes as soon as they arrive in their family's small village.

Amid the animated dinner chatter, Carlos notices that his parents have never been livelier. Everyone is impressed that he and his sisters are dressed nicely and can speak English. Papa tells them the schools in America are good and his children are getting a fine education, and that he has steady work in his new country. As Carlos and his sisters fall asleep that night under the stars, Mama and Papa come out of Grandfather's house and begin to dance, so pleased to be home, if only briefly. In that moment, Carlos understands that for his parents, Mexico will always be home. They left so their children could have "the opportunities." It's a perspective-changing insight.

SEVEN THINKING BOXES

Questions to ask about *Going Home* by Eve Bunting
SEL Competency: Social-Awareness   Focus: Perspective-Taking

PLAIN CARDBOARD BOX	BASIC THINKING
	Do the parents and the children in this story have the same opinion about going to Mexico for Christmas? What is the opinion of the children? What is the opinion of the parents?
PUZZLE BOX	PUZZLING DETAILS
	What details in the story best show that the children's perspective has changed by the <u>end</u> of the story? Why do you think it changed?
HEART BOX	FEELINGS
	What feeling (or feelings) do you think contributed to the parents' perspective about leaving Mexico to come to America? What details in the story show this?
UNUSUAL BOX	CREATIVE THINKING
	What could these parents have said to their children to help them understand their perspective about wanting to go back to Mexico for Christmas?
BROKEN BOX	PROBLEMS AND ISSUES
	What problem were the parents trying to solve by coming to America? What does this show about their <u>perspective</u>?
TREASURE BOX	SOMETHING TO TREASURE
	The word "opportunities" comes up quite often in this story. Explain how this word relates to the message of the book, and the perspective of both the parents and the children?
TOOL BOX	AUTHOR'S TOOLS
	How does the author use the illustrations to add to *your* <u>perspective</u> on life in Mexico and the parents' feelings about Mexico?

SEVEN THINKING BOXES

Questions to ask about *any* book for perspective-taking

PLAIN CARDBOARD BOX	**BASIC THINKING** • What is the main character's perspective at the beginning of this story? Does it change? How? • Does someone in this story have a perspective <u>different</u> from that of the main character? Explain.
PUZZLE BOX 	**PUZZLING DETAILS** • Find a quote in this book that best shows the main character's perspective. Why did you choose this quote? • Choose a quote in this book that best explains the reason behind this character's perspective. In your opinion, is it a good reason? Why or why not?
HEART BOX	**FEELINGS** • How were feelings important to this character's perspective at the beginning of the story? • What feelings were most important in this character's change of perspective?
UNUSUAL BOX	**CREATIVE THINKING** • In what ways was creative thinking important to changing a character's perspective in this story? • What creative solution could you have suggested to help to change this character's perspective?
BROKEN BOX	**PROBLEMS AND ISSUES** • What was the problem in this story and how did it relate to perspective-taking? • For whom was this perspective the biggest problem? Why?
TREASURE BOX	**SOMETHING TO TREASURE** • What does this character's perspective show about what he or she treasures? Explain. • What did <u>you</u> learn about understanding someone's perspective from reading this book?
TOOL BOX	**AUTHOR'S TOOLS** • How did the author make this character's perspective seem real? What crafts helped to develop this character? • How did the author show <u>conflict</u> in this story?

Empathy

Empathy is not just sensitivity, but the capacity to vicariously experience another person's situation. It's walking in someone else's shoes. You can imagine their feelings as if they were your own. You recognize why they respond to a problem as they do because you would likely react to it similarly. If your friend is excited to have been chosen as the captain of his baseball team, you are genuinely excited for him. You don't secretly wish the honor had gone to someone else.

WHAT WE HOPE TO SEE IN THE CLASSROOM REGARDING EMPATHY, AND WHAT WE SOMETIMES SEE INSTEAD

In the classroom we want to see students cheer each other on, handing out "atta girls" (or boys) when a compliment is in order. We want them to understand each other's tears when they are sad, and register concern when someone is going through a tough time. Empathy, like perspective-taking, is best comprehended when there's transparency about the situation at hand, so we need to help students build understanding of some of the complex issues that require sensitivity and kindness.

More awareness can lead to more sensitivity. Some students intuitively recognize the needs of other students and respond accordingly: "Come and sit at our table during lunch." "Hey, I'm a Patriots fan, too." There are other students who will help when requested: "Marcos, please pick Jeremy for your reading buddy today." But other kids focus only on *their* wants, never *others'* needs. When you ask everyone to find a turn-and-talk partner during a reading lesson, Liam turns to two friends who are already partners, forming a group of three, which leaves Noah (sitting next to him) with no partner at all. It's true that Noah is shy and doesn't express himself easily. But you wish *someone* would offer up a bit of kindness, unsolicited. In the meantime, you make a mental note to arrange for this *not* to happen to Noah next time.

ENHANCING CLASSROOM CULTURE: QUESTIONS FOR TEACHERS TO ASK THEMSELVES ABOUT EMPATHY

1. Which students in my class often show empathy? How do they show it?

2. Which students in my class seem the least empathetic? What seems to be responsible for this lack of empathy?

3. Do my students know the word empathy and what it means? How could I deepen their understanding of this?

4. What situations in our classroom, our school, our community, and our world would benefit from empathy? How could I connect these issues to my students' lives in a responsible way?

5. What role models in real life and in literature could I use to demonstrate the power of empathy?

6. What one problem inside or outside the classroom do I regard as needing the most empathy from my students? How could I address this?

WHAT TO LOOK FOR IN BOOKS ABOUT EMPATHY

There is no shortage of books related to empathy, though the term is seldom used in texts. Sometimes other words are substituted, like kindness or understanding. But most often, no label is provided at all. Students need to *infer* the presence of empathy, or its absence. I look for books in which the consequences of no empathy are clear, and other stories that are built around the power of empathy generously applied. I look for books that suggest the importance of empathy not just toward family and friends, but toward animals and situations beyond our classroom walls. I think it's especially important in today's world to include titles that relate to immigrants and their need for empathy. The five books described here in Chart 5.2: Books Aligned to Empathy each meet at least one of these criteria.

CHART 5.2: BOOKS ALIGNED TO EMPATHY

THE MESSAGE	THE BOOK
Lack of empathy is hurtful	*Each Kindness* by Jacqueline Woodson (primary and intermediate)
Empathy means caring about how others feel	*Four Feet, Two Sandals* by Karen Lynn Williams and Khadra Mohammed (primary and intermediate)
Animals need empathy, too	*Ivan: The Remarkable True Story of the Shopping Mall Gorilla* by Katherine Applegate
Countries and cultures can show empathy toward each other	*14 Cows for America* by Carmen Agra Deedy (intermediate)
Newcomers need lots of empathy	*The Journey* by Francesca Sanna (primary and intermediate)

Lack of empathy is hurtful

If there is one book that has come to exemplify the importance of empathy in our classroom it's *Each Kindness*. I've brought this book to many schools and the ensuing conversations have been enlightening. I'll first describe the story itself, and then my experience reading it to a class of third graders.

In the book, a girl named Maya joins a classroom, and the other students, particularly the girls, make a point of excluding her and treating her unkindly. They inch their desks away from her, rebuke her efforts to play together on the playground, and whisper mean comments behind her back. One day Maya is absent, and the teacher brings in a pot of water. As she drops a stone in, the ripples spread outward and she reminds her students that kindness is like that: One kind deed leads to another. She then challenges each child to share a kind act they they've performed as they drop their own stone into the pot. Chloe, the queen of the mean girls, can think of nothing to say, and gets the message right away: She will apologize to Maya and try to become her friend. But Maya's desk remains empty and eventually the teacher tells the class she has moved away. Then the story ends.

"You didn't read the last page," offered a third grader seated right in front of me. "Oh, I did," I assured her. "Sometimes you just don't get a second chance."

This illustrates a problem we often see with empathy. Too many kids think that an apology will make it all better. In this story, there was no opportunity for an apology, showing how important it is to be kind the first time. And even if Maya returned to the school and was treated more kindly, hurtful words and behavior make a lasting impact.

But I have a concern with this book: the way the teacher handled the situation. Surely, she saw the class's behavior toward Maya, but she waited to address it until too much time had passed, and the child was absent. Where was the pot exercise when it could have made a difference? Maya needed an advocate, and she needed her teacher to respond with courage—at a time when the class could have problem-solved together.

Empathy means caring about how others feel

For a true study in empathy, read *Four Feet, Two Sandals*. Not only does it give students a glimpse into life in a refugee camp in the Middle East, but also lets them view empathy in action. Lina and Feroza both dive for a pair of sandals that have been dropped off at their camp, among other used shoes and items of clothing. But they each emerge with only one of the sandals—not very useful, they conclude. Instead, they decide to share them. Lina will wear them one day, and then it will be Feroza's turn. The girls become friends as they honor this agreement, and all is well until Feroza receives word that she and her mother will be allowed to go to America. But what shall they do with the sandals? You will need to read the story yourself to learn its sweet ending. May our students be inspired by Lina and Feroza to emulate such empathy.

Animals need empathy, too

While many students are familiar with the Newbery medal winner *The One and Only Ivan,* fewer readers know its picture book counterpart, **Ivan: The Remarkable True Story of the Shopping Mall Gorilla,** written by the same author. While Ivan, a silverback gorilla, was born in a tropical forest, he was soon captured and brought to America. At first he lived in a home like a human child, wore cute outfits, and ate foods (like doughnuts) not suitable for gorillas. He was then sent to a shopping mall where he lived in a cage and entertained shoppers for 27 years until angry children and adults staged protests. Although Ivan was released, he was no longer acclimated to jungle survival. He spent his final years at Zoo Atlanta in a natural habitat.

Empathy for animals is an important concept to build in the classroom. Asking students how they show empathy toward their pets is a good place to begin. Talk about animals in the wild, too: Is it okay to keep a raccoon or another wild animal as a pet? How can they help the plight of endangered animals like the sea turtle?

Countries and cultures can show empathy toward each other

Empathy means concern for *all* creatures, especially when they are defenseless. Even countries can show kindness toward each other. One of the most powerful books I know, conveyed through both its narrative and illustrations, is **14 Cows for America**, the story of a Maasai village's response to the September 11 attacks. It seems unfathomable that anyone would be unfamiliar with this infamous day. But children in elementary school now were not even alive when it happened. For them, it's history. I can't imagine a more compassionate way of educating them about the horror of the day than through this story, which emphasizes the empathy that occurred in its aftermath.

Kameli, who is in the United States studying to become a doctor, returns home to his remote Kenyan village to the delight of his people, the Maasai. The Maasai are herders who treat their cows as honorably as the people in their family, and they are always eager for Kameli's stories of America. But this time, the young doctor says he has only one story, and it hurts his heart. As his tale of 9/11 unfolds, his audience listens intently, stunned, until one elder asks what they as a community can do.

An American diplomat is invited to come to the village, but this is no ordinary diplomatic visit. He is greeted by hundreds of Maasai in full tribal regalia, and as part of the ceremony is blessed with fourteen sacred cows for America: Even a powerful nation can be wounded. Even a small nation can offer comfort. You will need to read this book more than once to absorb all its visual details. Be sure to note the image on the last page of the Twin Towers reflected in eye of the Maasai.

Newcomers need lots of empathy

Recently, when I read the story **The Journey** to a group of fifth graders as part of a SEL workshop, the teachers observing the lesson were surprised by the students' level of background knowledge about immigration. They knew a lot. They knew what a refugee camp was, that people were probably there because their home country was at war and no longer safe, that they must wait there before being resettled in another country, and that their journey would likely be long and difficult. Today's students are citizens of the world. The challenge for us is to nurture their global knowledge, inspiring as much empathy as possible. *The Journey* is a wonderful resource to start this conversation.

According to the author's note, *The Journey* is the synthesis of many journeys, of many stories about the trauma that forces a family to flee their country and their suffering in pursuit of safety and freedom. The sparse text and vivid illustrations make this book meaningful for students of any age, and as I read it aloud, there is no shortage of concern for these travelers: "How could little kids ever be brave enough to hide out in the woods at night when they know guards are looking for them?" "What if their boat capsized?" We discuss these perils. But what I really want to talk about is the next part: what happens to the family after the book ends and these children become students in their classrooms, or in a classroom in another city or state.

"Why is empathy especially important when a newcomer is an immigrant from another part of the world?" I ask. "It's not just that they don't speak our language or have any friends," an articulate fifth grader once shared. "We can't know how bad it was for them before they got here. They are probably hurting bad inside." We concluded that discussion with a hypothetical question: "Right now in your classroom you don't have any classmates who have recently arrived from another country, but a new immigrant could walk through your door tomorrow. How would you respond with *empathy*?" Consider extending the discussion of this book even further with the questions that follow for Seven Thinking Boxes.

FEATURED BOOK FOR EMPATHY: *The Journey* by Francesca Sanna

SEVEN THINKING BOXES

Questions to ask about *The Journey* by Francesca Sanna
SEL Competency: Social-Awareness   Focus: Empathy

PLAIN CARDBOARD BOX	**BASIC THINKING** Name three difficulties this family experienced on their journey. Which one would have been the most difficult for you? Why?
PUZZLE BOX	**PUZZLING DETAILS** Did anyone show empathy toward this family during their journey? How?
HEART BOX	**FEELINGS** At what point could this family have really benefited from empathy? How might it have made a difference to their feelings?
UNUSUAL BOX	**CREATIVE THINKING** How was creative thinking important to this family's survival? What do you think mattered most to them? How important do you think empathy was to them during their journey? Explain.
BROKEN BOX	**PROBLEMS AND ISSUES** What do you consider to be the biggest problem in this story? How does empathy matter? Explain your thinking.
TREASURE BOX	**SOMETHING TO TREASURE** What can you learn from this family's journey? How will it make a difference to the empathy you show toward newcomers?
TOOL BOX	**AUTHOR'S TOOLS** In this story, the author/illustrator uses a lot of black in the illustrations. Why do you think she does this? Connect the use of this color to empathy.

SEVEN THINKING BOXES

Questions to ask about *any* book for empathy

PLAIN CARDBOARD BOX	BASIC THINKING
	• In your own words, explain the situation in this book where empathy was needed.
	• Who showed empathy in this story? Or, who did not show empathy? Explain.

PUZZLE BOX	PUZZLING DETAILS
	• What quote in this book do you think is the best example of empathy? Why?
	• What detail in this book will you remember most? Why?

HEART BOX	FEELINGS
	• What feelings resulted because of lack of empathy in this story? Explain.
	• What feelings resulted because characters in this story showed empathy? Explain.

UNUSUAL BOX	CREATIVE THINKING
	• Was creative thinking involved in helping anyone in this story understand the meaning of empathy? Explain.
	• How would you have solved the problem in this story by showing more empathy?

BROKEN BOX	PROBLEMS AND ISSUES
	• What problem(s) did lack of empathy create in this story?
	• What problems might the lack of empathy in this story create in the future? Explain.

TREASURE BOX	SOMETHING TO TREASURE
	• Who learned a lesson about empathy in this story? What was the lesson?
	• What lesson about empathy did you learn from this story? How will it make a difference in your life?

TOOL BOX	AUTHOR'S TOOLS
	• How do the illustrations in this story help to show empathy or the need for empathy?
	• How does the author <u>show</u> the need for empathy in this story? (It might be through the character's actions, words, or the thoughts in their head.)

Appreciating Diversity

As Queensborough Community College's website states,

> [D]iversity encompasses acceptance and respect. It means understanding that each individual is unique and recognizing our individual differences. These can be along the dimensions of race, ethnicity, gender, sexual orientation, socio-economic status, age, physical abilities, religious beliefs, political beliefs, or other ideologies. (2018)

In education when we speak of diversity, we are often referring to racial, ethnic, and cultural differences. That will be our emphasis here, as other differences will be addressed under other SEL focus areas.

Appreciating diversity is more than acknowledging that racial and ethnic differences exit. Appreciation means understanding how to relate to people and cultural norms different from those of our own group. It means recognizing when discrimination leads to privilege for some and disadvantages for others. At its best, appreciating diversity means working together to promote equity.

WHAT WE HOPE TO SEE IN THE CLASSROOM REGARDING APPRECIATING DIVERSITY, AND WHAT WE SOMETIMES SEE INSTEAD

Most classrooms that I visit in urban areas are racially and ethnically diverse, though the same is less likely to be true in suburban or rural districts. From what I observe, students communicate respectfully with each other, and there is no obvious racial or ethnic tension. But I am only a guest in these classrooms and don't know what lurks beneath the surface. What I would like to see, and seldom do, is open, forthright conversations between students and teachers about race and ethnicity. "We're all the same here," is the message conveyed in many classrooms. But is that really *appreciating* diversity?

ENHANCING CLASSROOM CULTURE: QUESTIONS FOR TEACHERS TO ASK THEMSELVES ABOUT APPRECIATING DIVERSITY

1. On a scale of 1-10, how comfortable do I feel talking about race and ethnicity with my students? What would help me feel more comfortable?

2. When was the last open, forthright conversation I had with my students about race or ethnicity? What were some of the take-aways?

3. Is there a disproportionate number of racially diverse students in my lowest reading group? Do they have access to the same literacy opportunities as students in other groups? If not, why?

4. To what extent do my students cross racial or ethnic boundaries when choosing partners for group work?

5. What is the best example of appreciating diversity that I have seen in my current class?

6. Have I ever witnessed an issue of racial or ethnic disrespect in my classroom? If so, how did I handle it? Would I handle it differently now?

WHAT TO LOOK FOR IN BOOKS ABOUT APPRECIATING DIVERSITY

I am always on the hunt for books that feature diverse characters engaged in situations where race or ethnicity is a critical component. When it comes to African American characters, this is easy. There are so many wonderful picture books about the Civil War era and the Civil Rights era that I could fill hundreds of pages featuring those stories alone. There are some twenty-first stories about African Americans, as well, but these may or may not be racially focused. Take *The Last Stop on Market Street,* for example. This is an amazing story (awarded both the Newbery and Caldecott top honor). But in this case, although the characters are black, race doesn't play a major role in the plot of the tale.

It's more difficult to find high quality picture books about non-white characters other than African-Americans who face discrimination, though some good ones certainly exist. As many ethnicities and races as possible should be present in the literature we read with students, not just so they can see faces like their own reflected back at them, but so they can ask questions about how we can right racial and ethnic wrongs and embrace diversity moving forward. In the books profiled here, listed in Chart 5.3: Books Aligned to Appreciating Diversity, I feature five issues to consider when building a greater appreciation of diversity—and characters that represent five different ethnicities. Of course, the issue is not intended to be specific to the particular ethnic or racial group.

CHART 5.3: BOOKS ALIGNED TO APPRECIATING DIVERSITY

THE MESSAGE	THE BOOK
Appreciating diversity begins with communication Featured: African Americans	*The Other Side* by Jacqueline Woodson (primary and intermediate)
Joining in promotes acceptance Featured: Middle Eastern Americans	*One Green Apple* by Eve Bunting (primary and intermediate)
Racial profiling is hurtful Featured: Asian Americans	*Heroes* by Ken Mochizuki (primary and intermediate)
Sometimes you need to fight for justice Featured: Mexican Americans	*Separate is Never Equal: Sylvia Mendez and Her Family's Fight for Desegregation* by Duncan Tonatiuh (intermediate)
Find strength within yourself to combat discrimination Featured: Native Americans	*Muskrat Will Be Swimming* by Cheryl Savageau (primary and intermediate)

Appreciating diversity begins with communication
Featured: African Americans

Many books address the day-to-day life of African Americans in the 1950s and 60s, especially the discrimination and segregation in the South. A book that continues to make my short-list of best titles in this area is **The Other Side**. Annie, a white child, lives on one side of a fence, and Clover, a black child, lives on "the other side." The fence divides their lives, both literally and symbolically. At first there is no common ground for these children. Then they become curious about each other, forming a friendship as they sit together on the fence. Eventually, other children come along and they all jump rope together. Afterward they sit on the fence and someone suggests that perhaps one day someone will come along and knock the fence down.

When we finish reading, I ask, When did these girls first begin to appreciate diversity? Was it when they became curious about each other? Sat side-by-side on the fence? When other children got involved? Or will there be no true appreciation of diversity until the fence comes down? As students respond, I get a closer look at their thinking about what it means to appreciate diversity. They recognize that turning the tide in race relations begins with communication.

Joining in promotes acceptance
Featured: Middle Eastern Americans

Students new to our classrooms from the Middle East may not be appreciated for reasons that have nothing to do with skin color. For this and other reasons, I love **One Green Apple**. In this book, Farah tells the story of her second day at her new American school. The class is visiting an apple orchard, and as they bump along in the hay wagon, she notes that some of her classmates smile friendly smiles, and others smile as if they don't mean it, mentioning her country in a "not fond" tone.

She realizes she's different in the language she speaks and in the dupatta that covers her head and shoulders. She is confused when her teacher speaks to her extra-loudly, as if she's incapable of hearing. She is perplexed, too, when her classmates try to stop her from tossing her green apple into the cider press along with their red ones. Will her green apple really make the cider taste different, as the other children fear? In the end, it's Farah's own efforts to get in on the action—helping other students push the heavy handle of the cider mill—that make her feel like part of the group, and like she is appreciated. Never underestimate the power of joining in! And be aware that tone of voice is extra important when the language is different.

Racial profiling is hurtful
Featured: Asian Americans

If ever there was a book perfect for demonstrating the hurt of racial profiling, it's **Heroes**. Set in an American neighborhood post-World War II, Donnie and a few of his buddies like to play war after school. The problem is that Donnie is Japanese American, and his friends always insist that he play the bad guy. Donnie hates this role and tells his friends repeatedly that both his dad and uncle fought for America and have plenty of medals to prove it. When Donnie's dad sees what's happening, he has an idea. The next day, he and Donnie's uncle arrive at school in time for dismissal with so many ribbons and medals that there's barely enough room on their uniforms. That afternoon, the boys decide to play football.

Students are quick to recognize the injustice in Donnie's "bad guy" role but are less inclined to see today's stereotypic "terrorist" view of Middle Easterners as inaccurate. We can't let this poison seep into students' minds if there's any hope of appreciating diversity within and beyond our classroom.

Sometimes you need to fight for justice
Featured: Mexican Americans

From where I sit in the eastern part of our country, Mexican Americans' plight to secure social justice seldom receives the attention it deserves. Students may be able to tell you about Ruby Bridges, a victim of school segregation in the south. But how many of them can tell you about Sylvia Mendez and her family's struggle to attend an integrated school in California? The book *Separate Is Never Equal: Sylvia Mendez and Her Family's Fight for Desegregation* brings Mexican American segregation to light.

When Sylvia and her brothers go to enroll in their new school in California in 1944, they are told they must go to the Mexican school instead, even though it's not in their neighborhood. The Mexican school, by contrast, is a shack in a cow pasture, so different from the new, modern building attended by non-Mexicans. The Mendez family is not satisfied by the school officials' explanation that the other school is "better" for Mexicans. Eventually, Sylvia's father gets a lawyer to help him and they file a lawsuit.

The trial is grueling, with numerous educational leaders openly claiming that Mexican children are inferior to their white peers. But at last two education specialists defend the need for children of all races and ethnicities to be educated together in order to understand each other. A year later, the judge rules in favor of the Mendez family on the grounds that separate is never equal. Children will never appreciate diversity unless they *experience* diversity.

FEATURED BOOK FOR APPRECIATING DIVERSITY: *Muskrat Will Be Swimming* **by Cheryl Savageau**

Find strength within yourself to combat discrimination
Featured: Native Americans

While every race and ethnicity experiences prejudices specific to their group, other issues are more universal. This is why I chose **Muskrat Will be Swimming** as the featured book for appreciating diversity. Jeannie is a young Abenaki girl who is tormented by her classmates for being a "lake rat." She lives down by the lake in a house that the other kids view as more of a shack, with old cars and appliances littering her yard. Jeannie tells her Grampa about this bullying, but what happens next isn't the expected fairy tale outcome, where everyone ultimately sees the error of their ways and by the last page, all is well. In this story, there's a different message.

Grampa tells Jeannie that although her classmates' behavior is unkind, it may not change. Still, he can help solve her problem. He tells her the legend of the muskrat, an animal that has brought great honor to the Abenaki people over the years. Rather than focusing on her classmates' mean-spirited remarks, he tells her she should instead be proud that she is a "lake rat," with esteemed ancestral connections. The message is clear: Your ethnicity can be a source of strength, and help you to stand up against ignorance. The questions that follow for Seven Thinking Boxes will help your students think more deeply about diversity.

SEVEN THINKING BOXES

Questions to ask about *Muskrat Will be Swimming* by Cheryl Savageau
SEL Competency: Self-Awareness   Focus: Appreciating Diversity

PLAIN CARDBOARD BOX	**BASIC THINKING** Why is Jeannie upset at the beginning of the story? What does her classmates' behavior show about their appreciation of her Native American heritage?
PUZZLE BOX	**PUZZLING DETAILS** What lines at the end of this story <u>best</u> show Jeannie's new appreciation of her Native American roots? Why did you choose these lines?
HEART BOX	**FEELINGS** Although her classmates didn't change their behavior, Jeannie was happier at the end of the story. What caused this change? What does this have to do with appreciating diversity?
UNUSUAL BOX	**CREATIVE THINKING** How was telling a story a creative way for Grandpa to help Jeannie solve her problem? How can stories help us appreciate diversity?
BROKEN BOX	**PROBLEMS AND ISSUES** Grampa tells Jeannie that he experienced a similar problem with name calling when he was a child. Why do you think he tells her this? What is he trying to show her about the problems she's experiencing because of her Native American roots?
TREASURE BOX	**SOMETHING TO TREASURE** What do you think Jeannie learned in this story about appreciating diversity? What do you think her classmates learned?
TOOL BOX	**AUTHOR'S TOOLS** This book contains a story within a story. Why do you think the author includes the folktale about the muskrat? How could you use this technique in your own writing?

SEVEN THINKING BOXES

Questions to ask about *any* book for appreciating diversity

PLAIN CARDBOARD BOX	**BASIC THINKING** • How was diversity important to this story? Explain. • Which character in this story showed the best (or least) appreciation of diversity? Explain.
PUZZLE BOX	**PUZZLING DETAILS** • Find a quote in this book that you think best shows an understanding of the importance of diversity? Why did you choose this quote? • At what point in the story did characters' feeling about diversity change? How did it change?
HEART BOX	**FEELINGS** • What feelings in this story did characters experience because there wasn't enough appreciation of diversity? What details support this? • How did the main character's feelings change when he or she felt more appreciated for their diversity?
UNUSUAL BOX	**CREATIVE THINKING** • Can you think of any creative solution to this diversity issue? Explain. • Was there a character in this story who thought creatively to solve this diversity problem? Explain.
BROKEN BOX	**PROBLEMS AND ISSUES** • What problem in this story made it clear that some characters didn't appreciate diversity? • Who <u>outside</u> of this story might have the power to change something about this diversity problem? What would they need to do?
TREASURE BOX	**SOMETHING TO TREASURE** • What lesson did the main character in this story learn about appreciating diversity? • What can you learn from this story about appreciating diversity? How will this make a difference in your life?
TOOL BOX	**AUTHOR'S TOOLS** • How did this author make this diversity issue seem real? What kind of details did the author use to show this problem? • What strong words did the author choose to convince you there was a diversity problem in this story?

Respect for Others

Respect can be a complicated concept for students. This definition might be a place to start:

> Having respect for someone means you think good things about who a person is or how he/she acts. You can have respect for others, and you can have respect for yourself. (Talking with Trees, n.d.)

While we want students to have respect for things like class rules and norms that might include listening politely to peers and addressing people by name, what I want to consider here is respect for differences beyond race, ethnicity, and culture. Here, let's consider differences that are cognitive, neurological, or physical—among others.

WHAT WE HOPE TO SEE IN THE CLASSROOM REGARDING RESPECT FOR OTHERS, AND WHAT WE SOMETIMES SEE INSTEAD

In the classroom we like to see children whose actions show positive regard for others' feelings and points of view, regardless of any differences that might be cognitive, neurological, or physical. We like to see respect for children who are younger and adults who are older. We like gender preferences to be respected, as well as family structures with varied configurations. And so much more!

We don't want students to be blind to these differences, but to embrace them. Show the child who is different from you that you appreciate her by choosing her for a turn-and-talk partner, or sitting next to her in the cafeteria. But also find something positive to say: "I really like both your moms, Emma." "You remind me of Emmanuel in that book we read because you never stop trying." Respect for differences will grow if we give students the opportunity to understand and talk about them. Begin with a book. Begin with a conversation.

ENHANCING CLASSROOM CULTURE: QUESTIONS FOR TEACHERS TO ASK THEMSELVES ABOUT RESPECT FOR OTHERS

Beyond race, culture, and ethnicity, what other differences are represented by the students in my classroom? (These could be any kind of learning difference or personal or family difference.)

1. How do my students respond to each other's differences: Respect? Disrespect? What is the evidence?

2. What have I done to help my students better understand their classmates' differences? What could I do?

3. How can I help my students understand the difference between *tolerance* and *respect*?

4. How can I help my students understand the difference between offering sympathy to people with differences (feeling sorry for) and offering respect (dignity and appreciation)?

5. What role models could I highlight to show the perseverance and achievements of people with learning or other differences?

WHAT TO LOOK FOR IN BOOKS ABOUT RESPECT FOR OTHERS

There are hundreds of great books that focus on differences beyond race, culture, and ethnicity. There are books that relate to sight and hearing loss, chronic and progressive illnesses, physical limitations, Down Syndrome, and autism—and these are just for starters. Most of these books (listed in Chart 5.4: Books Aligned to Respect for Others) build an understanding of the difference itself, with the hope that increased understanding promotes more respect. Building respect should not be left to chance. Use the story as a place to begin. Then take the conversation to the next level by talking with students about how they can *show* respect.

CHART 5.4: BOOKS ALIGNED TO RESPECT FOR OTHERS

THE MESSAGE	THE BOOK
We are *all* wonders—despite physical or other differences	*We're All Wonders* by R. J. Palacio (primary)
Respect gender preferences	*Julián is a Mermaid* by Jessica Love (primary and intermediate)
Respect families that may look different from your own	*Stella Brings the Family* by Miriam B. Schiffer (primary)
Think of autism as a *difference,* not a *disability*	*Uniquely Wired: A Story about Autism and Its Gifts* by Julia Cook (primary and intermediate)
Respect older family members and friends	*The Summer My Father Was Ten* by Pat Brisson (primary and intermediate)

We are *all* wonders—despite physical or other differences

If you only read one book on the topic of differences, *We're All Wonders* might be a good choice because it addresses differences in a generic way. It was written by R. J. Palacio, the same author who wrote the novel *Wonder*. The picture book is not a junior version of the chapter book about Auggie Pulman, but conveys the same message: Everyone deserves respect despite their differences. The main character in the story, who is not named (and could be any kid), says that people don't see that he's a wonder. Instead, all they see is that he looks different. There's a lot of staring and even some laughing and mean comments. He knows he can't change the way he looks, but hopes he can change the way people see him.

Yes, in the classroom kids sometimes stare at students who look different, or worse—they whisper about them or ostracize them. I notice in my visits to intermediate grades that Auggie Pullman from the *Wonder* chapter book has become a reference point for initiating discussions about respecting others. I expect *We're All Wonders* can do the same for younger students.

Think of autism as a *difference,* not a *disability*

Just like physical differences, cognitive and neurological issues are typically viewed by other students as disabilities, not differences. Can students respect the gifts that a child with Down Syndrome brings to their class? Can they appreciate the uniqueness of a peer with autism? We need to work on changing our own mindset about differences before we can change the perceptions of our students.

Uniquely Wired: A Story about Autism and Its Gifts can help. The story is told by Zak, a boy with autism. He explains that he doesn't see the world the way many people do. He has an amazing memory and learns everything he can about subjects that interest him, like trains or watches. Other people might get tired of Zak telling them about watches, but to Zak, watches hold endless fascination. Zak also explains that he'd rather do things by himself and doesn't like it when people get into his space. He especially doesn't like hugs. His hearing is super powerful and too much sound can flood his brain. Zak teaches us that we all learn, see, and hear differently. While we are all different in some ways, we are a lot alike in needing people to understand and respect us.

Respect gender preferences

Critical dialogue should address respect for other differences too—gender preferences, for example. I remember the long-ago album by Marlo Thomas (yes, an album; it was *that* long ago), with its song titled "William Wants a Doll." It offered a worthy defense of little William's desire for his own doll baby (after all, he would be a father one day). However, I hope we've moved on from *defending* gender preferences to *celebrating* them.

For a gem of a book that honors gender choices, choose *Julián is a Mermaid*. Unfazed by typical gender expectations, Julián is mesmerized by the ladies he's seen bedecked in beautiful flowing dresses, and dreams of dressing in similar attire himself to resemble a mermaid. When Abuela comes into the room where Julian has ripped the curtains from the windows to create his mermaid tail, the expression on her face is not a happy one. Is she displeased about his choice to be a mermaid or the mess?

It turns out that her concern is about the mess. In fact, she affirms Julián's choice to dress as a mermaid by offering him a necklace to complement his outfit. Together they go to a parade where everyone is sporting exotic attire. In the end, the story is about Julián's joy in behaving just like himself. It is not a story that gets preachy about the importance of accepting atypical gender preferences; it simply celebrates the choice Julián makes.

Respect families that may look different from your own

I notice that many teachers are more comfortable talking about physical and even cognitive differences than gender or sexual preferences. These may be topics that don't find a place in your curriculum until a related issue presents itself. But it's good to have a book handy to get the conversation going when needed.

Stella Brings the Family treats the topic of same-sex parents in a manner well-suited to primary students. Stella has two dads and is worried about the upcoming Mother's Day celebration at her school. She doesn't have a mom to bring. In the end, she brings Daddy and Papa and a few other relatives, as well. Her family fits right in with Howie and his two moms, and the families of other students who brought a grandparent instead of a parent. All family structures need to be respected.

FEATURED BOOK FOR RESPECT FOR OTHERS: *The Summer My Father Was Ten* by Pat Brisson

---

Respect older family members and friends

Students need to respect age as well as gender, and there are many books with age-related messages. I was tempted to feature a book about dementia and Alzheimer's, as there are so many children touched by this awful disease. But this is generally a personal issue more than a school-based one and seems better addressed at home. For this reason, a dementia-related title, *The Weeds in Nana's Garden,* is included among books listed on the Curated List of Books Aligned to SEL Skills under Respect for Diversity. Here, let's consider a story of an inter-generational friendship, a blessing we hope all students will experience.

I consider *The Summer My Father Was Ten* to be one of the most endearing stories in my library. A young girl recounts a story her father told her about the summer he was ten years old. It seems that he and his buddies got out of control one afternoon as they played baseball and destroyed the vegetable garden of an elderly neighbor, Mr. Bellavista, by tearing up tomatoes and throwing them at each other. When the older man returned home, he looked in dismay at his ruined garden. The other boys ran off, but not the narrator's dad. He owned up to the thoughtless deed and the next spring, helped Mr. Bellavista plant a new garden.

At summer's end, the boy and the man harvested the crop and shared a meal of pasta and garden-fresh tomato sauce. Planting, harvesting, and sharing a meal became an annual tradition, even when Mr. Bellavista was very elderly. When the girl's dad became an adult himself, he planted the garden alone and brought the pot of sauce to share at Mr. Bellavista's nursing home. So much respect here: taking responsibility for one's actions, providing help to an older generation when needed, and just being a caring friend. The following questions for Seven Thinking Boxes will help you and your students dig deeper into this story and the matter of respect.

SEVEN THINKING BOXES

Questions to ask about *The Summer My Father Was Ten* by Pat Brisson
SEL Competency: Social Awareness   Focus: Respect for Others

PLAIN CARDBOARD BOX	**BASIC THINKING** Summarize this story. Try to use the words *respect* and *disrespect* in your summary.
PUZZLE BOX	**PUZZLING DETAILS** What detail in this book stands out to you the most? Why? What does it show about respect?
HEART BOX	**FEELINGS** What feelings did the boys' actions in the garden create for Mr. Bellavista? Why do you think he felt this way?
UNUSUAL BOX	**CREATIVE THINKING** How else could the girl's dad have shown respect toward Mr. Bellavista after the garden incident?
BROKEN BOX	**PROBLEMS AND ISSUES** Why do you think the other boys ran off after destroying Mr. Bellavista's garden? What does this say about respect?
TREASURE BOX	**SOMETHING TO TREASURE** What message do you think the author wanted to share in this story related to respect? What does this message mean to you in your own life? How could *you* show respect?
TOOL BOX	**AUTHOR'S TOOLS** Perspective is important to a story. It's told by the daughter of one of the boys who destroyed the garden (now a dad), and you hear the dad's perspective. How might this story have been different if it was told from Mr. Bellavista's perspective? Retell or rewrite one of the pages from his perspective.

SEVEN THINKING BOXES

Questions to ask about *any* book for respect for others

PLAIN CARDBOARD BOX 	**BASIC THINKING** • What happens in this story that shows respect? • What happens in this story that shows disrespect?
PUZZLE BOX 	**PUZZLING DETAILS** • What detail in this story stands out to you the most? Why? What does it show about respect? • What character in this story was the *best* example of respect? How did this person show respect?
HEART BOX 	**FEELINGS** • In this story, whose feelings were hurt by someone's lack of respect? What made this situation so hurtful? • Did anyone in this story change to show more respect? Whose feelings were involved? How?
UNUSUAL BOX 	**CREATIVE THINKING** • Was creative thinking involved in solving the respect problem in this book? Explain. • What creative solution could *you* have offered to help solve this respect problem?
BROKEN BOX 	**PROBLEMS AND ISSUES** • Disrespect often leads to other problems. What problems did disrespect lead to in this story? • What kind of disrespect did this book feature? (It might be related to age, gender, physical differences, or something else.) Do we ever see the same problem in our daily lives? How? Why is this an important problem to solve?
TREASURE BOX 	**SOMETHING TO TREASURE** • Who learned a lesson about respect in this story? What lesson did *you* learn? How might it change your thinking or actions in the future? • If you could give someone in this story some advice about showing respect, what would you say?
TOOL BOX 	**AUTHOR'S TOOLS** • In a story about respect, perspective really matters. How might this story be different if it was told from a different character's perspective? • How does this author *show* respect or disrespect in this story—rather than just telling readers a character was respectful or disrespectful?

CLASSROOM READING TO ENGAGE THE HEART & MIND

CHAPTER 6
RELATIONSHIP SKILLS: THE POWER OF US

Relationships are the heartbeat of a classroom—relationships between the teacher and students, as well as student-to-student relationships. Surviving in a classroom requires cooperation, teamwork, listening, communicating with peers, and speaking up when needed. When relationships are strong, these interactions are positive. Weak or poor relationships can make the classroom difficult to navigate. Relationship skills might involve maintaining and growing positive relationships, altering strained relationships, and in some situations, moving away from unhealthy relationships.

CASEL defines relationships and social skills as "[t]he ability to establish and maintain healthy and rewarding relationships with diverse individuals and groups. The ability to communicate clearly, listen well, cooperate with others, resist inappropriate social pressure, negotiate conflict constructively, and seek and offer help when needed" ("Core SEL Competencies," n.d.).

The focus areas for relationships and social skills include: '

- Social engagement
- Relationship-Building
- Teamwork
- Communication

In all four focus areas, it's the "we" that matters most. *We* engage socially with each other to enjoy each other's company or provide mutual support. *We* try hard to build new relationships or rebuild relationships that need adjusting. *We* work as a team to accomplish more than each of us might achieve individually. *We* need to communicate in a manner that allows relationships to flourish and people to hear our message as we intended. As we delve into these focus areas and the books that support each one, notice the power of *us*.

Social Engagement

Plainly stated, social engagement means participating in a community. Even just two people can constitute a community, though more often, a community is a group of people, large or small. It is typically voluntary and involves interaction. Some people like extensive social engagement, and choose to be with other people as often as possible. For others, a little socializing goes a long way. Similarly, in social situations, some people like to take charge while others prefer to blend in, letting others do the leading.

WHAT WE HOPE TO SEE IN THE CLASSROOM FOR SOCIAL ENGAGEMENT, AND WHAT WE SOMETIMES SEE INSTEAD

In today's classrooms there are numerous opportunities for students to work together, often without direct teacher supervision. These might include group projects where three or four students work collaboratively to produce a single product, literature circles, or book clubs where students meet to discuss a book they are all reading. Sometimes working together is as simple as turning to talk with a partner for a minute or two about a question the teacher asked during a lesson. New teachers learn quickly (and often from group-work-gone-wrong) that students engage most productively in small groups or partner work when a culture of collaboration has been established in the classroom.

A collaborative culture is one where students work willingly with *all* peers, not just their best friends. They do not exclude less popular classmates, and especially do not convey that they dislike partnering with certain children. Collaborating means working *together*, and giving all group members the opportunity to be heard. No one dominates, and no one expects other group members to carry their weight. Students stay on topic and work toward the completion of mutual goals.

While having a class that measures up to these collaborative standards may be a pipe dream, the goal is a valuable one and worth the effort. But sometimes we pursue collaboration with a bit too much vigor. How can we also honor students who prefer to work independently, those for whom smaller doses of social engagement best meet their needs?

ENHANCING CLASSROOM CULTURE: QUESTIONS FOR TEACHERS TO ASK THEMSELVES ABOUT SOCIAL ENGAGEMENT

1. What do my students seem to understand about social engagement (getting along with each other)? What do my students *not* seem to understand about social engagement?

2. What opportunities do I provide in my classroom for students to interact with each other?

3. What have I done so far to build a culture of collaboration in my classroom? What else could I do?

4. How do I balance opportunities for my students to work collaboratively and work independently?

5. Have I talked with my students about what makes a good friend? What could I include in a conversation about friendship?

6. How can I help my students become more responsible when they collaborate with peers?

WHAT TO LOOK FOR IN BOOKS ABOUT SOCIAL ENGAGEMENT

Almost every story we read with students demonstrates social engagement in action. Sometimes the story is *about* the relationship, and other times the relationship supports or hampers the resolution of the character's problem. For this area we'll profile books *about* relationships, listed in Chart 6.1: Books Aligned to Social Engagement. Sometimes students believe that social engagement is about adventure, entertainment, or some other stand-out experience where the *activity* is the focus. To show how *not* true this is, I look for books that portray the simple pleasures of spending time with a friend, what it means to be a good friend, and what it means when someone is not your "good" friend. Notice the common ground here: friendship—social engagement at its best.

CHART 6.1: BOOKS ALIGNED TO SOCIAL ENGAGEMENT

THE MESSAGE	THE BOOK
Sometimes just "hanging out" with friends is the best fun	*The Relatives Came* by Cynthia Rylant (primary and intermediate)
When you are kind to your friends, they will be kind to you	*Mama Panya's Pancakes: A Village Tale from Kenya* by Mary and Rich Chamberlin (primary)
Friends help each other through tough times	*Rescue and Jessica: A Life-Changing Friendship* by Jessica Kensky and Patrick Downes (primary and intermediate)
Beware of false friends	*Fox* by Margaret Wild (intermediate)
Friends support and encourage each other in many ways	*Meet Danitra Brown* by Nikki Grimes (primary and intermediate)

Sometimes just "hanging out" with friends is the best fun

When I reflect on visits with special friends, what stands out is not the meals we ate or the things we did, but the conversations we had. I love when hours tick by with no agenda, and afterward I'm not even sure what we discussed. But I know I had fun. It's that message about the simple joy of hanging out with friends that I want to communicate to students.

The Relatives Came delivers this message perfectly. The relatives left Virginia in their old car and drove all day before they arrived at the home of their aunt, uncle, and cousins (some grandparents were there, too). What followed was hours of hugging, then a big supper that required they all take turns at the table (because there were so many relatives!). There weren't enough beds to go around, so they all slept side-by-side on the floor. And so it went, until the relatives packed up their old car for the trip back home. Notice there were no visits to Disney World, no major league baseball games, and not even any video games. Challenge your students to think about how they might have fun with a friend by doing something that doesn't require money and doesn't involve technology.

When you are kind to your friends, they will be kind to you

Mama Panya's Pancakes: A Village Tale from Kenya features pancakes as the key friend-making ingredient. In this story, Adika, Mama Panya's son, invites all his friends to supper as he and Mama walk to their village market to purchase what they need for pancakes. Mama is nervous because she has just a few coins, only enough to make a few pancakes. However, when the friends arrive, they all bring a little something to add to the meal, grateful for Adika's invitation. The friends enjoy the pancakes, but even more, they enjoy the fellowship with each other.

I love sharing this book with primary grade students, and after the story I always ask them to think about a time when they've done something kind for someone and been shown a kindness in return. It works the other way, too. I remind them: If your friend does something nice for you, surprise him with something nice when he least expects it.

Friends help each other through tough times

Friends are for having fun, but they can also offer support or help when times are tough. I love the book *Rescue and Jessica: A Life-Changing Friendship* for its message about the support of a good friend. I love it even more because in this story, the supporting friend is an animal—a service dog.

This story is based on a real-life friendship between Jessica Krensky, who was injured in the Boston Marathon bombing in 2013, and a black Labrador named Rescue who helped her adjust to her new life as a double amputee. He could open doors that were hard for her to reach, bring her things she needed, or simply offer a snuggle when Jessica needed comfort. Jessica thought Rescue was amazing. Although Rescue began his "career" as a guide dog, that didn't quite suit him. His trainer recognized that he would do better *beside* a partner instead of *leading* one—exactly what Jessica needed. Helpful friends are good at that: knowing just what someone needs at just the right moment.

Beware of false friends

Sometimes a friend *appears* to care about you, but their motives are questionable. We see this more than we'd like in the classroom. For example: the bully who gets another student to taunt a classmate with the promise "you'll be my best friend." Some kids have a talent for instigating a conflict, then disappearing while someone else takes the blame.

The book *Fox* will provide older elementary students and even middle schoolers with many talking points about false friends. In this story, intriguing even in its odd presentation on the page (handwritten paragraphs placed sideways, right-side-up and upside down), Dog finds Magpie and carries her to his cave to care for her burnt wing. The bird is frantic because she will no longer be able to fly, but Dog tries to cheer her up. He has one blind eye, but says life is still good. He even offers to let Magpie ride on his back. At first Magpie is pleased: She will be Dog's missing eye, and he will be her wings. But then Fox comes along.

Magpie is suspicious and fears Fox's sly eyes always watching her. She even warns Dog, though Dog is not concerned. One night, Fox whispers to the bird that he can run faster than Dog, fast like the wind. Magpie says she'll never leave Dog, but after repeated prodding, gives in. Atop Fox's back, Magpie does feel like she's flying, and they travel far. That's when Fox shakes Magpie from his back and says, "Now you and Dog will know what it is like to be truly alone." Magpie attempts the journey home, but whether she reaches her destination is uncertain as the story ends.

So many questions emerge from this fable, but one that I always ask is, "If Magpie recognized that Fox was trouble, why did she give in to him?" And then, "What can we learn from Magpie's experience?"

FEATURED BOOK FOR SOCIAL ENGAGEMENT: *Meet Danitra Brown* by Nikki Grimes

Friends support and encourage each other in many ways

Meet Danitra Brown isn't your garden-variety picture book. It's not a story with a problem and a solution. Instead, it is a set of 13 poems about the friendship between Danitra Brown and her friend Zuri Jackson that creates a montage of the many dimensions of friendship.

Zuri does the talking, but readers get to see what makes each girl special. For example, Zuri likes that Danitra is strong and independent—it gives her the strength to stand up to the class bully. Zuri is the kind of friend who's willing to spend the afternoon at Danitra's house when Danitra is taking care of her sick mom. Other times, the girls spend happy afternoons together, acting out plays and jumping rope.

Sometimes they cheer each other up: When Zuri is sad because she doesn't have a dad, Danitra tells her she's got it good; her mom loves her twice as much. Zuri returns the favor by sharing her ice cream money when Danitra doesn't have quite enough. Sometimes even good friends get angry with each other—like the time Zuri blabbed that Danitra was afraid of pigeons. But they don't stay angry long. There's so much to share, including their dreams for the future. Danitra says she's going to win the Nobel Prize. And Zuri is certain she'll make that happen.

If we're in need of role models to showcase positive social engagement, we couldn't find better examples than Danitra and Zuri. The questions that follow for Seven Thinking Boxes provide a place to begin that conversation.

SEVEN THINKING BOXES

Questions to ask about *Meet Danitra Brown* by Nikki Grimes
SEL Competency: Relationship Skills   Focus: Social Engagement

PLAIN CARDBOARD BOX	BASIC THINKING
	Name two things related to friendship that you know about Danitra. Name two things that you know about Zuri. From which poems did you get this information?
PUZZLE BOX	**PUZZLING DETAILS**
	Which of Danitra's character traits do you think was most important to being a good friend? Why? Which poem showed this?
HEART BOX	**FEELINGS**
	How did Zuri show that she was sensitive to Danitra's feelings? How did Danitra show that she was sensitive to Zuri's feelings? How was this important to their friendship? Which poems provided this evidence?
UNUSUAL BOX	**CREATIVE THINKING**
	In what ways was creative thinking important to these girls' friendship? Which poems best show creative thinking?
BROKEN BOX	**PROBLEMS AND ISSUES**
	What problems did each of these girls face? How did their friendship make a difference as they responded to these problems?
TREASURE BOX	**SOMETHING TO TREASURE**
	If you were Danitra, what would you most treasure about your friendship with Zuri? Why? If you were Zuri, what would you most treasure about your friendship with Danitra? Why?
TOOL BOX	**AUTHOR'S TOOLS**
	This author wrote this book as a set of poems rather than as a story. Why do you think she did this? How does it make a difference to the message about friendship?

SEVEN THINKING BOXES

Questions to ask about *any* book for social engagement

PLAIN CARDBOARD BOX	**BASIC THINKING**
	• What actions in the story show that someone was a good friend? What made this person a good friend? • What actions in this story show that someone was <u>not</u> a good friend? Why do you think this person acted this way?
PUZZLE BOX	**PUZZLING DETAILS**
	• Choose a quote about friendship from an online site. What character in this story do you think would have liked this quote? Why? • Who needed a friend in this story? Choose a quote that you think best shows this. Why did you choose this quote?
HEART BOX	**FEELINGS**
	• Whose feelings in this story were affected by someone being a good friend? Explain. • Whose feelings in this story were hurt by someone <u>not</u> being a good friend? Explain.
UNUSUAL BOX	**CREATIVE THINKING**
	• How could you have been a friend to this person? What kind of a friend did this person need? Why? • If a character in this story was <u>not</u> a good friend, what could you have said to her or him to change that behavior?
BROKEN BOX	**PROBLEMS AND ISSUES**
	• What problem was created in this story because someone was <u>not</u> a good friend? Explain. • Did the problem in this story get solved? Did friendship help? How?
TREASURE BOX	**SOMETHING TO TREASURE**
	• Who learned a lesson about friendship in this story? What did they learn? • After reading this book, is there something that <u>you</u> treasure more about friendship? How could you show this in your life?
TOOL BOX	**AUTHOR'S TOOLS**
	• What did this author do to make the friendship seem real? (It might be the kind of problems that were described. It might be the way the characters responded. Or, it might be something else.) • How might this story have been different if had been told from another character's point of view? Choose one page and rewrite it from this other point of view.

Relationship-Building

There are many relationships that are important to our students, both in and out of school. We see how complicated peer-to-peer relationships can be, as there are *many* students, each one unique. I've heard it said that if you have 20 students in your class and a new student arrives, you don't have *one* new student, you have *21* new students. Yes, even one child can change the entire classroom dynamic.

Then there are the relationships between students and teachers. Students must build relationships (and learn the rules) not just in their own classroom, but in the school library, the art and music rooms, and elsewhere in their school. Sometimes one teacher will have a great relationship with a student, but another will find him difficult: "I just love Jacob. His creativity shines through every time." Or, "Jacob can be so frustrating. No matter what the task is, he always has to do things his own way."

As teachers, we need to help students build relationships, not just with us and their peers, but with other people, too. Could there be a better place to explore relationship-building than in a classroom, where hundreds of possibilities present themselves every minute of every day?

WHAT WE HOPE TO SEE IN THE CLASSROOM REGARDING RELATIONSHIP-BUILDING, AND WHAT WE SOMETIMES SEE INSTEAD

In the classroom we'd like to see students partnering with lots of different classmates as well as groups of various sizes. It would be ideal if students chose to collaborate with peers they haven't worked with before. Or, even if the choice isn't theirs, it would be nice if they'd embrace—with a smile on their face—partnerships or groups determined by their teacher. Sometimes we *do* see this. But other times, students gravitate to the same friend or group of friends every time. This prevents new relationships from forming, or makes it difficult for previously negative relationships to become more positive.

ENHANCING CLASSROOM CULTURE: QUESTIONS FOR TEACHERS TO ASK THEMSELVES ABOUT RELATIONSHIP-BUILDING

1. What kinds of opportunities do I provide in my classroom for students to build relationships with each other?

2. How do I encourage students to work with classmates who might not be their first choice?

3. Have I discussed relationship-building with my students—what it means and why it's important? How could I engage my students in this conversation?

4. Which of my students build relationships easily? How do they achieve this?

5. Which of my students would most benefit from better relationship-building skills? How could I support them in developing these skills?

6. How can I model building positive relationships as I build relationships with them?

WHAT TO LOOK FOR IN BOOKS ABOUT RELATIONSHIP-BUILDING

Students need to build relationships with many different types of people in many different circumstances. I look for books that feature situations children are most likely to encounter. For example, sibling relationships are a frequent source of aggravation in many children's lives. Bullying is a common tension in many schools, and sometimes students need to form relationships with classmates who speak different languages. In some students' lives, family members come and go as the result of divorce, death, and so forth. All of these changes bring about new interpersonal dynamics. Most of all, I think we need to help students rethink relationships that may not have worked in the past: How can I learn to like this person who initially didn't seem very likable? If we want our students to build strong relationships, we must choose books that feature a range of social issues. Chart 6.2: Books Aligned to Relationship-Building lists titles that meet this criteria.

CHART 6.2: BOOKS ALIGNED TO RELATIONSHIP-BUILDING

THE MESSAGE	THE BOOK
Building a relationship with a sibling	*My Rotten Redheaded Older Brother* by Patricia Polacco (primary and intermediate)
Building a relationship with a bully	*The Recess Queen* by Alexis O'Neill (primary and intermediate)
Building a relationship in spite of language differences	*Sitti's Secrets* by Naomi Shihab Nye (primary and intermediate)
Building a relationship with a new family member	*Crow Call* by Lois Lowry (intermediate)
Building a relationship with someone we didn't like initially	*The Raft* by Jim LaMarche (primary and intermediate)

Building a relationship with a sibling

For children who have brothers or sisters, sibling relationships are ever-present in their lives. They may see their brother as the favored child who gets all the attention, lavish gifts, a later bedtime, and preferred treatment in sibling disputes: He is soooo annoying! Meanwhile, they get blamed for stuff they didn't do and never win a brother-to-brother argument. Of course, their sibling would report the situation differently. My go-to book for sibling rivalry used to be *The Pain and the Great One* by Judy Blume, in which a big sister and little brother each describe life in their family—from their point of view. Unfortunately, this book is no longer in print, but if you can find a copy, grab it.

Otherwise, I also love ***My Rotten Redheaded Older Brother***. In this story, author Patricia Polacco (Tricia) describes family life with Richard, her brother who is four years her senior. Richard can do *everything* better than Tricia (important things like spitting the farthest), and at every turn, gloats about his superiority. Tricia grows tired of this and vows to show Richard she can be best at something. One evening when they are at the fair, Tricia gets her big chance: They are riding the merry-go-round, and Tricia is determined to stay on longer than her brother.

She stays on so long, in fact, that she becomes dizzy and falls off. It's not until she regains consciousness the next day that she realizes it was Richard who came to her rescue, running to get help. It's a sweet reminder that although our siblings may seem to complicate our everyday lives in countless infuriating ways, love prevails in times of need. After reading this book, ask your students to remember an act of support that an otherwise annoying sister or brother (or cousin) performed for them.

Building a relationship with a bully

Bullying is a critical topic in all schools and a frequent focus of discussion. While these conversations are important, I worry about them for a couple of reasons. One relates to misinterpreting bullying, discussed below under the "communication" focus area. The other relates to common strategies for changing bullying behavior.

Our first goal when bullying occurs is to stop it in its tracks quickly. This is a legitimate response, and often achieves the desired outcome: the bully ceases bullying—at least in the short term. But too often it's the teacher who effects the change, which does nothing to empower student-victims, or dig deeper into the "why" behind the bully's behavior. ***The Recess Queen*** is a book that masterfully offers strategies to bullying victims, and also provides a closer look at the bully herself. Although it looks to be a story for younger students, its themes are appropriate for a wide age range.

The book's main character, Mean Jean, is the undisputed queen of the playground. She declares that *she* is first to use whatever playground equipment strikes her fancy and barks at anyone who dares challenge her. Then one day a new student arrives. Her name is Katie Sue, a teeny, tiny kid. Unfamiliar with Jean's rules, she gets to the swings and the soccer ball first, and the recess queen is *not* happy, yelling with increased ferocity. But little Katie is undeterred: "How *did* you get so bossy?" she asks—and then goes back to playing.

But Katie Sue does something else, too. She pulls out a jump rope and invites Mean Jean to jump with her. To everyone's surprise, Jean joins the game, and that becomes the beginning of a new Jean—one who has friends, and who is so busy having fun on the playground that she no longer has time for bullying. In the end, Katie Sue shows us that standing up to a bully is a first important step in curtailing their behavior. But maybe we should try harder to build relationships with bullies as well. There's a chance that the bullying is more a defense against loneliness than a symptom of inherent meanness. A friend might be just what a bully needs to behave differently.

Building a relationship when we don't speak the same language

Building a relationship with someone who speaks a different language offers another kind of relationship challenge. Since words are our communication life-line, we hardly know what to do when words fail us. This is often the case when new students come to our class with a first language other than English. Over time, non-English speakers will learn English. But right now, today, how can we and the other students in our class communicate with them?

Sitti's Secrets is a beautiful story of a girl who built a loving relationship with her grandmother despite their language differences. Mona visits her grandma (*sitti*, in Arabic) in Palestine. They use gestures to communicate needs like hunger and fatigue and play games such as marbles that don't require words. But their relationship grows most notably by paying attention to the small things that are important to each other.

Mona notices that Sitti likes to eat cucumber for breakfast and prefers to bake bread on a flat rock. Sitti likes her lemonade with mint and every time before drinking it, breathes in the pungent aroma. These are Sitti's "secrets" and Mona would not know them if she didn't look and listen carefully. The message for building relationships? Sometimes a person's character is better communicated through the details of our interactions with them rather than through their words. What small details have your students noticed about each other that could strengthen their relationships? What have *you* noticed?

Building a relationship with a new family member

When a new family member arrives on the scene, it's these nuances of our daily lives that the new person doesn't know. *Crow Call* is a book better suited to older elementary students, since the narrative is long for a picture book and the themes are more sophisticated. Although she looks to be about eight or nine years old, Liz is just getting to know her dad. He's been away at war (World War II, from the looks of the illustrations) and recently arrived home. They go to the diner for breakfast and Dad asks about her favorite food. Cherry pie, Liz tells him, thinking to herself that he'd already know this if he hadn't been away so long. But they are just getting to know each other and continue on their way to the remote wooded area where her dad will hunt for crows. The crows eat the crops, Dad tells her, and at this time of year their babies are grown and out of the nest, so no need to worry.

But Liz *is* worried, uncomfortable with the idea of hunting, despite her amusement with the crow whistle that magically brings out dozens of crows hidden among the trees. Dad senses Liz's reluctance and puts down his gun. They leave the forest hand in hand. Liz and Dad still have much to learn about each other. But Liz's honesty in telling her dad how she feels about hunting, and her dad's sensitivity to Liz's feelings, moved their relationship in the right direction. What does it take to build a relationship with a new family member? Can students offer any wisdom from their own lives?

Building a relationship with someone we didn't like initially

Building a relationship with a new person in your family is challenging, but maybe not as challenging as rectifying a relationship that has soured. "I don't like Jeremy," Mitchell announced. "We're enemies. Please don't make me sit next to him." "Hmmm, enemies," I replied. "That was last year in second grade. You're both older now, more mature. I'm counting on you to figure this out." At the end of third grade, Mitchell came to me again, begging to be placed in the same fourth grade class with Jeremy.

We need to help our students turn animosity toward someone into something more positive. That's what happens in *The Raft.* Nicky dreads spending the summer with his eccentric grandmother who spends her days carving bears in her remote cabin that doesn't even have a television. As the story begins, he makes a point of being unpleasant, and rejects Grandma's every effort to make their time together enjoyable.

Then a raft floats mysteriously down the river, and Nicky is intrigued. He discovers animals etched into its surface and begins to imagine the fun that awaits him. Grandma doesn't seem surprised by the raft's appearance but delights in the way Nicky now enjoys all the river has to offer. She often joins him and shares stories of the summers she spent on the river, when she was Nicky's age. In the end, Nicky is pleased that he's becoming a "river rat," just like Grandma. Sharing interests with someone builds bridges and fortifies a relationship. The questions that follow for Seven Thinking Boxes focus on improving a relationship that needs strengthening.

FEATURED BOOK FOR BUILDING RELATIONSHIPS:
The Raft by Jim LaMarche

SEVEN THINKING BOXES

Questions to ask about *The Raft* by Jim LaMarche
SEL Skill: Relationships and Social Skills   Focus: Relationship-Building

PLAIN CARDBOARD BOX	**BASIC THINKING** What do you think changed Nicky's relationship with Grandma the most? Choose one specific event in the story and explain your thinking.
PUZZLE BOX	**PUZZLING DETAILS** What details show Nicky's feelings toward Grandma at the beginning of the story? What do these details show about Nicky's efforts to build a relationship with his grandmother?
HEART BOX	**FEELINGS** Whose feelings were you concerned about in this story? Why? Can feelings have an effect on a relationship? How?
UNUSUAL BOX	**CREATIVE THINKING** We can tell from this story that Grandma is a very creative person. She was a good artist and carved many animals into the raft. How else does Grandma show her creativity? How did it help her build a relationship with Nicky?
BROKEN BOX	**PROBLEMS AND ISSUES** Grandma recognized that there was a problem with Nicky's attitude at the beginning of the story. Do you think she handled the situation well? Would you have handled it similarly or differently? Explain.
TREASURE BOX	**SOMETHING TO TREASURE** By the end of the story, Nicky and Grandma have a strong relationship. Do you think this will change the way Nicky approaches people in the future? Why or why not? How could *you* form a stronger relationship with someone you may not have liked in the past?
TOOL BOX	**AUTHOR'S TOOLS** The author tells this story from <u>Nicky's</u> point of view. Choose a page that shows something about Nicky's and Grandma's relationship and retell it from <u>Grandma's</u> point of view.

SEVEN THINKING BOXES

Questions to ask about *any* book for relationship building

PLAIN CARDBOARD BOX	**BASIC THINKING** • What evidence in this story showed that people needed to build a stronger relationship? Which characters were involved? • What actions in the story helped to build a positive relationship?
PUZZLE BOX	**PUZZLING DETAILS** • What quote best shows that someone in this story worked hard to build a strong relationship? • What quote best shows the need for a stronger relationship? Explain this quote in your own words.
HEART BOX	**FEELINGS** • Whose feelings were involved in resolving the relationship problem in this story? How did people feel at different points during the story? • Imagine yourself as one of the characters in this story before the relationship problem was solved. Would your feelings have been the same or different from those of the character? Explain.
UNUSUAL BOX	**CREATIVE THINKING** • If it had been up to you to solve the relationship problem in this story, how would you have handled it? Why would this have been a good solution? • Was there a character in this story who used creative thinking to solve a relationship problem? Explain.
BROKEN BOX	**PROBLEMS AND ISSUES** • What situation led to the relationship problem in this story? Explain in your own words. • If this relationship problem was not resolved, what might have happened next? Why?
TREASURE BOX	**SOMETHING TO TREASURE** • Did anyone in this story learn a lesson about building relationships? What was the lesson? • What did this story teach *you* about building relationships in your own life? What will this story help you remember about building relationships?
TOOL BOX	**AUTHOR'S TOOLS** • In a story about relationships, there are often two characters involved. How does the author <u>show</u> the relationship between these characters? (The author might use dialogue, internal thoughts, description, body language, or something else.) • Rewrite a scene in this story from a different character's point of view to show his or her perspective.

Teamwork

So far in this chapter we've examined social engagement, where person-to-person dynamics impact the quality of a relationship, and relationship-building, which emphasizes how to initiate or enhance a relationship. But teamwork is something more. Teamwork is the willingness of someone to work together with a group to achieve a common aim. Teamwork is typically more focused on achieving specific outcomes than on either social engagement or relationship-building.

WHAT WE HOPE TO SEE IN THE CLASSROOM REGARDING TEAMWORK, AND WHAT WE SOMETIMES SEE INSTEAD

When students hear the word "team," it's the image of sports teams that usually come to mind. The term may also play a role on the playground, where kids form teams to play games like kick ball and four-square. (Playground games haven't changed much through the decades.) Inside the classroom, we're more inclined to label activities in which students work together as "group work" rather than "teamwork," though the intent of the work is about the same. In both cases, however, the teacher is not be directly involved (excluding reading groups, where the teacher is part of the mix, and usually the de facto group leader).

What we'd like to see in the classroom in the name of teamwork are opportunities for students to work with lots of different groups to collaborate on tasks like science experiments, social studies projects, literature studies, and more. Groups might be interest-based, or configured so that students with different skills are represented across groups. (For instance, each group might include someone who likes to take notes, likes to design graphics, or likes to identify resources.) There might also be times when groups are organized by the level of support they'll need from the teacher.

I wish I could report more of *any* kind of teamwork present in the classrooms I visit. To be fair, I visit mostly during the literacy block where the opportunity for working in groups may not be as great as during other areas of instruction. But typically, I see students working by themselves. It's important to build students' independence, so some of this alone time is appropriate. But *interdependence* will be key to solving many real-world 21st-century problems, and students need to build these skills as well.

ENHANCING CLASSROOM CULTURE: QUESTIONS FOR TEACHERS TO ASK THEMSELVES ABOUT TEAMWORK

1. What opportunities for teamwork do I regularly provide to students in my classroom?

2. Among the opportunities for group work I've provided recently, how have teams (or groups) been determined? How else could my students be placed into groups?

3. How would I define an appropriate balance between working independently and working interdependently? What factors are responsible for this balance?

4. How well do my students function in groups? What factors contribute to their success? What factors contribute to ongoing problems?

5. Have I had a conversation with my students about how to work successfully as a team? What could I include in a conversation on this topic?

6. Have I had a conversation with my students about how to be a good team leader? What would I include under the heading of qualities of a good team leader?

WHAT TO LOOK FOR IN BOOKS ABOUT TEAMWORK

For books about teamwork I sought stories about *groups* of characters as opposed to single main characters, in which those characters pursue a clearly defined *goal*. Locating books that met these criteria was a bit more challenging than I anticipated because the theme was often similar from story to story: Sticking together solves problems. It's a valuable message, but I wanted students to relate it to different situations. I looked for stories with a focus on teamwork in sports, and scenarios where the "team" was a family. I wanted students to see how team members support each other emotionally, and the way team leaders guide and motivate. The books listed in Chart 6.3: Books Aligned to Teamwork demonstrate these more nuanced messages.

CHART 6.3: BOOKS ALIGNED TO TEAMWORK

THE MESSAGE	THE BOOK
We're stronger together	*Goal!* by Mina Javaherbin (intermediate)
A family is a team	*Brothers at Bat: The True Story of an Amazing All-Brother Baseball Team* by Audrey Vernick (primary and intermediate)
Families work together to solve problems	*A Chair for My Mother* by Vera B. Williams (primary)
Team leaders provide guidance	*Swimmy* by Leo Lionni (primary and intermediate)
Being part of a team provides emotional support	*Baseball Saved Us* by Ken Mochizuki (intermediate)

We're stronger together

Set in South Africa, **Goal!** will immediately attract sports-minded students with the over-sized soccer ball that dominates the cover illustration. They will predict that the story is about making a goal in soccer—and to some extent, they will be right. But in this story, the real "goal" is to outsmart a group of bullies who threaten to steal a soccer ball from a team of younger boys.

It's one of the younger boys who tells this story. He is proud to have won a regulation ball for his excellent grades, and asks his friends to join him for a soccer game, called football in South Africa. Ever mindful that the streets in their community are not safe, one member of the team must always stand guard atop a building, eyes peeled for the band of bullies that roams the alleys. Sure enough, the bullies arrive. But just in time, the younger kids shove the new ball under a bucket. It's only a small plastic ball that the bullies see, and they are quick to grab it. The younger teammates hope the bullies will not kick the plastic ball toward the bucket, which will reveal the new ball if it topples. Luck is on their side and they make a great show of crying about their lost plastic ball as the bullies carry it off.

After reading this story, talk with students about the challenges faced by the younger boys and the way teamwork helped them succeed: What did they do to stick together? How did sticking together make a difference?

A family is a team

I like the idea of helping students recognize that a family is a kind of team. Family members work together toward common goals that help their family flourish, and they play together to enjoy each other's company. To showcase the power of a family that plays together, try *Brothers at Bat: The True Story of an Amazing All-Brother Baseball Team*. It's the story of the Acerra brothers—all 12 of them, though there were 16 children in the family in all. Not only were they the longest-playing family team in history, these boys were also wonderful examples of how teammates (and family members) support each other. There was no jealousy, rivalry, or poor sportsmanship. No stomping off the field.

The Acerra brothers played baseball in the 1930s, nearly 100 years ago. Although it's unlikely that one family today could staff an entire baseball team, this story could be used to launch a discussion of the ways that families have fun together, what "family" means to students, and how *their* family functions as a team.

Families work together to solve a problem

Families work together in countless ways. Sometimes kids do chores around the house to lighten the parents' load and to earn a bit of spending money. Sometimes, when money is tight, everyone in a family makes sacrifices so there will be enough food on the table. Sometimes families save up to take special vacations together or enjoy some other treat. I especially love *A Chair for My Mother* for its portrayal of a family that rallies around a problem and solves it together.

Rosa and her mom return from shopping one day to find two fire trucks parked outside their apartment building, flames leaping from the roof. Rosa frantically tries to find her grandma, who, thankfully, turns out to be safe. But the apartment is destroyed, and its contents are lost. Eventually the family moves into the downstairs apartment, but the rooms are empty. Especially missed is a comfortable chair for Mama to sit in when she returns from her waitressing job. Mama brings home a large jar, and bit by bit, fills it with the tip money she receives at work. Rosa and Grandma contribute, too. When the jar is full, they take the coins to the bank, convert them to ten-dollar bills, then head for the department store in search of the perfect arm chair. They find one with pink roses, and it really *is* perfect—perfect for Mama to rest on when she gets home from work. Perfect for Grandma to sit and chat with friends. And perfect for Rosa to cuddle on with a book. Have your students worked alongside their family to solve a problem as a team? What was the problem? How did teamwork help?

Team leaders provide guidance

Teams often need leaders to get them organized for action and to keep everyone motivated until the goal is reached. There are many people students can read about to identify leadership skills, but fewer books that highlight how the leader works with members of their team. For this, I defer to a fish. His name is **Swimmy** (from a book of the same name). Swimmy loses several fishy friends to a large tuna and is elated when he encounters another school of fish hiding among the weeds. He invites them to come and play, but they decline, fearful of the big fish that will gobble them up.

That's when Swimmy thinks of a plan. He decides they will all swim together in one extra-large fish shape, each fish in his own place with Swimmy as the eye. Now *they* are the ones to chase the big fish away. If I was sharing this book simply as a "cute story," it would be most appropriate at the primary grade level. But when you think about its message—how an effective team leader can devise a plan and enlist the cooperation of all the teammates to reach a goal—you can see how it's also a terrific tale for older students, too.

FEATURED BOOK FOR TEAMWORK: *Baseball Saved Us* by Ken Mochizuki

---

Being part of a team provides emotional support

By contrast, **Baseball Saved Us**, the featured book for teamwork, might be best suited to students in the intermediate grades. It's about life in a Japanese internment camp during World War II and requires some background knowledge of the political climate at that time. It was an ugly period in our country's history for Japanese Americans, and to ease the trauma of their imprisonment in barracks surrounded by barbed wire, the young narrator's dad decided the community needed a baseball field. Soon, everyone was playing.

Baseball saved them from endless days of sitting around and contemplating all they had lost, and gave them back some self-esteem. The narrator, nicknamed Shorty by his teammates, wasn't much of a ball player at first, but scored the winning run at the end of the season. Success! But being part of a team is about more than winning. It can give you a sense of belonging. Feeling like you belong helps ease emotional pain in turbulent times. Check out the questions for Seven Thinking Boxes to start your classroom conversation about the emotional value of teamwork.

SEVEN THINKING BOXES

Questions to ask about *Baseball Saved Us* by Ken Mochizuki
SEL Skill: Relationships and Social Skills   Focus: Teamwork

PLAIN CARDBOARD BOX	**BASIC THINKING** What living conditions in the internment camp showed that the people who lived there might benefit from being on a team?
PUZZLE BOX	**PUZZLING DETAILS** Which detail do you think *best* shows the difficulty of living in an internment camp? Why did you choose this detail?
HEART BOX	**FEELINGS** How did being part of a team change Shorty's feelings about himself? Why?
UNUSUAL BOX	**CREATIVE THINKING** Shorty's dad decided to make a baseball field to help members of his community feel better about themselves. What might have been another creative solution to this problem?
BROKEN BOX	**PROBLEMS AND ISSUES** What was the problem that Japanese Americans faced—beyond being forced to live in internment camps? How could teamwork make a difference?
TREASURE BOX	**SOMETHING TO TREASURE** The title of this book is *Baseball Saved Us*. How did baseball save Shorty and other Japanese Americans in this camp?
TOOL BOX	**AUTHOR'S TOOLS** Notice the colors the illustrator used in this book. How do they change from the beginning to the end of the story? Why do you think the illustrator chose them? How do they contribute to the mood throughout the story?

SEVEN THINKING BOXES

Questions to ask about *any* book for teamwork

PLAIN CARDBOARD BOX	**BASIC THINKING**
	• What kind of teamwork was involved in this story? What details show this? • Were all members of the group (or team) team players? That is, did they all work together to support the team? Explain.
PUZZLE BOX	**PUZZLING DETAILS**
	• How did teamwork help? Choose a quote that best shows the power of teamwork in this story. • Find a quote from this story that best shows the need for teamwork. Why did you choose this quote?
HEART BOX	**FEELINGS**
	• Whose feelings changed by being part of this team? How did they change? • If you had been in the same situation as these characters, would your feelings have been the same or different? Explain.
UNUSUAL BOX	**CREATIVE THINKING**
	• How did creative thinking help solve the teamwork problem in this story? Explain in your own words. • How might *you* have solved this problem if you were the team leader?
BROKEN BOX	**PROBLEMS AND ISSUES**
	• What situation in this book led to the need for teamwork? (It might have been something that occurred before the story began.) • Do you think the problem in this story has been solved forever or will more teamwork be needed to resolve it? Explain.
TREASURE BOX	**SOMETHING TO TREASURE**
	• What do you think this author wanted you to understand about teamwork from this story? • In the future, how might this story make a difference to you? How could teamwork be important in your own life?
TOOL BOX	**AUTHOR'S TOOLS**
	• How do the illustrations in this book show the value of teamwork? It might relate to the colors in the illustrations, the expressions on characters' faces, or something else. • Choose one scene from this story that shows teamwork. Add description, dialogue, or some other craft to make the scene even more interesting.

Communication

CASEL places *communication* first among its focus areas for relationship skills. However, I choose to list it last, because communication is the glue that holds relationships together—whether you are just engaging socially, building a relationship, or working as a team. When it comes to communication, we may not think much about it unless it's not going well: When people misinterpret what we say, for example. Or, when we realize we've neglected to share something that should have been explained and the result is confusion rather than clarity. Or, when we should have spoken up to advocate for ourselves, and now it's too late. Of course, there are other scenarios, as well, and teachers deal with many of them on a regular basis. Children often speak before they think—among other issues that derail their communication.

WHAT WE HOPE TO SEE IN THE CLASSROOM REGARDING COMMUNICATION, AND WHAT WE SOMETIMES SEE INSTEAD

Above all, we would like to see students communicate with kindness, both verbally and nonverbally, and with a sense of what is appropriate in the moment—kind words that show empathy and body language that conveys openness and acceptance. Instead, we often get attitude (insert eye roll), a lack of tact, kids who use their words to hurt, and students who remain silent when they should speak up. We spend plenty of time talking with students about choosing kind words rather than hurtful ones, but could we do more to focus their thinking on what it means to communicate well? Get started by considering these questions.

ENHANCING CLASSROOM CULTURE: QUESTIONS FOR TEACHERS TO ASK THEMSELVES ABOUT COMMUNICATION

1. What are my communication strengths? My weaknesses? How do they impact my work with students?

2. Which of my students communicate well? What are some examples? What accounts for their good communication skills?

3. Which of my students are not good communicators? What do I see in the classroom that shows me this? What seems to be the root of the problem?

4. What would I include in a conversation with my students about the importance of communicating well, and *how* to communicate well?

5. What real-life examples could I share with students that would demonstrate the benefits of good communication? Who do my students know outside of our classroom who are models of good communication?

6. How can I help my students understand that people communicate in *many* ways—not just with words?

WHAT TO LOOK FOR IN BOOKS ABOUT COMMUNICATION

There are many picture books suitable for the elementary grades that demonstrate the power of communication—how good communication helps to improve a situation, and the ways poor communication creates problems. These books generally address other themes, too, but the importance of communication is evident in its impact on the story's characters. I chose books that can help students see the way they communicate (or should).

Do students realize that a poor choice of words can turn a small problem into a major crisis? Do they consider others' feelings when making a point? Do they see that there are times when it is important to speak up and defend themselves, and times when its more important to build a relationship? Do they recognize that actions communicate as well as words, and that there are other modes of communication, too? I selected books (listed in Chart 6.4: Books Aligned to Communication) that represent all of these messages.

CHART 6.4: BOOKS ALIGNED TO COMMUNICATION

THE MESSAGE	THE BOOK
The words you choose matter—a lot	*The Sandwich Swap* by Queen Rania of Jordan Al Abdullah (primary)
Consider other people's feelings when communicating	*The Honest-to-Goodness Truth* by Patricia C. McKissack (primary and intermediate)
It's important to speak up for yourself	*My Name Is Sangoel* by Karen Lynn Williams and Khadra Mohammed (primary and intermediate)
Communication involves sharing the real you	*Marianthe's Story: Painted Words and Spoken Memories* by Aliki (primary and intermediate)
Communication builds relationships	*The Day You Begin* by Jacqueline Woodson (primary and intermediate)

The words you choose matter—a lot

Conflicts between students can begin with a single hurtful word. Maybe Ryan didn't *mean* to insult Thomas when he said he was a "computer nerd," but that hurt Thomas's feelings, so now Thomas retaliates by l calling Ryan a "loser." Would there have been a better way to express that Thomas has a lot of knowledge about technology and can always fix the classroom Chromebooks? Because then they wouldn't have gotten into this war of words that is spiraling out of control.

This is essentially what happens in **The Sandwich Swap**. Two girls, Salma and Lily, are besties until they each feel compelled to comment on each other's sandwich. Lily calls Salma's chick pea paste sandwich *yucky*, which prompts Salma to declare that Lily's peanut butter and jelly sandwich is *gross*. Soon the words become more hurtful—weird, stupid, dumb—and other kids in the class become involved, choosing sides. What began as one poorly chosen word erupts into a full-out food fight in the cafeteria—and a trip to the principal's office for Salma and Lily. After a major clean-up operation, the two girls decide to sample each other's sandwiches. And what do you know: They like what they taste.

There are numerous themes here, including openness to new experiences and other cultures. But I also like to use this book as an example of how poor communication, even a single wrong word, can lead to tons of trouble. Instead of calling her sandwich "gross," what else could Lily have said to Salma to show that she didn't know what was in her sandwich, but would like to understand? Help students rethink *how* they communicate: You don't have to agree, but can you disagree respectfully?

Consider other people's feelings when communicating

It's the art of speaking *honestly* but *kindly* that's at the heart of **The Honest-to-Goodness Truth**. I use this book frequently, and it never disappoints. As the story begins, Libby is caught telling a lie by her mom. She is reprimanded and vows never to lie again. "This is easy," students tell me, "the theme is always tell the truth."

But then truth-telling gets trickier. Libby *does* tell the truth: She tells her little friend at church that her dress is pretty, but she has a hole in her sock. She announces that another friend cried in front of all the parents. She tells her elderly friend Miz Tusselbury that her garden is over-run with weeds. Libby's friends are disappearing, and she doesn't understand why. She finally recognizes the problem when someone treats her in a similar fashion, criticizing her ancient but beloved horse. It's never wrong to tell the truth, she recognizes, but the *way* you tell it matters. What a valuable lesson for our students.

It's important to speak up for yourself

I think teachers sometimes do a better job of getting students to be quiet than encouraging them to speak up. We tell them not to tattle or complain about unimportant things—the kid who cuts ahead of them in line or won't share the yellow highlighter. Bullying is an exception; we always want them to speak up about that, and of course we want them to tell us when they are hurt, or when something happens that is dangerous or seriously wrong. But how do we explain the difference between problems they could solve themselves, and issues that require speaking up? Where is that fine line? Beginning with the story *My Name is Sangoel* might get this conversation started.

My Name is Sangoel is the beautiful story of a young refugee who leaves behind his homeland of Sudan to come to America. He brings with him little other than his Dinka name, and is sad when everyone he meets, including his new teacher and classmates, mispronounces it. At first the boy just mumbles the correct pronunciation, but no one seems to hear. He doesn't give up. On the front of his white shirt, he draws a picture of a sun, and under it, a soccer goal. Oh, respond his friends, your name is "Sun-goal." They finally understand.

What if Sangoel hadn't spoken up? His name, like almost everything else from his past, would have been gone forever. When his words didn't work, he found another way to communicate. This required courage and persistence, but Sangoel was brave and didn't quit. Our students shouldn't give up either. Talk with them about situations when it might be important for them to speak up. Who would be a trusted listener? How could they communicate if they didn't have the words?

Communication means sharing the real you.
Marianthe's Story: Painted Words and Spoken Memories takes Sangoel's experience one step further. Like Sangoel, Marianthe (Mari) is new to America, and arrives with a similar life story and language barrier. But from the beginning, Mari paints what she cannot express verbally. At first her "painted words" describe her feelings—a sad heart to show her distress over her classmates' unwelcoming treatment of her. And her teacher wastes no time setting everyone on a different path. But what makes the biggest difference is the other pictures Marianthe paints, and the simple words she uses to share her story—her life story.

This is when readers flip the book over and hear Marianthe's spoken memories. She paints the home where she lived with her family, and her village where many people were killed, while others died from famine. She describes how she went to school, two hours away, though no one but her parents understood why a *girl* needed an education. Still, her parents wanted more for her. Her father left for America first and she missed him a lot. But soon she followed, and began her new life. She finishes her story and her classmates cheer. They are then eager to share *their* stories.

What is most significant here is that Marianthe willingly shares who she really is—her story. Of course, it's a work of fiction and she achieves (almost seamlessly) the happily-ever-after ending we'd like for all our newcomers. But if students when they are ready, are willing to share even a small piece of themselves or their journey, perhaps the outcome would be greater empathy all around.

FEATURED BOOK FOR COMMUNICATION: *The Day You Begin*
by Jacqueline Woodson

Communication builds relationships

The need for communication is a common theme in books about newcomers, and in **The Day You Begin**, the author (Jacqueline Woodson) is honest about the bravery it requires. Because fitting in doesn't come easily. Your classmates share tales of exotic summer travels to distant countries and glorious beaches—while you spent your days caring for your little sister and reading books during her naptime. Who'd want to hear about that? Your clothes and hair are different, and even when you speak your new language, your words sound different from those of your classmates.

This is the way it will be until you take that big step and begin to tell your *own* story: Although you never left your block, all those naptime books you read transported you to exotic destinations, too. Then somehow your new classroom starts to feel a little more welcoming. Someone says something kind to you, like they mean it. You begin to make a friend.

I like that this story is narrated in the second person, told directly to "you," the newcomer. *You* need to take some responsibility for building relationships. Yes, we expect other students to show kindness toward classmates who are new. But kindness and friendship are not the same. Building a relationship with someone requires communication from both parties. The questions that follow for Seven Thinking Boxes focus not just on enlisting the kindness and generosity of classmates, but on empowering newcomers to take an active role in building relationships—through a willingness to communicate.

SEVEN THINKING BOXES

Questions to ask about *The Day You Begin* by Jacqueline Woodson
SEL Skill: Relationships and Social Skills   Focus: Communication

PLAIN CARDBOARD BOX	**BASIC THINKING** • What are some of the ways the author says you (a newcomer) might be different from your classmates?
PUZZLE BOX	**PUZZLING DETAILS** • Which sentence in this book was most helpful to you as a newcomer? Why?
HEART BOX	**FEELINGS** • Have you ever felt like one of the children in this story? When? Did communication help?
UNUSUAL BOX	**CREATIVE THINKING** • How could you communicate something about yourself that you feel comfortable sharing even if you don't know all the words to say what you mean?
BROKEN BOX	**PROBLEMS AND ISSUES** • How does it make it even more of a problem to make new friends if you don't try to communicate something about yourself?
TREASURE BOX	**SOMETHING TO TREASURE** • What do you think the author is trying to help you understand about how to make new friends?
TOOL BOX	**AUTHOR'S TOOLS** • Why do you think the author wrote this story as if she is speaking directly to "you?"

SEVEN THINKING BOXES

Questions to ask about *any* book for communication

PLAIN CARDBOARD BOX	BASIC THINKING
	• What are some examples of good communication in this story? How is it helpful to the characters? • What are some examples of poor communication in this story? What happens because of this poor communication?
PUZZLE BOX	PUZZLING DETAILS
	• Find a quote in this book that you think helped another character understand the importance of good communication? How did it help? • Find a quote in this book that best shows what can happen when someone doesn't communicate or doesn't communicate well.
HEART BOX	FEELINGS
	• Whose feelings were hurt because of poor communication? • Did better communication change anyone's feelings in this story? How?
UNUSUAL BOX	CREATIVE THINKING
	• How else could this communication problem have been solved? Who could have helped? What could the person have said? • Did anyone in this story use creative thinking in order to communicate? Explain.
BROKEN BOX	PROBLEMS AND ISSUES
	• What caused the communication problem in this story? • What problem occurred because of poor communication?
TREASURE BOX	SOMETHING TO TREASURE
	• What did the character in this story learn about the importance of communication? How will that help you when you are in a similar situation? • What do you treasure most from this story? How does it relate to communication?
TOOL BOX	AUTHOR'S TOOLS
	• Choose a place in the story where the main character was not able to communicate well. Add a couple of sentences showing the thoughts in her/his head. • How do the illustrations in this story show good communication? How do they show poor communication?

CHAPTER 7
RESPONSIBLE DECISION-MAKING: CHOICES AND CONSEQUENCES

Could there be anything more important than the decisions we make? Our choices typically affect us personally, impact the people closest to us, and often lead to far-reaching consequences that we may or may not anticipate. It's where personal behavior and social behavior intersect. This makes *responsible* decision-making essential. CASEL defines responsible decision-making as the "ability to make constructive choices about personal behavior and social interactions based on ethical standards, safety concerns, and social norms. The realistic evaluation of consequences of various actions, and a consideration of the well-being of oneself and others" ("Core SEL Competencies," n.d.).

CASEL identifies six focus areas for responsible decision-making:

- Identifying problems
- Analyzing situations
- Solving problems
- Evaluating
- Reflecting
- Ethical responsibility

Like some other SEL competencies, the designated focus areas for responsible decision-making are highly interdependent. Good decisions begin with the identification of a problem, and along the way, there is an analysis and evaluation of the situation. At the end comes a solution, and ideally reflection on the decision-making process. Throughout, decision-makers should never lose sight of the ethics embedded in the choices they make. For the purposes of this chapter, I believe analysis and evaluation of situations to be so dependent on each other that they will be examined together.

Identifying Problems

Identifying a problem means you know you have a problem, you can name it, and you recognize the need to do something about it. It sounds simple enough, but personal problems mess with our dignity, self-esteem, and sense of control over our destiny. Maybe if you deny that you have a problem it will simply go away on its own (that rash that appeared out of nowhere on your arms). Or, if you admit reading is difficult for you, you'll somehow be sentenced to a lifetime of low-paying jobs. (And if your teacher can't help you fix your reading problem, you'll feel like an even bigger failure.) We can't help our students solve a problem until they have acknowledged that there *is* a problem, as well as what might have caused it.

WHAT WE HOPE TO SEE IN THE CLASSROOM REGARDING IDENTIFYING PROBLEMS, AND WHAT WE SOMETIMES SEE INSTEAD

Teachers are adept at identifying academic problems, and students can generally tell you if they're "good at reading" or "bad at math." But when the issues are social or emotional, recognizing problems gets more complicated. Some kids interpret *everything* as a problem (even a crisis), even when something is not a *real* problem. (They didn't get their last turn to kick the ball during recess.) Other children see nothing as a problem: They do *not* interrupt too much. They do *not* bully. It is *not* a problem that they don't follow through on responsibilities. This section can't list every social emotional problem that students face (that would be an endless task), so instead it explores how to help students recognize when a legitimate problem exists. Use the questions below to guide you.

ENHANCING CLASSROOM CULTURE: QUESTIONS FOR TEACHERS TO ASK THEMSELVES ABOUT IDENTIFYING PROBLEMS

1. What kinds of problems do my students typically identify for themselves? Are they academic problems, personal, or social?

2. What kinds of problems would I *like* my students to be able to identify for themselves? Try to be specific.

3. Which of my students are *not* good at identifying problems for themselves? How does this impact them academically, socially, and emotionally?

4. Have I talked with my students about what it means to identify a problem and how this can be the first step toward solving their problem? What would I include in a discussion about problem identification?

5. What might be getting in the way of my students' ability to identify problems? Am I contributing to this in any way?

6. Other than talking with students about identifying problems, how else could I support their development in this area?

WHAT TO LOOK FOR IN BOOKS ABOUT IDENTIFYING PROBLEMS

Choosing books for identifying specific problems would be hopeless. Almost all stories have a problem, so selecting a few at random would serve no purpose in most classrooms. Instead, let's think about *how* problem identification works: When is a problem truly a problem, and when is it not a problem at all? How do you know if you've identified the *real* problem—or if the symptom springs from another cause entirely? When is a problem so complex that to solve it, you need to identify all the smaller pieces within it? Are you being honest with yourself about your problem? (That's often the first step.) When should you ask for help to better understand your problem? I look for books that touch upon all these components of problem identification, five of which are listed in Chart 7.1: Books Aligned to Identifying Problems.

CHART 7.1: BOOKS ALIGNED TO IDENTIFYING PROBLEMS

THE MESSAGE	THE BOOK
Not a problem, but an opportunity	*Beautiful Oops!* by Barney Saltzberg (primary and intermediate)
Don't rush to judgment about a problem you face with another person	*Enemy Pie* by Derek Munson (primary)
Some problems are complex; you need to recognize all the pieces	*A Thirst for Home: A Story of Water Across the World* by Christine Ieronimo (intermediate)
Being honest with yourself can help you identify a problem	*Marisol McDonald Doesn't Match/ Marisol McDonald no combina* by Monica Brown (primary)
Recognize when you need help to understand your problem	*Thank You, Mr. Falker* by Patricia Polacco (primary and intermediate)

Not a problem, but an opportunity

There are students who regard every small hiccup in and out of school as a major calamity. For these kids, there's no such thing as a *little* problem. Many crumpled papers later, they continue to wail that their story "stinks," or that their drawing of the Great Pyramid of Giza just doesn't look right. Step back, you advise these students. Look at the drawing from a different angle and maybe you'll see a possibility you overlooked.

For the children in your class who need to see problems as possibilities, read *Beautiful Oops!* While its board-book format would suggest more relevance for the primary grades, even older students will love the interactive pages that magically transform from oops to amazing. A torn piece of paper becomes the mouth of a friendly-looking monster. A blob of spilled paint is the start of a purple elephant. In fact, some "problems" are not problems at all, but the opportunity for an otherwise-unimagined new beginning. I'm reminded of those wrong turns I occasionally(?) make when driving, and the lovely sights I'd miss if I paid closer attention to my GPS. How can we help our students decide that some of their perceived crises aren't crises at all? That they can make different choices about how they view them, and how they proceed?

Don't rush to judgment about a problem you face with another person

With so much focus on bullying in schools, we sometimes over-identify problems between children as bullying even when that's not the issue. Remember that bullying involves a real or perceived imbalance of power: one person has the upper-hand and dominates, while the other is victimized. Some disagreements between students are not about the suppressor and the suppressed. Kids disagree. They argue. Maybe the winner had more convincing arguments. Maybe the supposed victim misread the behavior of their classmate. It can be complicated.

For problems that might be misinterpreted as bullying, check out *Enemy Pie*. The boy who narrates the story is eager to get rid of his #1 enemy, new neighbor Jeremy Ross. Apparently, Jeremy once failed to invite the narrator to his trampoline party, and then there was the vaguely-remembered time Jeremy struck the narrator out in a baseball game and laughed. The boy's dad says he has the perfect solution: enemy pie. He won't say what's in it, but for it to work, the two boys must spend the day together.

They do, but a strange thing happens as they make water balloons, play basketball, and eat lunch at Jeremy's house: the narrator decides his #1 enemy isn't so bad after all. In fact, he likes him. Now the boy is worried Jeremy will eat the pie (which smells delicious) and his hair will fall out, or there will be some other enemy-provoked consequence. Don't eat the pie, he warns. But Jeremy is undeterred and eats it anyway.

His hair does *not* fall out. In the end, the narrator realizes he's lost his best enemy and looks forward to the next play date with his new friend.

A too-quick judgment of Jeremy based on a first impression made the narrator believe that Jeremy wasn't a very nice kid. But first impressions aren't always reliable. Help your students see that they shouldn't be too fast to identify something or someone as a problem (especially as a bully) until they've taken a closer look.

Some problems are complex; you need to recognize all the pieces

Sometimes we identify situations as problems when they aren't, or rush to judgment after misreading a situation as a problem. But there are also problems that are more complex than we may at first recognize, and require us to sort out all the pieces. *A Thirst for Home: A Story of Water Across the World* is a good example.

I was inspired to include this book under "identifying problems" because in these last few years, I've used it to model close reading with many classes—it presents a problem with many bits and pieces that require extremely close attention.

The story is told in the voice of Alemitu, now named Eva, who once lived in a village in Ethiopia and currently lives with her adopted family in America. As the story begins, Alemitu is walking with her mama (her emaye) to the watering hole where they go each day to fill their jug. The water is dirty and contaminated, but it is all they have. Their food runs out, and the roar of hunger in Alemitu's stomach is fierce. With little hope for her daughter's survival amid such drought and famine, Emaye makes an adoption plan for Alamitu. As the little girl leaves, there are many tears from both mother and daughter.

"What?" students exclaim. "Her mother gave her away?" They are horrified. To them, this is cruel and unforgivable. But then we look more closely at the problems that led to the mother's choice: no food and no clean drinking water. How long can a child survive under such conditions? As the story continues, there are the further complications that spring from Eva adjusting to a new life and learning a new language. But at least with her new family, she is safe. A part of her will always be Alemitu, from a land far away. It is the same sun that shines on both sides of the world, and the same water that connects us all. Once students see all of the pieces of this problem, they are better equipped to consider the wisdom of Emaye's difficult decision.

Being honest with yourself can help you identify a problem

Alemitu's mom was able to assess her problem honestly, and plan accordingly. But Marisol McDonald is not so forthright about her situation, at least not initially. *Marisol McDonald Doesn't Match / Marisol McDonald no combina* is a delightful story for younger students told in both English and Spanish. Marisol is part Peruvian, part Scottish, and part American, and she likes to mix all her cultures together. She eats peanut butter and jelly burritos for lunch, speaks English and Spanish (sometimes in the same sentence), and thinks polka-dots and stripes are perfect together.

When a classmate criticizes her for never matching, she takes up the challenge, wearing matching clothes to school the next day, eating a peanut butter and jelly sandwich on bread, and only speaking one language. This is boring, she thinks, and then decides *not* matching is exactly right for her. In the end, Marisol's problem was not about matching or mismatching, but about fooling herself into believing that others should get to define her. Honesty helped her recognize the root of her problem.

FEATURED BOOK FOR IDENTIFYING PROBLEMS: *Thank You, Mr. Falker*
by Patricia Polacco

Recognize when you need help to understand your problem

Of all the books about enlisting support to understand a problem, perhaps none is more powerful than **Thank You, Mr. Falker.** This is another of Patricia Polacco's autobiographical tales, this time focusing on Trisha's struggles to read. Trisha was great at art, and her classmates looked admiringly at her drawings, but sounding out words remained difficult for her, not just in first grade, but all the way to grade four. She felt dumb. She hated school. The other kids laughed at her.

When Trisha started fifth grade, her new teacher Mr. Falker didn't seem to care who was cutest or smartest or who could read best. For a while she got really good at disguising her problem, hiding out under the stairwell during reading time. But eventually Mr. Falker caught up with her and the truth was apparent to both of them: Trisha could not read. Trisha was tired of running from her problem and agreed to let Mr. Falker help. And help her, he did. Not only did Trisha learn to read that year, but Patricia Polacco has now written over 100 picture books for children, spreading the joy of reading to millions of young readers. The questions that follow for Seven Thinking Boxes will encourage students to explore Trisha's problem in more depth.

SEVEN THINKING BOXES

Questions to ask about *Thank You, Mr. Falker* by Patricia Polacco

SEL Competency: Responsible Decision-Making   Focus: Identifying Problems

PLAIN CARDBOARD BOX	**BASIC THINKING** What were some of the early signs that Trisha was having trouble with reading? Why do you think no one helped her sooner?
PUZZLE BOX	**PUZZLING DETAILS** What do you think Grandpa meant when he said "knowledge is like the bee that made that sweet honey, you have to chase it through the pages of a book!"?
HEART BOX	**FEELINGS** How did Trisha's feelings get in the way of her asking for help?
UNUSUAL BOX	**CREATIVE THINKING** How did Mr. Falker show that he was a creative teacher as he tried to figure out Trisha's reading problem?
BROKEN BOX	**PROBLEMS AND ISSUES** How did Trisha make her problem worse for a while? How did she finally solve it?
TREASURE BOX	**SOMETHING TO TREASURE** Why do you think Patricia Polacco wrote about this experience? How does she want her experience to help other children?
TOOL BOX	**AUTHOR'S TOOLS** Reread the last page of this story. Why do you think Patricia Polacco chose to end the story in this way?

SEVEN THINKING BOXES

Questions to ask about *any* book for identifying problems

PLAIN CARDBOARD BOX 	**BASIC THINKING** • What problem did this character face? Explain it in your own words. • What were the early signs of this problem? At the beginning of the story, did the character realize it was a problem? What is the evidence?
PUZZLE BOX 	**PUZZLING DETAILS** • Was this character honest with himself about this problem? Find a quote that shows either that the character recognized the problem, or that the character denied the problem. • What is the turning point in this story, the place where the character recognized the problem?
HEART BOX 	**FEELINGS** • How did feelings affect the identification of this problem? Did feelings help the character acknowledge the problem? • Did identifying the problem lead to different feelings at the end of the story? Explain.
UNUSUAL BOX 	**CREATIVE THINKING** • How did creative thinking make a difference in identifying this problem? • How would you have used *your* creative thinking to help the character identify this problem?
BROKEN BOX 	**PROBLEMS AND ISSUES** • In what ways was this problem complex? What were the different parts of the problem that needed to be identified? • Did this problem have an effect on anyone other than the main character? Explain.
TREASURE BOX 	**SOMETHING TO TREASURE** • What did the character in this story learn about identifying a problem? What did you learn? • Who might benefit from reading this book? Why?
TOOL BOX 	**AUTHOR'S TOOLS** • How does the author introduce readers to the problem-causing situation? How does the author end the story? Why do you think the author began and ended the story in this way? • How do the illustrations in this story show the problem? Find one illustration that really shows the problem and explain why you chose it.

Analyzing and Evaluating Situations

Analysis is the process of breaking a problem down into smaller pieces to understand it better, while evaluation means making a judgment based on the merits of one choice over another. Analysis should precede evaluation, but for decision-making they generally go hand-in-hand. Once you've examined all the choices, problem-solvers select the most promising path and move forward toward their goal.

The gray walls in my living room are a case in point. When I decided to change the paint color from yellow to gray, I wanted to make an informed choice. My husband was onboard because he was tired of repainting rooms after I whined that the color looked nothing like it did on the paint chart. So we purchased a bunch of those little sample cans (despite the ridiculous price)—turns out there are way more than "50 shades of gray." We were in it for the long haul, slapping blobs of "Misty Gray," "Stonington Gray," "Drifting Snow," and countless other grays on patches of wall.

We analyzed our options: Some grays were darker than others. Several had tints of different colors. Then we evaluated: Which grays were too dark, too light, too blue, not blue enough? Eventually, we had to choose one. We weren't certain we were making the perfect choice, but our research had at least pointed us in the right direction. End of story: We like our new Misty Gray living room. I'm glad we analyzed and evaluated before buying the first gray that struck our fancy.

WHAT WE HOPE TO SEE IN THE CLASSROOM REGARDING ANALYZING AND EVALUATING SITUATIONS, AND WHAT WE SOMETIMES SEE INSTEAD

Making decisions too quickly without the benefit of systematic analysis and evaluation is a common kid problem. Why waste time on analysis and evaluation, they reason, when they could go with their instincts and finish the job sooner? This accounts for lots of those wrong answers to comprehension questions (and our pleading with students to go back to the text for evidence). But they instead think that relying on their memory will be sufficient. It also explains some of the need for revision in students' writing. They plop down the first word that pops into their head rather than taking the extra few seconds to ponder the most *precise* language. On the flip side are students who spend so much time examining the pros and cons of something that making any kind of decision is painfully slow. What follows are questions to help you think more systematically about your students' analysis and evaluation.

ENHANCING CLASSROOM CULTURE: QUESTIONS FOR TEACHERS TO ASK THEMSELVES ABOUT ANALYZING AND EVALUATING SITUATIONS

1. Which of my students are good analyzers and evaluators? What behaviors do I see in the classroom that indicate this?

2. Which of my students rush to begin a task without thinking it through before getting started? How does that impact their performance?

3. How can I model good analytic and evaluative thinking to make this process visible to my students?

4. How could I help my students better understand what it means to analyze and evaluate a situation before moving forward toward their goal? What would I include in this conversation?

5. How can I help my students analyze and evaluate the evidence as objectively as possible before making a decision?

6. What kinds of tasks could I give my students that would help them see the need for analyzing all their options before deciding on a plan of action?

WHAT TO LOOK FOR IN BOOKS ABOUT ANALYZING AND EVALUATING SITUATIONS

This is one of those SEL areas that students may understand more easily by examining nonexamples—the kinds of problems that can arise when a person's actions precede thoughtful analysis and evaluation. So, some of the books I chose for this section (listed in Chart 7.2: Books Aligned to Analyzing and Evaluating Situations) are ones in which characters make impulsive, rather than strategic, decisions. Mostly, though, I want students to recognize that situations calling for analysis and evaluation are seldom clear-cut. They need to learn to weigh the evidence carefully, and understand that even then, they can't be certain that they've chosen the best path until the situation works itself out, for better or worse. I placed books in this category that include plenty of evidence for students to consider. Sometimes the implications are personal, impacting only their own well-being. Other times, there's more at stake: the welfare of an entire people or community. In all cases, I want students to consider not just the decision the character made, but how *they* would have moved forward in the same situation.

CHART 7.2: BOOKS ALIGNED TO ANALYZING AND EVALUATING SITUATIONS

THE MESSAGE	THE BOOK
Acting before thinking can lead to problems	*Too Many Tamales* by Gary Soto (primary)
You can often reverse a bad decision	*Those Shoes* by Maribeth Boelts (primary and intermediate)
Choosing between personal safety and a personal goal	*Freedom School, Yes!* by Amy Littlesugar (intermediate)
Choosing between following the rules and following your heart	*The Yellow Star: The Legend of King Christian X* by Carmen Agra Deedy (primary and intermediate)
Choosing what's *most* important	*The Three Questions: Based on a Story by Leo Tolstoy* by Jon J. Muth (primary and intermediate)

Acting before thinking can lead to problems

In the story **Too Many Tamales,** Maria and her mom are making tamales for their holiday family dinner. Her mom removes her diamond ring to keep it away from the sticky massa, and when she leaves the room for a moment, Maria can't resist trying it on for "just a minute." But she forgets to take it off as she continues kneading the dough and doesn't think about the ring again until her cousins arrive. She looks at her hand: no ring. What to do! The ring must be inside one of the 24 tamales awaiting the dinner guests, Maria reasons. She and her cousins begin eating them, one by one. No one bites into anything suspicious, but the littlest cousin thinks he might have swallowed something hard. Everyone gets a stomach ache. (The picture on this page is priceless.) As Maria runs to her mother to confess, she sees something shiny on her finger. Indeed, the ring had already found its way home. The family works together to make a second batch of tamales—though the children say they've already had way too many.

Had Maria been more thoughtful about her decision regarding the ring, she probably wouldn't have tried it on at all: It wasn't her ring; she hadn't asked permission; her hands were sticky. But there was no forethought that preceded the choice she made. And it didn't end there. Not only was *she* upset, but her cousins became unwitting accomplices in her plot to retrieve the missing ring. She eventually goes to her mom to confess, but could she have done this sooner? This is a great example to share with young children about what can happen when we don't think through (analyze and evaluate) a situation sufficiently before diving in. One careless step often leads to a string of other unfortunate events.

You can often reverse a bad decision

Jeremy nearly gets caught in a similar cycle of misdeeds in *Those Shoes*. "Those shoes" are black high-tops with two white stripes, and all the cool kids in Jeremy's class have them. Jeremy wants them, too. Grandma informs him there's no place for "want" in their house, only "need." But Jeremy is so insistent that she eventually gives in, taking him downtown to the thrift store. He spies "those shoes" in the window and couldn't be more excited. They look great, but Grandma won't buy them because Jeremy can barely squeeze his feet inside: they're much too small. Jeremy realizes this, too, but wants the shoes so badly that he buys them with his own money. Maybe the high-tops will stretch, he hopes. But they don't stretch, and the pain is nearly unbearable.

The decision to buy the high-tops was not a good one, and didn't show enough analytic thinking. But a new thought begins to take shape, and this time Jeremy is more reflective: His friend Antonio has feet that are smaller than his. Antonio's old shoes are ripped and falling apart, and moreover, he was the only kid who didn't laugh at Jeremy's uncool shoes earlier. Jeremy weighs his options: Should he keep the shoes and endure excruciating pain? Or, give his way-cool shoes to Antonio? He chooses the latter and on the first day it snows, he's pretty happy with the boots his grandma bought for him—which he *needed*!

I love this story for its message about turning around a bad decision. You may start down the wrong path, but don't be afraid to reverse direction. As in Jeremy's case, it took some courage. He needed to sacrifice what he *wanted* to consider someone else's *need*. Children aren't quick to make the distinction between want and need. Is there anything they could give up that could make life a little better for someone else?

Choosing between personal safety and a personal goal

One of the factors we always want students to consider when analyzing and evaluating a situation is the risk involved: What is the possible danger to you or someone else? We need to acknowledge that this is a personal choice, and there should be no value judgment. For some people, the potential for harm might make the risk too great. For others, the perceived value of the goal may outweigh the risk. *Freedom School, Yes!* is a perfect opportunity for students to consider the choice the main character makes against the choice they might have made.

This is a book of historical fiction based on the 1964 Mississippi Freedom Summer Project. Nineteen-year-old Annie was the Freedom School teacher, newly arrived from up north to teach young African Americans about their history and heritage. But before Freedom School even began, someone threw a brick through Annie's bedroom window in the house where she was staying. A threatening note attached to the brick told her to "Go home or else!!" Then the church that was to be the site of the summer school was set afire. Nonetheless, Annie did *not* go home, and school *did* begin the next day—under an old hickory tree.

Ask your students: If you had been Annie, would you have stayed to teach Freedom School, or would you have returned north? If you had been one of the children in this community, would you have risked attending the school, or stayed home due to the hostility and violence? There are no right or wrong answers here, just multiple opportunities to analyze and evaluate. The same evidence can yield so many different responses.

Choosing between following the rules and following your heart

Sometimes the stakes are even higher, and involve not just a community's fate, but the fate of an entire country. Such is the case in *The Yellow Star: The Legend of King Christian X of Denmark.* The story is set in Denmark in 1940 as the Nazis invade Copenhagen. Denmark's beloved King Christian does his best to keep all Danes safe, though the Nazi soldiers don't make it easy. They hoist the Nazi flag where the Danish flag once stood, prompting the king to remove it against the soldiers' orders. Even worse, the Nazis command all Jews to wear a yellow star so that they can be easily identified.

The king wanted his countrymen to remain Danes, not be divided into Jews or Christians. But what could he do? He found his answer in the stars. He realized it would be almost impossible to identify one star amid thousands. So King Christian's tailor sewed him a yellow star, which he wore defiantly as he rode his horse through the streets of the city. His subjects saw him and knew just what to do. The last page of the story needs no explanation—readers realize that *everyone* is wearing a yellow star. Once again, there were only Danes in Denmark.

While Nazis did terrorize the Jews in Denmark during this time in history, remember that this story is a *legend*. The events as they're narrated here didn't really happen (although it is true that King Christian was much admired for his charisma and courage). Still, there's food for thought here: What's worth fighting for? When is it appropriate to stand up against an oppressor? What would *your* students have done if confronted with the dilemma faced by this leader?

FEATURED BOOK FOR ANALYZING AND EVALUATING SITUATIONS:
The Three Questions: Based on a True Story by Leo Tolstoy by Jon J. Muth

Choosing what's *most* important

With so many choices available and so many people weighing in (with often conflicting advice), how is a child to decide which path to take? For responding to this dilemma, I love the book ***The Three Questions***. Nikolai, the main character, admits that he's often uncertain about the right way to act, but thinks he'll feel more confident if only he can get the answer to three simple questions: When is the best time to do things? Who is the most important one? What is the right thing to do? He asks three friends but is dissatisfied with their answers, eventually stumbling upon Leo, a very old but wise turtle.

Leo only smiles, but Nikolai stays around to help him dig his garden. As a fierce storm approaches, Nikolai hears a cry for help and finds an injured panda that he brings back to Leo's house to heal. The mama panda has lost her baby in the storm. Nikolai braves the storm again to find the panda's child. By the next morning, the storm is over, and the pandas are recovering. But Nikolai remains disappointed that his questions still have not been answered.

The old turtle disagrees: If Nikolai had not been in the turtle's garden, he wouldn't have heard the panda's cries. So, the most important person right then was the turtle, and the most important thing was to help with the garden. No matter the situation, the most important time is always *now*. The most important person is the one you're with, and the most important thing is to do good for the one at your side. I'd say this is great advice. You could, without a doubt, spend several minutes on every page of this book, getting students to understand and then respond to the author's words. You could also get your classroom conversation started with the following questions.

SEVEN THINKING BOXES

Questions to ask about *The Three Questions: Based on a Story by Leo Tolstoy* by Jon J. Muth
SEL Competency: Responsible Decision-Making   Focus: Analyzing and Evaluating Situations

PLAIN CARDBOARD BOX	**BASIC THINKING** What were Nikolai's three questions? Why did he want to answer them?
PUZZLE BOX	**PUZZLING DETAILS** Which detail do you think best proves old turtle's advice to Nikolai? Why did you choose this detail?
HEART BOX	**FEELINGS** How were Nikolai's feelings the same or different from your feelings when you're not sure what to do? Explain.
UNUSUAL BOX	**CREATIVE THINKING** Did solving Nikolai's problem involve creative thinking? If not, what kind of thinking was needed?
BROKEN BOX	**PROBLEMS AND ISSUES** Do you think Nikolai could have solved his problem on his own, or did he need someone to help him? Explain your thinking.
TREASURE BOX	**SOMETHING TO TREASURE** Do you think Nikolai will treasure the response that he received from old turtle? Why or why not? What do *you* treasure from old turtle's advice? Why?
TOOL BOX	**AUTHOR'S TOOLS** Why do you think the author included <u>three</u> examples from Nikolai's friends to each of his questions?

SEVEN THINKING BOXES

Questions to ask about *any* book for solving problems

PLAIN CARDBOARD BOX	**BASIC THINKING** • What was the situation that needed to be analyzed and evaluated? • Who was responsible for the situation that needed to be analyzed and evaluated? In what way?
PUZZLE BOX	**PUZZLING DETAILS** • What do you think were the most important pieces of evidence that this character needed to consider when dealing with this situation? Why? • Did the author leave out any important pieces of evidence that *should* have been included in order to evaluate the situation?
HEART BOX	**FEELINGS** • How were feelings involved in this situation? Did the character's feelings prevent her or him from seeing the situation clearly? • How did the character's feelings change at the end of this story based on the outcome of the situation?
UNUSUAL BOX	**CREATIVE THINKING** • Did someone in this story need to think creatively as they analyzed and evaluated their situation? Explain. • How might you have analyzed and evaluated this situation differently? Why?
BROKEN BOX	**PROBLEMS AND ISSUES** • What problems did the character face in analyzing and evaluating this situation? • For whom was this situation the biggest problem? Why?
TREASURE BOX	**SOMETHING TO TREASURE** • What did the character learn from analyzing and evaluating this situation? Do you think he or she will ever face a similar situation in the future? How do you think the character might respond? • What did you learn from this story about analyzing and evaluating situations? How might it change your life in the future?
TOOL BOX	**AUTHOR'S TOOLS** • In stories where there is an important situation to be analyzed and evaluated, there is usually a lot of tension or suspense. How did the author build tension or suspense in this story? • Do you think the author made this story realistic? Would "real people" (not just story characters) act this way? Explain.

Solving Problems

Solving social emotional problems with students is more difficult than we often acknowledge, not just because there are so many problems to solve, but because our first impulse is to treat the symptom. Whatever it takes, just make it stop. We have all kinds of strategies to eradicate issues like bullying, name-calling, and other bad behavior, and they often do work in the short term. But perhaps we need to think more about the *cause* than the symptom.

A social emotional problem with a student is like an iceberg. At the tip, you may see anger. But what's below the surface that you can't see? Stress, frustration, grief, something else? Whatever is going on underneath needs to be addressed before the problem is truly solved.

WHAT WE HOPE TO SEE IN THE CLASSROOM REGARDING SOLVING PROBLEMS, AND WHAT WE SOMETIMES SEE INSTEAD

There are many programs available to schools that target social emotional problem solving. They're designed to proactively develop children's skills for recognizing and managing their emotions, as well as building positive relationships, empathy, and respect. If these programs make the necessary difference when real problems arise, then that's great. But it seems to me that we still have too many kids who listen patiently during class meetings, but then demonstrate the same impulsive behavior (or whatever) 20 minutes later. Where's the transfer? This tells me we keep applying band aids when we should be having deeper conversations. Ask yourself some of the questions below to reimagine your approach to problem solving in your classroom.

ENHANCING CLASSROOM CULTURE: QUESTIONS FOR TEACHERS TO ASK THEMSELVES ABOUT SOLVING PROBLEMS

1. Does my school have a program or a prescribed approach for resolving students' social emotional problems? If so, does it work? What is the evidence?

2. What is my typical response to social emotional problems in my classroom?

3. Which of my students seem most capable of resolving their social emotional issues? How do they do this?

4. Which of my students have the most difficulty resolving social emotional issues? What do I see? What issues seem to lie beneath the surface for these students?

5. What would I include in a conversation with my students about solving social emotional problems so that they could be better equipped to handle them?

6. How will I know when my students have made progress in this area? What is reasonable to expect at this grade level regarding their ability to solve social emotional problems?

WHAT TO LOOK FOR IN BOOKS ABOUT SOLVING PROBLEMS

For books about problem solving, I look for stories that go beyond "sounds good" solutions. It sounds good to say that students should think before they act. It sounds good to tell them that they should speak kindly to their classmates and stick with a problem until they solve it. But how can we get at the heart of the matter, and help them develop strategies with more punch? I look for stories that offer specific strategies: Work *together*. Ask for help when you need it. Find a creative outlet that channels your "problem energy" into positive energy. Find common ground, a shared interest that builds connections. Take a first step; the solution may still be far away, but every next step brings you closer to your goal. These are the messages I want to share with students about solving problems. And these are the messages in the books profiled here in Chart 7.3: Books Aligned to Solving Problems.

CHART 7.3: BOOKS ALIGNED TO SOLVING PROBLEMS

THE MESSAGE	THE BOOK
Working together helps to solve a problem	*Charlie Anderson* by Barbara Abercrombie (primary and intermediate)
Find common ground in order to solve a problem	*Drawn Together* by Minh Lê (primary and intermediate)
Know when to ask for help to solve a problem	*Maddi's Fridge* by Lois Brandt (primary and intermediate)
Expressing yourself creatively can help reduce the stress of a problem	*Dave the Potter: Artist, Poet, Slave* by Laban Carrick Hill (intermediate)
Changing a heart is the first step in solving a problem	*The Promise* by Nicola Davies (primary and intermediate)

Working together helps to solve a problem

In any kind of dispute between students, the "combatants" become very competitive: *My* interests are the most important. We need to do this *my* way. Sometimes, in fact, it seems more important to win than to follow through on whatever the win represents. Jacob lobbied (loudly) to be the secretary of his science project group. However, when the team began to do their research, he had no interest in taking the notes. Could the problem be solved through compromise, where everyone involved gets something but also gives something up?

I know a couple of sisters who would support the notion of working together to solve a problem. They are the characters in the story *Charlie Anderson,* a book simple enough for primary grades, but with enough layers of meaning that it works for older students, too. A cat appeared on the girls' doorstep one evening and quickly became part of their lives. They named him Charlie. They fed him dinner and let him sleep at the end of their beds. This was a well-loved cat, and they didn't mind a bit when he got plumper and plumper. One night, Charlie didn't come home, and the girls were frantic.

The next day they knocked on every door in their neighborhood: Had anyone seen their cat, Charlie? When they reached the very last house, the owners said they hadn't seen him either. But just then the cat appeared from behind the door. "Charlie!" the girls exclaimed. No, the neighbors corrected, our cat's name is Anderson. Apparently, this kitty was spending his nights with one family, and his days with another—and eating his meals at both places. They agreed that Charlie Anderson could have two homes. Both families loved him. This was the best solution.

I appreciate this story for its focus on compromise and solving problems together, but also for what it says about being loved by two families in two places. Another piece of this book's plot is that the sisters live with their mom during the week, but spend the weekends with their dad in a different house. What a gentle way of sharing the message that though your time may be divided, your love can be multiplied. They had two homes, just like Charlie Anderson.

Find common ground in order to solve a problem

When students face problems with each other, sometimes they can only see their differences. We don't agree on *anything*, they think. They may, in fact, agree on many things, but in that moment, they just can't see it. Quite by chance and desperate for any solution to the snarky comments two fourth grade girls often made to each other about who had the coolest clothes, I invited them both to share lunch with me one day. It was awkward at first, but it turned out they both adored Peeps, those Easter marshmallow chicks, found their younger brothers outrageously annoying, and watched the same TV show every Friday night. In the thirty minutes we spent eating cafeteria chicken nuggets and applesauce, no one mentioned designer labels or lectured about kindness.

But by the end of lunch, the snark had melted away, and was replaced by laughter and conversation about shared interests.

Drawn Together makes a similar point. In this story, a young boy dislikes visiting his grandfather, not because he dislikes Grandpa, but because they don't speak the same language and it's difficult to communicate. But to the boy's surprise, the grandfather reveals "a world beyond words." He shows the boy his drawings and the boy is fascinated, for he loves to draw, too. The things they couldn't *say* emerge in their art, and their illustration styles even begin to blend together.

Beyond the incredible illustrations in this book, I also like that it is nearly wordless (in keeping with its message). We can all communicate our story in our own way. I envision teachers reading this book aloud, inviting children to help tell it along with them, then following up with an activity that allows students to work with a classmate they barely know to identify a common interest. I wonder what new connections would emerge.

Know when to ask for help to solve a problem

The decision-making component of solving problems is especially evident in *Maddi's Fridge*. This is another book that *looks* like it's intended for young kids, but the message also works for older students. The topic is timely, too—unfortunately, far too many families don't have enough to eat.

Sofia and Maddi are friends, and enjoy playing together at the playground in their urban neighborhood. Maddi is better at the climbing wall, which makes Sofia envious. Sofia suggests they take a snack break and races to Maddi's apartment where she flings open the refrigerator door to find. . .not much. When Sofia asks Maddi why her mom doesn't just go to the store, Maddi confides that they don't have enough money. She makes Sofia promise not to tell.

Sofia doesn't tell. But she does try to help by sneaking the leftover fish from dinner into her backpack to deliver to Maddi the next day. By the time Maddi sees it, however, no one would want to eat it. Ditto for the eggs and burritos that follow. Sofia doesn't want to break her promise, but she can't help Maddi all by herself. So she tells her mom, and together they go to the grocery store and bring food to Maddi's. Maddi reminds Sofia that she broke her promise, which Sofia acknowledges—but helping her friend was more important. Maddi is fine with that.

So many conversations can begin with this story: the fact that 20% of children in the United States don't have enough food in the fridge, the importance of asking for help when you can't solve a problem yourself, and the complicated issue of when it's okay to break a promise. No matter what grade I share this book with, it's a hit every time. And teachers enjoy it as much as their students.

Expressing yourself creatively can help reduce the stress of a problem

Some problems students face will be fixable. They might require working together, as in *Charlie Anderson*, or finding a shared interest as we saw in *Drawn Together*. Other problems require a long time to fix—not enough food in the fridge is an example of that. But still other problems are unfixable (like a terminal illnesses) or cannot be resolved in the foreseeable future. It was the relentlessness of slavery that was the issue for ***Dave the Potter: Artist, Poet, Slave.***

This is an amazing book. The sparse narrative about Dave, an extraordinary artist, poet, and potter who lived in South Carolina in the 1800s, reflects the free verse poetry of the inscriptions on Dave's pots. The full-page paintings by Bryan Collier are so incredible that you'll want to hang them in your living room—the intensity of Dave's passion for his work leaps off each page. It's like observing a craftsman in action. First, you see the clay itself, then Dave pulling the shape of a jar from his wheel, and lastly his words, etched with a stick:

"I wonder where is all my relation
Friendship to all—and, every nation"
—August 16, 1857

Through his potter's wheel, Dave was able to turn the ugliness of bondage into something beautiful, the inscribed lines of poetry adding heart to his finished pieces. I think about students who come to school every day with problems that they can't solve either: a difficult home life, few friends, low self-esteem, or a hundred other things. What creative outlet might provide them with a new window on their world? What could we do to help them discover this outlet?

FEATURED BOOK FOR SOLVING PROBLEMS: *The Promise* by Nicola Davies

---

Changing a heart is the first step in solving a problem

For our darkest moments, when even our creative genius fails us, we must hold tight to the promise of a better tomorrow. ***The Promise*** is a modern fable that shows us how. It begins on a mean street in a mean city where everything is broken. The narrator survives by stealing, and one night, attempts to snatch a bag from a frail old woman. The woman is stronger than she looks, however, and doesn't let go until the thief promises to plant what's inside. The girl agrees, eager to empty the bag of its food and money. Imagine her surprise when the contents are only acorns!

Yet the girl feels fortunate. She now understands the promise, for in her hands she holds a forest. She begins to plant. She plants all over that mean city, and while nothing changes at first, tiny green shoots eventually sprout from cracks in the pavement. Finally, there are trees, and the broken people begin to smile. They start planting, too, moving on to more cities to heal more brokenness.

There's so much to love about this story. It helps students see that only one small glimmer can be enough to change a person's perspective, and that "the forest" may not appear overnight, but even a small green sprout is a promise of better things to come. What seeds might take root in our students' minds today that may someday lead to their own garden of wishes-come-true? See the questions for Seven Thinking Boxes to begin that conversation.

SEVEN THINKING BOXES

Questions to ask about *The Promise* by Nicola Davies
SEL Competency: Responsible Decision-Making   Focus: Solving Problems

PLAIN CARDBOARD BOX	**BASIC THINKING** What evidence does the author provide to show that the story takes place in a mean city?
PUZZLE BOX	**PUZZLING DETAILS** What do you consider to be the turning point in this story for solving the problem? It could be different places based on your point of view. Be sure to defend your answer with good evidence.
HEART BOX	**FEELINGS** What do you think was responsible for the girl's negative feelings at the beginning of this story? How did her feelings change by the end of the story? Why did they change?
UNUSUAL BOX	**CREATIVE THINKING** In what ways was this story a creative way to teach a lesson about solving problems? Can you think of another creative way to teach this same lesson?
BROKEN BOX	**PROBLEMS AND ISSUES** What was the problem that needed to be solved in this story? Why do you think no one had fixed it before?
TREASURE BOX	**SOMETHING TO TREASURE** This story is a modern-day fable that teaches a lesson. What lesson does the girl in this story learn about solving problems? How can this lesson help you solve problems in your own life?
TOOL BOX	**AUTHOR'S TOOLS** The author of this story (Nicola Davies) is well-known for using language that paints a very clear picture. What words or phrases did she use in this story that painted a picture in your mind?

SEVEN THINKING BOXES

Questions to ask about *any* book for solving problems

PLAIN CARDBOARD BOX	BASIC THINKING
	• What was the problem in this story that needed to be solved?
	• How was the problem solved? Who was responsible for solving it?
PUZZLE BOX	**PUZZLING DETAILS**
	• What do you consider to be the turning point for solving this problem? What detail in the story shows this?
	• What detail in this story best shows the kind of problem that needed solving? (Was it a problem where people needed to work together, where they needed to find common ground, or something else?)
HEART BOX	**FEELINGS**
	• How did feelings make a difference to the way the problem got solved in this story? How did characters' feelings change from the beginning to the end of the story?
	• How did *you* feel about the way the problem was solved in this story? Why?
UNUSUAL BOX	**CREATIVE THINKING**
	• In what ways was creative thinking or creativity important to solving this problem? Explain.
	• What creative solution could you have offered to solve this problem? What else could the characters have tried?
BROKEN BOX	**PROBLEMS AND ISSUES**
	• Did the problem that needed solving in this book begin *during* the story, or *before* the story began? Explain your thinking.
	• What might have happened if the problem in this story had not been solved? How would this have affected the characters?
TREASURE BOX	**SOMETHING TO TREASURE**
	• What lesson about solving problems did the author want readers to learn from this story? How might it make a difference to the way you solve problems in your own life?
	• Who might benefit from reading this book? Why?
TOOL BOX	**AUTHOR'S TOOLS**
	• How do the illustrations in this book help to show how the problem was solved? What do you find especially meaningful about these illustrations?
	• Look back at the beginning of this story (the problem). Now look at the end (the solution). How do they fit together?

Ethical Responsibility

Ethical decisions are not about following or breaking laws. If you do something unethical, but not illegal, you most likely won't be arrested or sent to jail. It's *your* choice, based on what *you* value: But will you be able to live with yourself afterward? Will you feel good about your choice, or will you have regrets? Ethical decisions stem from being on your best behavior, from trying to do the "right" thing. Whoa, what a tall order!

It gets complicated because people don't always agree on what is "right." Initially, some of this discrepancy might come from a young child's stage of moral development. But then other factors kick in: motivation, experience, and things such as cultural norms and political ideologies. Still, we wish our students would subscribe to at least a few basic ethical principles—concern for others, trustworthiness, honesty, and integrity.

WHAT WE HOPE TO SEE IN THE CLASSROOM REGARDING ETHICAL RESPONSIBILITY, AND WHAT WE SOMETIMES SEE INSTEAD

Mostly, I think we do see ethical behavior from students. Yes, there are outliers who concoct weird stories about what happened to their homework, and some kids who always make a beeline for the birthday cupcake with the most frosting. And there are more serious offenders who steal money, phones, or other personal items from their classmates or teachers. There are also the dozens of little annoying infractions: kids who walk angelically down the hall when you can see them but take off like it's the Indy 500 as soon as they turn the corner. For the most part, this is common kid behavior (not the stealing part. . .). But I also think that we could do more to help students understand what ethical decision-making *is*, and how they can be ethical decision-makers. Ask yourself the questions below to help set your course.

ENHANCING CLASSROOM CULTURE: QUESTIONS FOR TEACHERS TO ASK THEMSELVES ABOUT ETHICAL RESPONSIBILITY

1. What ethical elements do I consider most important to students at my grade level?

2. Do I generally consider ethical decision-making to be valued by the students in my class, or does it seem to be a problem? For whom does it seem to be a problem?

3. Would my students benefit most from a discussion about honesty, honor, confidentiality—or some other ethical consideration?

4. What would I include in a discussion about ethical decision-making? How could I help them understand what ethical behavior is?

5. *Integrity* is an especially important ethical element. How could I make this visible to my students?

6. How could I help my students understand why ethical behavior is important?

WHAT TO LOOK FOR IN BOOKS ABOUT ETHICAL RESPONSIBILITY

There are a few things I look for in books that address ethical decision-making. First, does the story reflect a problem that students of this age are likely to encounter? Topics that apply to most elementary grades might include telling the truth, returning things you find that don't belong to you, and caring about others' needs, not just their own. I also want students to see that making these decisions is often not easy because in order to do the "right" thing, you sometimes have to sacrifice something you really want. This can leave you with mixed feelings about your ethical decision, even when you know you made the best choice. Finally, I look for books in which the choice isn't clear-cut: Is it ever okay to lie? When does hard work *not* pay off? While I've listed a message for each story profiled under this focus area in Chart 7.4: Books Aligned to Ethical Responsibility, for some students these stories will lead to more questions than answers.

CHART 7.4: BOOKS ALIGNED TO ETHICAL RESPONSIBILITY

THE MESSAGE	THE BOOK
Doing the right thing by respecting nature	*Fireflies* by Julie Brinckloe (primary)
Doing the right thing by caring about others' needs over your own	*The Can Man* by Laura E. Williams (intermediate)
Doing the right thing to protect someone	*Up the Learning Tree* by Marcia Vaughan (intermediate)
Doing the right thing when you find something that doesn't belong to you	*A Bike Like Sergio's* by Maribeth Boelts (primary and intermediate)
Doing the right thing, even when no one is looking	*The Empty Pot* by Demi (primary and intermediate)

Doing the right thing by respecting nature

Fireflies is a wonderful little story that fits many of the criteria I seek in books about ethical decision-making. First, young children can relate to it. Told from a young boy's point of view, it describes his excitement over the simple joy of catching fireflies. He finds a firefly catching jar and dutifully pokes holes in the top to let them breathe. Then he and his buddies go out into the night, and he is thrilled to catch not just one firefly, but hundreds. Later that night he places his firefly jar next to his bed, but notices they are falling to the bottom of the jar, and that their lights are becoming dimmer and dimmer. The boy squeezes his eyes closed to shut out what he knows is happening—he *wants* those fireflies. But suddenly, while they're still flickering, he runs to his open window and takes off the lid. He sheds some tears for his lost fireflies, but at the same time, feels himself smiling.

The boy knows he has done the right thing, the respectful thing, by letting the fireflies go. But simultaneously, he worked hard to get those fireflies and wanted to keep them. The right choice isn't always easy. This is a good conversation to have with students, and is also a reminder that the animals they may find outside like turtles and rabbits are not meant to be house pets.

Doing the right thing by caring about others' needs over your own

Caring for others' needs over your own is also a theme of **The Can Man**, though this story is more complex, with many sophisticated ideas running through it. Tim lives in an urban neighborhood. His birthday is approaching and he wants a skateboard, though he knows his parents can't afford to buy it for him. He'll earn the money to buy the skateboard himself, he decides. Very mature and responsible, students think at this point during the read aloud.

Moreover, Tim has a plan. There is a homeless man, the Can Man, on his street who travels the neighborhood with his shopping cart, collecting empty soda cans that he then turns in for money. Tim decides this would be a great job for him as well, and goes out at the crack of dawn every day. One morning he encounters the Can Man and is proud to tell him he now has seven large bags of empties, and that he'll turn them in so he can buy a skateboard. He asks the Can Man if he's collecting for something special. He answers that he would like a heavier coat, as winter is coming. But lately, he hasn't found many cans.

I always pause here to ask students what they think will happen next. Many predict exactly what does happen: Tim gives the money from his cans to the Can Man. But no one ever guesses the ending to the story. On the morning of his birthday, Tim opens his front door to find a large plastic bag with an empty can attached to the drawstring. He opens it: a skateboard. It's not new, but it's been freshly painted, the wheels oiled. On the back is his name in bright, bold letters. Just then the Can

Man rattles past with his cart and shouts Happy Birthday. The Can Man is wearing a new coat.

One of the questions students always raise when we finish this story is: Why didn't Tim's parents stop him from collecting the cans since they knew it would take business away from the homeless man? We can't be sure, I respond, but how do you think Tim would have reacted if his parents had been the ones to put a stop to this business venture? He would have been mad at them, students say. He wouldn't have understood because they probably tell him he should work hard if he wants to be successful. This way, Tim learned the lesson on his own and it was *his* choice to turn the money over to the Can Man. There is so much to discuss in this book. Beyond the story itself, there's the issue of homelessness and how to address it within a community.

Doing the right thing to protect someone

The characters in *Up the Learning Tree* face even greater ethical dilemmas: Is it ever right to disobey the law? Can telling a lie ever be the right thing to do? This is the story of Henry Bell, a (fictitious) young slave child, and he tells the tale himself. He's never been allowed to go to school. In fact, Master Grismore has threatened to cut off his finger if he even touches a book. However, Mistress has asked him to walk Master Simon to and from the schoolhouse each day.

On one of these trips, Henry arrives early and scrambles up into the branches of a sycamore tree right next to the schoolhouse. The teacher is *reading*, fascinating to a child who has never held a book or experienced the magic that the squiggly marks inside could deliver. He returns to his "learning tree" day after day, even etching letters into the limbs as the teacher introduces them to her students.

Later in the year, Master Simon stays home from school to avoid "the sickness" and it's Henry's job to carry Simon's assignments back and forth. On one of these trips, he finds an old book in the trash and is about to leave when Miss Hattie, the teacher, catches him. She reminds him how dangerous it could be if Master finds out, but says she doesn't believe in slavery and allows Henry to keep the book. In fact, she helps Henry with his reading each day after school.

But then disaster strikes. From his perch in the learning tree, Henry watches as three angry men storm into the schoolhouse. They demand to know if Miss Hattie has been teaching a slave. Yes, she admits. But when they ask who, the teacher gives the name of another slave who Henry knows died earlier that week from "the sickness." The men order Miss Hattie to be gone by the next afternoon—or else. As the teacher packs up her desk, Henry asks why she taught him. Everyone has the right to learn, she answers.

I've read this book to many classes and it always leads to animated discussions. It's not just the ethics of our decisions that matter, but the implications of those decisions:

Why did Miss Hattie lie about the name of the slave? Do you think she would have taught Henry if she thought she'd lose her job? What do you think would have happened to Miss Hattie if she didn't leave? Should she have let the men treat her this way?

Doing the right thing when you find something that doesn't belong to you
Sometimes honesty can be painful, which Ruben learns firsthand in ***A Bike Like Sergio's***. Ruben's best friend Sergio has a great bike, and he'd like one, too. He thinks about it as the lady in front of him at the grocery store opens her purse to pay the cashier and a dollar falls out. Ruben scoops it up without looking at it closely and stuffs it in his pocket. Later that night he unfolds the crinkled bill and discovers it's not one dollar, but one *hundred* dollars. The boy can hardly stop thinking about the bike that this money could buy him, though he does experience a few pangs of guilt as he watches his mom cut corners on their grocery list. When she asks him to go back to the store where he found the bill, he's extra worried. What if the lady is there again?

The lady *is* there, and Ruben follows her out of the store. He finds the courage to stop her and explain that he found her hundred-dollar bill. The lady is surprised, then joyful, but mostly grateful as she whispers her thanks. Ruben feels both full and empty, thinking about what's right, but also what's gone.

I like that this book acknowledges the difficulty of doing the *right* thing. It also leads to other conversations about finding money. What if you just find a penny or a nickel or a quarter? Is it equally wrong to keep *any* amount of money, or does the amount of money matter? Many children have found (or lost) money, so they'll likely have thoughts to share.

FOCUS BOOK FOR ETHICAL RESPONSIBILITY: *The Empty Pot* by Demi

Doing the right thing, even when no one is looking
A step beyond honesty is integrity. I define this to students as doing the right thing even when no one is looking. The fable of **The Empty Pot**, our featured book for ethical responsibility, is the best resource I've found to illustrate this concept to students of any age.

Many years ago in China, there was a very old emperor who needed to find a successor. He loved flowers and decided to let the flowers choose. He would give all the children in the land some seeds, and the one who returned the following year with the most beautiful flowers would be the next emperor. Young Ping was pleased, as he was known for the beautiful flowers he grew. He watered his seeds every day, but no sprouts appeared. He got better soil, a different pot, but still—nothing.

At the end of the year, Ping was ashamed to stand before the emperor with his still empty pot, even more so when every other child arrived with pots of lush blooms. The emperor looked at the beautiful pots but was not pleased. Then he came to Ping and asked why he'd brought an empty pot. The boy began to cry, saying he'd done the best he could. He was startled when the emperor smiled and announced to everyone that he'd found the one person worthy of his throne. The seeds he gave the children had been cooked and would never grow. Ping had the courage to come back with his empty pot, showing the integrity so important to leadership.

So, the other kids cheated? students always ask. Indeed, they did, I confirm. They didn't think anyone would find out, so they planted different seeds in their pots. Ping was the only one with *integrity,* because he followed the emperor's directions even when he could have been dishonest.

SEVEN THINKING BOXES

Questions to ask about *The Empty Pot* by Demi
SEL Competency: Responsible Decision-Making   Focus: Ethical Responsibility

PLAIN CARDBOARD BOX	BASIC THINKING
	In your own words, explain how the emperor planned to choose a successor to his throne. Do you think this was a good way to choose a new emperor? Why or why not?
PUZZLE BOX	PUZZLING DETAILS
	In your opinion, what is the quote in *The Empty Pot* that <u>best</u> shows the importance of ethical decision-making? Why did you choose this quote?
HEART BOX	FEELINGS
	Why did Ping feel so ashamed to bring his empty pot to the emperor? Should he have felt ashamed? Explain.
UNUSUAL BOX	CREATIVE THINKING
	This emperor chose a very creative way to choose his successor. Do you think it was a good plan? Why or why not?
BROKEN BOX	PROBLEMS AND ISSUES
	How did the other children (not Ping) solve their problem with the emperor's seeds? What does this show about the way they made decisions?
TREASURE BOX	SOMETHING TO TREASURE
	What lesson did the author want readers to learn from this story? How will this lesson affect the way *you* make decisions?
TOOL BOX	AUTHOR'S TOOLS
	Why do you think the author chose to write this story as a <u>fable</u>?

SEVEN THINKING BOXES

Questions to ask about *any* book for ethical responsibility

PLAIN CARDBOARD BOX	BASIC THINKING
	• What was the situation in this story that required someone to make a decision? • What decision did the main character make? Do you consider this to be an ethical decision? Explain.
PUZZLE BOX	PUZZLING DETAILS
	• What quote in this story do you think <u>best</u> shows the meaning of ethical decision-making? Why? • What do you think is the most important detail in this story? Why?
HEART BOX	FEELINGS
	• How did the character feel about the decision she or he made? Why? • Was this an easy decision to make? What feelings got in the way of this decision?
UNUSUAL BOX	CREATIVE THINKING
	• Did the character in this story use creative thinking to solve this problem? If not, what helped to solve this problem? • Think about all the stories we've read about ethical decision-making: Which character was the <u>most</u> creative in solving his or her problem?
BROKEN BOX	PROBLEMS AND ISSUES
	• Was the problem in this story a clear-cut matter of right and wrong? Explain. • Why was the problem in this story a difficult one to solve?
TREASURE BOX	SOMETHING TO TREASURE
	• What did the character in this story learn about ethical decision-making? What did *you* learn? • Would you want to be friends with the main character in this story based on the decision he or she made? Explain.
TOOL BOX	AUTHOR'S TOOLS
	• Is this story a fable, realistic fiction, or some other genre? Why do you think the author chose this genre to write a story focusing on ethical decision-making? • Stories about ethical decision-making often focus a lot on the <u>character</u>. How did the author of this story show what was important to this character?

Reflecting

Finally, we come to that place where all teaching and learning should culminate—reflection. I like to think of reflecting as the art of looking back in order to look ahead. These questions seem to serve both teachers and students equally well:

- What did I do?
- How did it go?
- Why did it go that way?
- What will I do tomorrow?

Reflection has the potential to inform *tomorrow* through today's successes and challenges linking our past and present with the future. In school this process often relates to cognitive goals, but when the focus is social and emotional, there needs to be more. More than self-awareness and self-management. More than social awareness and relationship skills. Even more than the aspects of responsible decision-making that we've already described. Who are our students in relation to their own past, their family's history?

Many stories profiled in this book portray multicultural characters or characters from different countries, but the impact of heritage has been addressed only incidentally. While we hope that students reflect on *all* the decisions they make, here I choose to feature characters for whom family history matters in making life choices.

WHAT WE HOPE TO SEE IN THE CLASSROOM REGARDING REFLECTING, AND WHAT WE SOMETIMES SEE INSTEAD

In the classroom and throughout a school we often see lots of nods to students' heritage. I've been lucky to arrive at some schools on International Foods Day and have enjoyed numerous tasty treats. Other days celebrate clothing from around the globe, and some students wear their native dress daily. We honor holidays from different cultures and invite students to tell us about their family's cultural traditions.

Still, I wonder how many students think about the many ways their family's history matters in their day-to-day lives—beyond holidays, foods, and clothing. What are the tokens of their everyday life that will one day bring a smile to their faces as they reflect on the small moments of their childhood?

I speak from experience, having recently uncovered bundles of old letters when I cleaned out the attic in our century-old home that's been in our family for generations. What fun I had reading through them—letters I'd written home to my parents during college (hilarious now in their accounting of dorm life in an all-girls school), greeting cards my grandmother had received from relatives now long-deceased, and even a letter written to my grandfather (then a young boy) by my great uncle, his brother, when he was stationed overseas during World War I. None of these were intended to become historical documents, but I sure was happy to have discovered them. In some cases, I got to reminisce about old experiences one more time. In others, I got to stitch together pieces of our family's past that I was encountering anew. Could we spend more time in our classroom building our students' awareness of the impact of family memories? Think about the questions below as you initiate this reflection in your classroom.

ENHANCING CLASSROOM CULTURE: QUESTIONS FOR TEACHERS TO ASK THEMSELVES ABOUT REFLECTING

1. What do I know about the heritage and family memories of the students in my class?

2. How could I learn more about my students' heritage and family memories in a way that is not invasive?

3. What do I want my students to understand about the importance of reflecting on heritage and family memories, and what might a discussion of this include?

4. How could I model this reflective thinking for my students by sharing with them some of my special family memories?

5. How could I help my students reflect more on how their family's history and their own memories are important to them?

6. How could I use the books about reflection to generate memory projects that might be meaningful to my students?

WHAT TO LOOK FOR IN BOOKS ABOUT REFLECTING

For this focus area I look for books that emphasize small moments and small mementos that may seem entirely insignificant until they take on personal meaning. It might be a "lucky" item of clothing, a scent that brings back memories of a special place, familiar landmarks that let you know you're getting closer to your favorite vacation destination, or scraps so inconsequential that they seem more trash than treasure. For many students, this "blast from the past" is a new area of self-discovery. Chart 7.5: Books Aligned to Reflecting lists some wonderful examples.

CHART 7.5: BOOKS ALIGNED TO REFLECTING

THE MESSAGE	THE BOOK
Small keepsakes from our past become our legacy for future generations	*The Lotus Seed* by Sherry Garland (primary and intermediate)
It's the little things that make our heart happy when we think about our past	*The Matchbox Diary* by Paul Fleischman (primary and intermediate)
Sometimes a special item of clothing has wonderful memories attached to it	*The Dress and the Girl* by Camille Andros (primary and intermediate)
Sometimes we hardly notice the pieces of our family's history that are such a big part of us	*The Fish House Door* by Robert F. Baldwin (intermediate)
Old family memories blend with new family experiences to build a stronger sense of who we are	*A Different Pond* by Bao Phi (primary and intermediate)

Small keepsakes from our past become our legacy for future generations

The story of *The Lotus Seed* shows children that even something as tiny as a seed can hold a lifetime of memories. The tale begins in Vietnam many years ago, when the grandmother of the narrator plucks a seed from a lotus pod to remember the last day of her emperor's rule. It becomes a symbol of bravery throughout her life and she carries it inside her pocket for good luck. When bombs fall during the war, she grabs the seed, leaving more precious heirlooms behind. She carries it all the way across the ocean to a bewildering new country, and it is there one night that the narrator's little brother discovers it and drops it into the mud—he's not sure where. Grandmother is distraught until one day the following spring, she sees a beautiful pink lotus sprouting in the garden. It is the flower of her country, and when the blossom fades, she gives a seed to each of her grandchildren so that one day they can give a lotus seed to their grandchildren. May Vietnam live forever in their hearts.

A seed symbolizes life. What kind of seed might symbolize life for each of your students? It might be the seed of a flower from their family's heritage. Or, it might be a flower that is meaningful to them right now, something they'd like to share with their own children one day. Then again, maybe it's not a flower at all, but some other token with special significance Why would they want to pass this to future generations?

It's the little things that make our heart happy when we think about our past

Sometimes it's not *one* special thing that's important, but a collection of memorabilia so small that it seems better suited to the dumpster than the family archives. I was reminded of this as I lured my adult daughter back to her childhood bedroom to clean it out. I would have made short work of the task armed with plenty of heavy-duty garbage bags, but she had other ideas, reminiscing about each item as she uncovered it: "Wow, the poster I made in eighth grade. I have to keep that." "I can't throw these away, my first pair of ballet shoes." Then my personal favorite: "Oh, look, my fake ID."

There were no contraband keepsakes in *The Matchbox Diary.* Great-Granddad's cigar box held a "diary" of small treasures collected first in Italy when he was a young boy, and then from his early days in America. He couldn't read or write, so the boxes were perfect for storing his memories. Each one told a story. There was the olive pit in one matchbox reminiscent of his hard life in Italy. His mom would give him an olive pit to suck when he was hungry. In another box was a single piece of macaroni, to remember the year with no rain and no wheat. When he came to America his first job was cutting fish in a factory. That box held a fish bone. Great-Grandpa opened each box in turn, explaining its contents, item by item.

But it wasn't just the items in the boxes that were important, it was the stories behind them. What if our students created their own matchbox diary (no actual matchboxes needed)? Could they find five objects of no monetary value, significant to them in some way? Could they tell the story behind each item? Whatever it takes, we need to remind our students that it's often the small details of our lives that matter and that we'll want to remember for a very long time.

Sometimes a special item of clothing has wonderful memories attached to it

You can extend the idea of memorable personal items to favorite pieces of clothing. This will resonate with many students who say they have a "lucky jersey," a "good luck necklace," or some other personal effect to which they are emotionally connected. For me it's my old Ugg slippers. Comfort food for my feet, perhaps too literally, with their smatterings of sauces, batter, and pan juices that sneak out of their respective baking dishes and land on the now-dull brown suede. But we continue to love each other, those old slippers and I; we've been through a lot together.

Meet *The Girl and the Dress.* This is a story about a girl and her favorite dress. They spent much of her childhood together in a country far away, enjoying an ordinary life of picking flowers and staring at the stars, while always wishing for something more spectacular. Then life changed. The girl sailed across the sea to America and grew up, the dress outgrown and somehow lost to her. Many years later, the girl has a daughter of her own, and as they walk together through the streets of their city, they pass a second-hand store. What's in the window? The dress! Just looking at it brings a flood of memories, spectacular in their simplicity. And the size is just right for the girl's daughter.

Where had that dress traveled in the years in between? What becomes of our one-time treasures when we move on? Students might use their imagination to envision the journey of their something-special, an icon of their youth. The point is to recognize how these simple items *do* somehow make life a little more spectacular.

Sometimes we hardly notice the pieces of our family's history that are such a big part of us

If we don't take note of family history as we're living it, it will pass us by and disappear forever. This is the message conveyed in **The Fish House Door**, a favorite in part because of the personal connections it evokes for me. This book was a gift from a former graduate student, and every time I read it, I think of her.

The story takes place on an island in Maine and features a family of lobster fishermen. One day, a "summer person" arrives to buy a couple of lobsters and, in passing, mentions that he likes the fish house door. This makes no sense to the son who is the story's narrator. For years, his dad has used the door to wipe off excess paint from brushes after repainting their lobster buoys, and now it's covered with large streaks of yellow and red.

As the weeks pass, the boy begins to ask questions about the door, its layers of color and the scribbles etched into its old wood. His father tells him tales of his grandfather and great grandfather, their connection to the island, and the boy listens thoughtfully. Meanwhile, the summer person, an art dealer, comes by for lobsters a few more times. He loves the door. He offers $500 for it, then $1,000, then $2,000. Although the family could use the money, Dad shakes his head no. It's the boy who speaks up: The door is not for sale for any price. It's his family's fish house door. When we view old relics through the lens of our past, they take on new meaning.

Old family memories blend with new family experiences to build a stronger sense of who we are

It's only a fishing trip. But to the boy and his dad in this Caldecott Honor book, **A Different Pond,** it's a time to connect past and present. The father and son leave before dawn, not for sport, but to put the next meal on their table. The dad works multiple jobs, and it's the only time he can spare. The father and son do ordinary things together, arranging twigs to build a fire and eating bologna sandwiches for breakfast. As they cast their fishing lines, the dad tells the boy about a different pond far away (in Vietnam) where he once fished with his brother, until the war took the brother away. With a few fish in their bucket, father and son pack up to return home. Do the trees near that faraway pond look the same or different, the boy wonders? That night he will dream of faraway fish, too.

It's only a fishing trip. But this gentle story brings together so much of what we want students to ponder for social emotional learning. First, there's the father's reflection on that "different pond" and the opportunity to pass along a glimpse of his heritage to his son. There's acknowledgement of his emotions, the sadness he continues to feel over the loss of his brother, and the boy's curiosity about the place that is a part of his family's past, but only in small ways a part of his own. Their time together strengthens their individual identities and builds the relationship between them.

Choose this book to help students recognize that while we may "fish in different ponds," all of us are connected—through our willingness to reflect on our past, the emotions derived from our life experiences, our ever-strengthening senses of self, and the relationships we build along the way. The questions that follow for Seven Thinking Boxes can help your students become more reflective about this story and their own.

FEATURED BOOK FOR REFLECTING: *A Different Pond* by Bao Phi

SEVEN THINKING BOXES

Questions to ask about *A Different Pond* by Bao Phi

SEL Competency: Responsible Decision-Making   Focus: Reflecting

PLAIN CARDBOARD BOX	**BASIC THINKING** What details in this book connect the past to the present? Find at least three examples.
PUZZLE BOX	**PUZZLING DETAILS** What details in this story would you <u>not</u> know if the story wasn't told from the boy's perspective? What do these details show about the boy's understanding of his family's past?
HEART BOX	**FEELINGS** In this story, family members really care for each other. What is it about their <u>past</u> and their <u>present</u> that makes this family so compassionate?
UNUSUAL BOX	**CREATIVE THINKING** What else do you think the father in this story could do to make the family's past more real to his son?
BROKEN BOX	**PROBLEMS AND ISSUES** What problems does this family face in their <u>present</u> life? What is the evidence? What problems did this family face in the <u>past</u>? Which problems do you think would be the most difficult to face? Why?
TREASURE BOX	**SOMETHING TO TREASURE** What do you think the boy treasures most from his family's past? What do you think his father treasures most? Why?
TOOL BOX	**AUTHOR'S TOOLS** If the author wanted us to know about this family's past, why do you think he chose to tell the story from the *son's* point of view? (Remember that the son never lived in Vietnam.)

SEVEN THINKING BOXES

Questions to ask about any book for reflecting

PLAIN CARDBOARD BOX	**BASIC THINKING** • What did reflecting have to do with this story? Explain in your own words. • How did this story end? How did reflecting make a difference to the outcome?
PUZZLE BOX	**PUZZLING DETAILS** • Find a quote in this book that you consider to be a good example of reflecting. Why did you choose this quote? • What detail in this story showed that characters needed to do more reflecting?
HEART BOX	**FEELINGS** • How did the main character's feelings change throughout the story based on reflection? • What feeling comes to mind when you think about this story? What did that feeling have to do with reflecting?
UNUSUAL BOX	**CREATIVE THINKING** • If *you* were reflecting on the situation in this story, how would you have handled it? • Based on what happens in this story, what could you reflect on in your own life in a similar way?
BROKEN BOX	**PROBLEMS AND ISSUES** • Was <u>not</u> reflecting a problem in this story? How? • Rewrite the ending of this story to show what might have happened if characters had not been reflective: What other problems might have occurred?
TREASURE BOX	**SOMETHING TO TREASURE** • What do you think this author wanted readers to understand about reflecting? How might reflecting help you in our own life? • What advice might you have offered this character about how to be more reflective, and why reflection is important?
TOOL BOX	**AUTHOR'S TOOLS** • How important is the <u>setting</u> of this story in characters' reflection? How does the author use the setting to show the importance of reflecting? • Does the author of this story build an understanding of setting as <u>time</u>, <u>place</u>, or <u>both</u>? Explain.

APPENDIX

Ten SEL Books for the Principal's Office

The classroom teacher can start this process, but it can be enhanced by others in the learning community too. How could school counselors, social workers, and psychologists use these books? How could administrators use them?

There are many reasons why students get sent to the principal's office. Sometimes the reason is positive—they might go to show off work that is spectacular or vastly improved over their previous products. But often they end up going due to situations that involve unacceptable behavior. Not all SEL focus areas correlate to why a student might find themselves in the principal's office. Failure to set personal goals, a lack of self-confidence, and other pervasive matters need attention that could potentially involve the principal, but probably not in her office in the next 10 minutes. These visits are often reserved for infractions that erupt spontaneously, that add up to one violation too many: "I told you that the next time you spoke unkindly to anyone, you could discuss it with the principal."

Below are 10 books that address typical issues that get kids "sent to the principal," which could help support these meetings in several ways. Kids often wait a few minutes in the outer office before their meeting with the principal begins. While they wait, hand them a book related to why they're there—speaking unkindly to classmates, bullying on the playground, or whatever. Ask them to read the book and be ready to talk about how it applies to them. As they read, they'll calm down a bit, and hopefully become distracted by the character and the problem in the story. Then begin the conversation with the character, and her problem: *What did Mean Jean learn about playground behavior by the end of the story?* This feels like less of a personal attack than leading with: *Why did you yell at the other kids on your team at recess again?* After sorting out Mean Jean's behavior, make the connection to their own behavior.

For the best success, choose easy-to-read books that have a straightforward message. The books should also be short, ideally with interesting illustrations. The goal is not for students to become lost in the nuances of the plot or the author's beautiful language, but to quickly identify the big idea. For younger children or struggling readers, the principal may need to read the story aloud at the start of their meeting.

The same basic questions can apply every time:

- **What happened in this story?** Check for understanding before asking about the big idea. If the student is unsure, quickly flip through the book to review it.

- **What did the character learn?** It's fine to help students with this. You might go back to a page where the lesson is revealed.

- **How does this lesson apply to you?** Be sure to focus on the central message, not some insignificant detail. ("The character is a boy and I'm a boy.")

- **What will you try to remember from this story the next time you are in a situation like this?** This is the key question and you may want to suggest some follow-up—a little accountability, a little cheerleading: *Stop by my office after recess tomorrow and let me know how it went. I know you can handle this.*

Any suitable books you already have will work. To get you started, I've identified 10 books (profiled in greater depth in Chapters 3–7) that reflect some of the most common reasons a student gets sent to the principal. Because the focus here is the story's message, even books typically used in the primary grades can be used with older students.

Anger, flaring temper: *When Sophie Gets Angry—Really, Really Angry* by Molly Bang

This book shows that anger can be a legitimate response, but there are appropriate ways of handling it.

Seeking attention in the wrong way, how to get noticed for good behavior: *Millie Fierce* by Jane Manning

At first, Millie thinks even negative attention is better than no attention. She learns that this doesn't really work.

Bad behavior choices, impulsive behavior: *The Snurtch* by Sean Ferrell

This book addresses significantly bad behavior, like ripping up a classmate's paper. It makes the point that *you* are not a bad person. Your "snurtch" made a bad choice, and you need to control your snurtch.

Lack of empathy, importance of apologizing: *Each Kindness* by Jacqueline Woodson

Through mostly passive aggressive behavior, the main character is excluded by other girls in her class. By the time they recognize the error of their ways, the girl has moved, with no opportunity for an apology.

Disrespect for individual differences: *We're All Wonders* by R. J. Palacio

This story encourages respect for and appreciation of everyone, despite individual differences. It's our uniqueness that makes us special.

Bullying, playground problems, importance of reaching out: *The Recess Queen* by Alexis O'Neill

This book makes two critical points: There is no place for bullying on the playground. Also, reaching out to a bully might change his behavior.

Poor choice of words leads to problems,; little problems can escalate into big problems: *The Sandwich Swap* by Her Majesty Queen Rania Al Abdullah of Jordan

There are a couple of strong messages here: It's our poor choice of words that sometimes leads to problems. Simple problems can quickly escalate when other people take sides.

Get to know people before you judge them; give new people a chance: *Enemy Pie* **by Derek Munson**

Sometimes first impressions aren't reliable. Get to know someone better before rushing to judgment.

The importance of finding a connection with someone; communicating when there are language barriers: *Drawn Together* **by Minh Lê**

If you think you don't have anything in common with someone, or disagree over something, look for a way to connect—even when you speak a different language.

The importance of honesty, the meaning of integrity: *The Empty Pot* **by Demi**

This is a great story for students who have been caught cheating, lying, or behaving inappropriately when out of your sight.

REFERENCES

4Rs (Reading, Writing, Respect, and Resolution). (n.d.). Retrieved from https://casel.org/guideprograms4rs-reading-writing-respect-and-resolution/

6 Things Everyone Believes About Thanksgiving that Are Absolutely Untrue. (n.d.). Retrieved from https://www.rd.com/culture/thanksgiving-myths/

Ackerman, C. (2019). 25 fun mindfulness activities for children and teens (+tips!). [Blog post]. Retrieved from https://positivepsychologyprogram.com/mindfulness-for-children-kids-activities/#mindfulness-activities-children

Bandura, A. (1977). *Self-efficacy: Toward a unifying theory of behavioral change. Psychological Review, 84*(2), 191–215.

Boyles, N. (2014). *Closer reading grades 3-6: Better prep, smarter lessons, deeper comprehension.* Thousand Oaks, CA: Corwin.

Brackett, M. (2018). The emotional intelligence we owe students and educators. *Educational Leadership, 76*(2), 12–18.

CASEL. (n.d). Retrieved from https://casel.org/

Cherry, K. (2019). The five levels of Maslow's hierarchy of needs: How Maslow's famous hierarchy explains human motivation. [Blog post]. Retrieved from https://www.verywellmind.com/what-is-maslows-hierarchy-of-needs-4136760

Core SEL Competencies. (n.d.). Retrieved from https://casel.org/core-competencies/

Costa, A.L., & Kallick, B. (2000). Habits of mind. Retrieved from https://www.chsvt.org/wdp/Habits_of_Mind.pdf

Durlak, J.A., Weissberg, R.P., Dymnicki, A.B., Taylor, R.D., & Schellinger, K.B. (2011). The impact of enhancing students' social and emotional learning: A meta-analysis of school-based universal interventions. *Child Development, 82*(1), 405–432.

Hampton, D. (2015). What's the difference between feelings and emotions? [Blog post]. Retrieved from https://www.thebestbrainpossible.com/whats-the-difference-between-feelings-and-emotions/

Maslow, A. (1943). A theory of human motivation. *Psychological Review, 50*(4), 370–396.

National Commission on Social, Emotional, and Academic Development. (n.d.). Retrieved from https://www.aspeninstitute.org/programs/national-commission-on-social-emotional-and-academic-development/

National Governors Association Center for Best Practices, Council of Chief State School Officers. (2010). Common Core state standards. Washington, DC: National Governors Association Center for Best Practices, Council of Chief State School Officers.

Partnership for Assessment of Reading for College and Careers. (2012). PARCC model content frameworks: English language arts/literacy, grades 3–11. Retrieved from https://parcc-assessment.org/content/uploads/2017/11/PARCCMCFELALiteracyAugust2012_FINAL.pdf

Perception. (n.d.) In *Merriam-Webster online.* Retrieved from https://www.merriam-webster.com/dictionary/perception

Queensborough Community College. (2018). Definition for diversity. Retrieved from http://www.qcc.cuny.edu/Diversity/definition.html

Stress Management. (n.d.). Retrieved from https://www.mayoclinic.org/tests-procedures/stress-management/about/pac-20384898

Talking with Trees. (n.d.). What is respect. [Blog post]. Retrieved from https://talkingtreebooks.com/definition/what-is-respect.html

Taylor, R.D., Oberle, E., Durlak, J.A., Weissberg, R. (2017). Promoting positive youth development through school-based social and emotional learning interventions: A meta-analysis of follow-up effects. *Child Development, 88*(4), 1156–1171.

Webb, N. (2009). Webb's Depth-of-Knowledge guide: Career and technical education definitions. Retrieved from http://www.aps.edu/sapr/documents/resources/Webbs_DOK_Guide.pdf

BIBLIOGRAPHY OF CHILDREN'S LITERATURE

Abdullah, R. A. (2010). *The sandwich swap*. New York, NY: Disney-Hyperion.

Abercrombie, B. (1995). *Charlie Anderson*. New York: Aladdin Paperbacks.

Adler, D. A. (2001). *Lou Gehrig: The luckiest man*. San Diego: Voyager Books.

Alexie, S. (2016). *Thunder Boy Jr*. New York: Little, Brown Books for Young Readers.

Aliki. (1998). *Marianthe's story: Painted words and spoken memories*. New York: Greenwillow Books.

Allsburg, C. V. (1990). *Just a dream*. Boston, MA: Houghton Mifflin Harcourt.

Allsburg, C. V. (1991). *The wretched stone*. Boston, MA: Houghton Mifflin.

Anda, D. D. (2019). *Mango moon*. Chicago, IL: Albert Whitman & Company.

Andreae, G. (2001). *Giraffes can't dance*. New York: Scholastic.

Andros, C. (2018). *The dress and the girl*. New York: Abrams Books for Young Readers.

Anholt, L. (2007). *Degas and the little dancer: A story about Edgar Degas*. Hauppauge, NY: Barron's Educational Series.

Applegate, K. (2014). *Ivan: The remarkable true story of the shopping mall gorilla*. New York: Clarion Books.

Baldwin, R. F. (2010). *The fish house door*. Yarmouth, ME: Islandport Press.

Bang, M. (2004). *When Sophie gets angry—Really, really angry*. New York: Scholastic.

Barnes, D. D. (2017). *Crown: An ode to the fresh cut*. Chicago: Bolden, an Agate imprint.

Bartone, E. (1997). *Peppe the lamplighter*. New York, NY: HarperCollins.

Bates, A. J., & Bates, J. (2018). *The big umbrella*. New York: Simon & Schuster Books for Young Readers.

Bates, K. L. (2013). *America the beautiful: Together we stand*. New York: Orchard Books.

Beaty, A. (2017). *Rosie Revere, engineer*. New York, NY: Abrams Books for Young Readers.

Berne, J. (2016). *On a beam of light: A story of Albert Einstein*. Chronicle Books.

Boelts, M. (2009). *Those shoes*. Somerville, MA: Candlewick Press.

Boelts, M. (2012). *Happy like soccer*. Somerville, MA: Candlewick Press.

Boelts, M. (2016). *A bike like Sergio's*. Somerville, MA: Candlewick Press.

Bosak, S. V. (2004). *Dream: A tale of wonder, wisdom & wishes*. Toronto: TCP Press.

Bradby, M. (1995). *More than anything else*. New York: Orchard Books.

Brandt, L. (2014). *Maddi's fridge*. Flashlight Press.

Bridges, S. Y. (2004). *Ruby's wish*. New York: Scholastic.

Brinckloe, J. (1986). *Fireflies!* New York: Aladdin Books.

Brisson, P. (1999). *The summer my father was ten*. Honesdale, PA: Boyds Mills Press.

Brisson, P. (2006). *Melissa Parkington's beautiful, beautiful hair*. Honesdale, PA: Boyds Mills Press.

Brown, M. (2011). *Marisol McDonald doesn't match / Marisol McDonald no combina*. New York: Lee & Low Books.

Browne, A. (2001). *Voices in the park*. New York: DK Children.

Bruchac, J. (2007). *Squanto's journey: The story of the first Thanksgiving*. New York: Houghton Mifflin Harcourt.

Bunting, E. (1989). *The Wednesday surprise*. New York: Clarion Books.

Bunting, E. (1990). *How many days to America?: A Thanksgiving story*. New York: Clarion Books.

Bunting, E. (1993). *Fly away home*. New York: Clarion Books.

Bunting, E. (1998). *Going home*. New York, NY: HarperCollins.

Bunting, E. (2006). *One green apple*. New York: Clarion Books.

Bunting, E. (2006). *Pop's bridge*. Boston, MA: Houghton Mifflin Harcourt.

Bunting, E. (2015). *The memory string*. Boston, MA: Houghton Mifflin Harcourt.

Burleigh, R. (2005). *Home run: The story of Babe Ruth*. San Diego: Silver Whistle.

Burleigh, R. (2012). *Night flight: Amelia Earhart crosses the Atlantic*. New York, NY: Simon & Schuster.

Byers, G. (2018). *I am enough*. New York, NY: HarperCollins.

Chamberlain, M., & Chamberlain, R. (2006). *Mama Panya's pancakes*: A village tale from Kenya. Bath: Barefoot Books.

Choi, Y. (2013). *The name jar*. Columbus, OH: Zaner-Bloser.

Clark-Robinson, M. (2018). *Let the children march*. Boston, MA: Houghton Mifflin Harcourt.

Clinton, C. (2017). *She persisted: 13 American women who changed the world*. New York: Philomel Books.

Cole, H. (2012). *Unspoken: A story from the Underground Railroad*. New York: Scholastic Press.

Coleman, E. (1996). *White socks only*. Morton Grove, IL: Albert Whitman & Company.

Coles, R. (2010). *The story of Ruby Bridges*. New York: Scholastic.

Collaço, J. (2014). *Firenze's light*. Shine Your Light Books.

Cook, J. (2008). *My mouth is a volcano!* Chattanooga, TN: National Center for Youth Issues.

Cook, J. (2018). *Uniquely wired: A story about Autism and its gifts*. Boys Town, NE: Boys Town Press.

Cooney, B. (1982). *Miss Rumphius*. New York: Viking Press.

Cosmo, A. J. (2018). *Little star*. Thought Bubble Publishing.

Crews, D. (1998). *Bigmama's*. New York: Greenwillow Books.

Crimi, C. (2017). *There might be lobsters*. Somerville, MA: Candlewick Press.

Curtis, G. (2001). *The bat boy & his violin*. New York: Simon & Schuster.

Davies, N. (2014). *The promise*. Somerville, MA: Candlewick Press.

Deedy, C. A. (2000). *The yellow star: The legend of King Christian X of Denmark*. Atlanta, GA: Peachtree Publishing Company.

Deedy, C. A. (2009). *14 cows for America*. Atlanta, GA: Peachtree Publishing Company.

Demi. (1996). *The empty pot*. New York: Square Fish.

Denos, J. (2017). *Windows*. Somerville, MA: Candlewick Press.

DeRolf, S. (1997). *The crayon box that talked*. New York: Random House.

Díaz, J. (2018). *Islandborn*. New York, NY: Dial Books for Young Readers, imprint of Penguin Random House.

Doerrfeld, C. (2018). *The rabbit listened*. New York, NY: Dial Books for Young Readers.

Drachman, E. (2010). *A frog thing*. Boulder, CO: Imagine Nation Books.

Egan, T. (2007). *The pink refrigerator*. Boston, MA: Houghton Mifflin Harcourt.

Engle, M. (2015). *Drum dream girl: How one girls courage changed music*. Boston, MA: Houghton Mifflin Harcourt.

Ferrell, S. (2016). *The Snurtch*. New York: Atheneum Books for Young Readers.

Ferri, G. (2016). *Brick by brick*. Minedition.

Ferry, B. (2015). *Stick and stone*. Boston, MA: Houghton Mifflin Harcourt.

Ferry, B. (2019). *Ten rules of the birthday wish*. New York, NY: G.P. Putnam's Sons.

Fleischman, P. (2002). *Weslandia*. Cambridge, MA: Candlewick Press.

Fleischman, P. (2016). *The matchbox diary*. Somerville, MA: Candlewick Press.

Fleming, C. (2003). *Boxes for Katje*. New York: Farrar, Straus and Giroux (BYR).

Forest, H. (2005). *Stone soup*. Little Rock, AR: August House.

Fox, M. (2019). *Koala Lou*. Hawthorn: Penguin Books Australia.

Frankel, E. (2013). *Dare! A story about standing up to bullying in schools (The Weird! Series)*. Minneapolis, MN: Free Spirit.

Frankel, E. (2013). *Tough! A story about how to stop bullying in schools (The Weird! Series)*. Minneapolis, MN: Free Spirit.

Frankel, E. (2013). *Weird! A story about dealing with bullying in schools (The Weird! Series)*. Minneapolis, MN: Free Spirit.

Gandhi, A., & Hegedus, B. (2014). *Grandfather Gandhi*. New York: Simon & Schuster.

Garland, S. (1997). *The lotus seed*. Boston, MA: Houghton Mifflin Harcourt.

Gerstein, M. (2004). *The man who walked between the towers*. New York: Scholastic.

Gillen, L. (2012). *Good people everywhere*. Portland, OR: Three Pebble Press, LLC.

Giovanni, N. (2008). *Rosa*. New York, NY: Square Fish.

Golenbock, P. (1992). *Teammates*. Boston, MA: Houghton Mifflin Harcourt.

Goodhart, P. (2017). *My very own space*. London: Flying Eye Books.

Grimes, N. (1997). *Meet Danitra Brown*. New York: HarperCollins.

Harrison, K. (2016). *Weeds in Nana's garden: A heartfelt story of love that helps explain Alzheimer's disease and other dementias*. Cobourg, Ontario: Flipturn Publishing.

Henkes, K. (1996). *Lilly's purple plastic purse*. New York: Greenwillow Books.

Henkes, K. (2008). *Chrysanthemum*. New York: Greenwillow Books.

Hest, A. (2007). *Mr. George Baker*. Cambridge, MA: Candlewick Press.

Higgins, C. (2018). *Everything you need for a treehouse*. San Francisco, CA: Chronicle Books.

Higgins, R. T. (2018). *We don't eat our classmates*. New York: Disney-Hyperion.

Hill, L. C. (2011). *Dave the Potter: Artist, poet, slave*. New York: Little, Brown Books for Young Readers.

Hoffman, M. (2000). *Boundless Grace*. New York: Puffin Books.

Hoffman, M. (2005). *Amazing Grace*. London: Frances Lincoln.

Hong, J. (2017). *Lovely*. Berkeley, CA: Creston Books.

Hood, S. (2018). *Ada's violin: The story of the recycled orchestra of Paraguay*. New York: Simon & Schuster.

Hood, S. (2018). *Shaking things up: 14 young women who changed the world*. New York: HarperCollins.

Hoose, P. M., & Hoose, H. (1998). *Hey, little ant*. Berkeley, CA: Tricycle Press.

Hopkinson, D. (2016). *Steamboat school*. Jump at the Sun Books.

Howard, E. F. (2000). *Virgie goes to school with us boys*. New York: Simon & Schuster.

Ieronimo, C. (2014). *A thirst for home: A story of water across the world*. New York: Bloomsbury USA Childrens.

Inserro, J. (2018). *Nonni's moon*.

Javaherbin, M. (2010). *Goal!* Somerville, MA: Candlewick Press.

Jonas, A. (1987). *Reflections*. New York: Greenwillow Books.

Jordan, D., & Jordan, R. M. (2003). *Salt in his shoes: Michael Jordan in pursuit of a dream*. New York: Simon & Schuster.

Kamkwamba, W. (2012). *The boy who harnessed the wind*. New York, NY: Dial Books for Young Readers.

Karst, P. (2000). *The invisible string*. Camarillo, CA: DeVorss & Company.

Kensky, J., & Downes, P. (2018). *Rescue & Jessica: A life-changing friendship*. Somerville, MA: Candlewick Press.

Kraus, R. (2008). *Leo the late bloomer*. New York: Windmill Books.

Kroll, V. (1997). *Masai and I*. New York, NY: Aladdin Paperbacks.

Krull, K. (2000). *Wilma unlimited: How Wilma Rudolph became the world's fastest woman*. San Diego, CA: Harcourt.

Krull, K. (2003). *Harvesting hope: The story of Cesar Chavez*. Boston, MA: Houghton Mifflin Harcourt.

Kuntz, D., & Shrodes, A. (2017). *Lost and found cat: The true story of Kunkush's incredible journey*. New York: Crown Books for Young Readers.

LaMarche, J. (2002). *The raft*. New York, NY: HarperCollins.

Laminack, L. L. (2004). *Saturdays and teacakes*. Atlanta, GA: Peachtree Publishing Company.

Larson, K., & Nethery, M. (2008). *Two Bobbies: A true story of Hurricane Katrina, friendship, and survival*. New York: Walker & Company.

Lê, M. (2018). *Drawn together*. Los Angeles, CA: Disney-Hyperion.

Leaf, M. (2011). *The story of Ferdinand*. New York: Penguin Group (USA).

Lester, H. (2010). *Tacky the penguin*. Boston, MA: Sandpiper.

Lionni, L. (1963). *Swimmy*. New York: Alfred A. Knopf.

Lionni, L. (2014). *Frederick*. New York: Random House USA.

Litchfield, D. (2016). *The bear and the piano*. New York: Clarion Books.

Littlesugar, A. (2001). *Freedom school, yes!* New York: Philomel Books.

Love, J. (2018). *Julián is a mermaid*. Somerville, MA: Candlewick Press.

Lovell, P. (2002). *Stand tall, Molly Lou Melon*. New York: Scholastic.

Lowry, L. (2009). *Crow call*. New York: Scholastic.

Ludwig, T. (2013). *The invisible boy*. New York: Alfred A. Knopf.

Luque, C. P. (2018). *A handful of buttons: Picture book about family diversity*. CreateSpace Independent Publishing Platform.

Maier, B. (2018). *The little red fort*. New York: Scholastic.

Manning, J. (2012). *Millie Fierce*. New York: Philomel Books.

Markel, M. (2013). *Brave girl: Clara and the shirtwaist makers' strike of 1909*. Balzer Bray.

Martin, J. B. (2009). *Snowflake Bentley*. Boston, MA: Houghton Mifflin Harcourt.

Martinez-Neal, J. (2018). *Alma and how she got her name*. Somerville, MA: Candlewick Press.

May, P. (2018). *Find your happy: A kids self love book*. CreateSpace Independent Publishing Platform.

McBrier, P. (2004). *Beatrice's goat*. New York: Aladdin Paperbacks.

McCully, E. A. (2007). *Mirette on the high wire*. New York: G.P. Putnam's Sons.

McCutcheon, J. (2017). *Flowers for Sarajevo*. Atlanta, GA: Peachtree Publishing Company.

McDonnell, P. (2014). *Me . . . Jane*. New York: Little, Brown Books for Young Readers.

McGhee, H. M. (2017). *Come with me*. New York: G.P. Putnam's Sons.

McKissack, P. C. (2003). *The honest-to-goodness truth*. New York: Aladdin Paperbacks.

McLerran, A. (2004). *Roxaboxen*. New York, NY: HarperCollins.

Meddour, W. (2019). *Lubna and Pebble*. New York, NY: Dial Books for Young Readers.

Michelson, R. (2013). *As good as anybody: Martin Luther King Jr. and Abraham Joshua Heschel's amazing march toward freedom*. New York: Dragonfly Books.

Miller, P. Z. (2018). *Be kind*. New York, NY: Roaring Brook Press.

Mitchell, M. K. (1998). *Uncle Jed's barbershop*. New York: Aladdin Paperbacks.

Mochizuki, K. (1993). *Baseball saved us*. Lee & Low Books.

Mochizuki, K. (1997). *Heroes*. Lee & Low Books.

Mochizuki, K. (2010). *Passage to freedom: The Sugihara story*. National Geographic School.

Mollel, T. M. (1999). *My rows and piles of coins*. New York: Clarion Books.

Mora, P. (2000). *Tomás and the library lady*. New York: Dragonfly Books.

Morales, Y. (2018). *Dreamers*. New York: Neal Porter Books/Holiday House.

Munsch, R. N. (1981). *The paper bag princess*. Toronto: Annick Press.

Munson, D. (2000). *Enemy pie*. San Francisco, CA: Chronicle Books.

Muth, J. J. (2002). *The three questions: Based on a story by Leo Tolstoy*. New York: Scholastic.

Nance, A. J. (2016). *Puppy mind*. Berkeley: Plum Blossom.

Napoli, D. J. (2010). *Mama Miti: Wangari Maathai and the trees of Kenya*. London: Simon & Schuster.

Nelson, K. (2013). *Nelson Mandela*. New York, NY: Katherine Tegen Books.

Nye, N. S. (1997). *Sitti's secrets*. New York: Aladdin Paperbacks.

O'Brien, A. S. (2015). *I'm new here*. Watertown, MA: Charlesbridge.

O'Malley, K. (2005). *Once upon a cool motorcycle dude*. Bloomsbury U.S.A. Children's Books.

O'Neill, A. (2002). *The recess queen*. New York: Scholastic.

Palacio, R. J. (2017). *We're all wonders*. New York: Alfred A. Knopf.

Palatini, M. (2009). *The perfect pet*. New York, NY: Katherine Tegen Books.

Park, F., & Park, G. (2003). *Good-bye, 382 Shin Dang Dong*. National Geographic Society.

Pearson, E. (2002). *Ordinary Mary's extraordinary deed*. Layton, UT: Gibbs Smith.

Peña, M. D. (2017). *Last stop on Market Street*. London: Puffin.

Penn, A. (2009). *The kissing hand*. Indianapolis: Tanglewood.

Pett, M. (2014). *The girl and the bicycle*. New York: Simon & Schuster.

Pett, M., & Rubinstein, G. (2011). *The girl who never made mistakes*. Naperville, IL: Sourcebooks Jabberwocky.

Phi, B. (2017). *A different pond*. North Mankato, MN: Picture Window Books, a Capstone imprint.

Pinkney, A. D. (2009). *Sojourner Truth's step-stomp stride*. New York: Jump at the Sun Books.

Pinkney, A. D. (2010). *Sit-in: How four friends stood up by sitting down*. New York: Little, Brown Books for Young Readers.

Piper, W. (2001). *The little engine that could*. New York: Scholastic.

Polacco, P. (1994). *Pink and Say*. New York: Philomel Books.

Polacco, P. (1998). *My rotten redheaded older brother*. New York: Simon & Schuster.

Polacco, P. (2001). *Thank you, Mr. Falker*. New York: Philomel Books.

Polacco, P. (1997). *Thunder cake*. Boston: National Braille Press.

Rabinowitz, A. (2014). *A boy and a jaguar*. Boston, MA: Houghton Mifflin Harcourt.

Raven, M. T. (2002). *Mercedes and the Chocolate Pilot: A true story of the Berlin airlift and the candy that dropped from the sky*. Chelsea, MI: Sleeping Bear Press.

Reynolds, P. H. (2018). *The word collector*. New York: Orchard Books.

Robinson, S. (2009). *Testing the ice: A true story about Jackie Robinson*. New York: Scholastic.

Rocco, J. (2014). *Blizzard*. New York, NY: Disney-Hyperion.

Ross, T. (1997). *Eggbert, the slightly cracked egg*. New York: Puffin Books.

Ryan, P. M. (2003). *When Marian sang*. New York: Scholastic.

Rylant, C. (1982). *When I was young in the mountains*. New York, NY: Puffin Books.

Rylant, C. (2001). *The relatives came*. New York: Atheneum Books for Young Readers.

Saltzberg, B. (2010). *Beautiful oops!* New York: Workman Publishing Company.

Sanna, F. (2016). *The journey*. London: Flying Eye Books.

Santat, D. (2017). *After the fall: How Humpty Dumpty got back up again*. New York, NY: Roaring Brook Press.

Sauer, T. (2018). *Wordy birdy*. New York: Doubleday.

Savageau, C. (2006). *Muskrat will be swimming*. Gardiner, ME: Tilbury House.

Say, A. (2009). *Tea with milk.* Boston, MA: Houghton Mifflin Harcourt.

Sayre, A. P. (2000). *Turtle, turtle, watch out!* New York: Orchard Books.

Schertle, A. (2000). *Down the road.* Boston, MA: Houghton Mifflin Harcourt.

Schiffer, M. B. (2015). *Stella brings the family.* San Francisco, CA: Chronicle Books.

Schroeder, A. (2000). *Minty: A story of young Harriet Tubman.* New York: Puffin Books.

Scieszka, J. (1996). *The true story of the 3 little pigs.* New York: Puffin Books.

Scillian, D. (2010). *Memoirs of a goldfish.* Ann Arbor, MI: Sleeping Bear Press.

Shannon, D. (1998). *No, David!* New York: Blue Sky.

Shannon, D. (2004). *A bad case of stripes.* New York: Scholastic.

Shetterly, M. L. (2018). *Hidden figures: The true story of four black women and the space race.* New York: Scholastic.

Snicket, L. (2013). *The dark.* New York: Little, Brown Books for Young Readers.

Soto, G. (1996). *Too many tamales.* New York: Puffin Books.

Spires, A. (2017). *The most magnificent thing.* Toronto: Kids Can.

Stead, P. C. (2010). *A sick day for Amos McGee.* New York: Roaring Brook Press.

Steig, W. (1986). *Brave Irene.* Boston, MA: National Braille Press.

Stein, D. E. (2012). *Interrupting chicken.* Somerville, MA: Candlewick Press.

Thermes, J. (2018). *Grandma Gatewood hikes the Appalachian trail.* New York, NY: Abrams Books for Young Readers.

Thompson, L. A. (2015). *Emmanuel's dream: The true story of Emmanuel Ofosu Yeboah.* New York: Schwartz & Wade Books.

Tonatiuh, D. (2014). *Separate is never equal: Sylvia Mendez and her family's fight for desegregation.* New York: Abrams Books for Young Readers.

Uegaki, C. (2014). *Sukis kimono.* Toronto: Kids Can.

Vaughan, M. (2003). *Up the learning tree.* New York: Lee & Low Books.

Vernick, A. (2012). *Brothers at bat: The true story of an amazing all-brother baseball team.* New York: Clarion Books.

Viorst, J. (1993). *Earrings!* New York: Aladdin Books.

Viorst, J. (2004). *Super-completely and totally the messiest.* New York: Atheneum Books for Young Readers.

Waber, B. (1973). *Ira sleeps over.* Boston, MA: Houghton Mifflin Harcourt.

Walden, B. (2018). *Seeds and trees: A children's book about the power of words.* Redding, CA: The Treasured Tree, LLC.

Wild, M. (2001). *Fox.* La Jolla, CA: Kane/Miller Book.

Wiles, D. (2005). *Freedom Summer.* New York: Atheneum Books for Young Readers.

Willems, M. (2012). *Knuffle bunny free: An unexpected diversion.* New York: Balzer Bray.

Williams, K. L. (1991). *Galimoto.* New York: HarperCollins.

Williams, K. L., & Mohammed, K. (2007). *Four feet, two sandals.* Grand Rapids, MI: Eerdmans Books.

Williams, K. L., & Mohammed, K. (2009). *My name is Sangoel.* Grand Rapids, MI: Eerdmans Books for Young Readers.

Williams, L. E. (2010). *The can man.* New York: Lee & Low Books.

Williams, V. B. (2007). *A chair for my mother.* New York: Greenwillow Books.

Winter, J. (2009). Sonia Sotomayor: *A judge grows in the Bronx.* New York: Atheneum Books for Young Readers.

Winter, J. (2005). *The librarian of Basra: A true story from Iraq.* Boston, MA: Houghton Mifflin Harcourt.

Winter, J. (2019). *The sad little fact.* New York: Schwartz & Wade Books, an imprint of Random House Childrens Books.

Wood, D. (2002). *A quiet place*. New York: Simon & Schuster.

Woodson, J. (2001). *The other side*. New York: G.P. Putnam's Sons.

Woodson, J. (2012). *Each kindness*. Nancy Paulsen Books.

Woodson, J. (2013). *This is the rope: A story from the Great Migration*. New York, NY: Nancy Paulsen Books, an imprint of Penguin Group (USA).

Woodson, J. (2018). *The day you begin*. New York, NY: Nancy Paulsen Books.

Worthington, M. (2015). *Noah chases the wind*. Saint Paul, MN: Redleaf Lane, an imprint of Redleaf Press.

Wyeth, S. D. (2002). *Something beautiful*. New York, NY: Random House USA.

Yolen, J. (1996). *Encounter*. New York: Houghton Mifflin Harcourt.

Yolen, J., & Stemple, H. E. (2010). *Not all princesses dress in pink*. New York: Simon & Schuster.

Yoo, P. (2010). *Sixteen years in sixteen seconds: The Sammy Lee story*. New York: Lee & Low Books.

INDEX